Aborted State?
The UN Initiative and New Palestinian Junctures

Aborted State?
The UN Initiative and New Palestinian Junctures

EDITORS

Noura Erakat
Mouin Rabbani

CONTRIBUTORS

Richard Falk

Noura Erakat

Raja Khalidi

Salim Tamari

Lisa Hajjar

Dena Qaddumi

Nimer Sultany

Samar Al-Bulushi

Sharon Weill

Naseer Aruri

Seif Da'na

Lauren Banko

Rashid Khalidi

Camille Mansour

Mouin Rabbani

Darryl Li

Ahmad Barclay

Asli Bâli

Susan Akram

Ryvka Barnard

Anthony Alessandrini

Sherene Seikaly

Karma Nabulsi

Dana Erekat

Nadia Hijab

TADWEEN PUBLISHING
Washington, DC

This publication is produced in part with the support of the Middle East Program at George Mason University, with which the Arab Studies Institute is affiliated.

Contents

Foreword   10

Richard Falk

Introduction   19

Noura Erakat and Mouin Rabbani

I | National Liberation Struggles   24

On the Possible Recognition of a Palestinian State at the United
Nations   25

Rashid Khalidi

Can the Palestinian Leadership Pave the Way from Statehood to
Independence?   29

Noura Erakat

Palestinian Options at the United Nations   35

Camille Mansour

Going to the United Nations, Sanctions, and the Tick-Tock of the
Palestinian Spring   41

Raja Khalidi

Palestine at the UN . . . Again   50

*O.I.L. Editors (Noura Erakat, Lisa Hajjar, Mouin Rabbani, Sherene
Seikaly, Max Ajl)*

Abbas's Next Move   53

    Mouin Rabbani

Is There a Palestinian Strategy?   55

    Salim Tamari

II | International Law and Statehood   62

Occupation Law and the One-State Reality   63

    Darryl Li

Roundtable on Occupation Law: Part of the Conflict or Part of the Solution?   70

    Noura Erakat, Lisa Hajjar, Dena Qaddumi, Ahmad Barclay, Aslı Bâli, Nimer Sultany, and Darryl Li

The Palestinian Statehood Strategy in the United Nations: Lessons From Namibia   97

    Susan Akram

ICC Rejects Palestine Bid   108

Imagining Justice Beyond the ICC   111

    Samar Al-Bulushi

Israel and Palestine: International Law Updates   116

    Sharon Weill

III | US Foreign Policy   123

Obama's Palestine Problem, and Ours   124

    Anthony Alessandrini

United States Should Step Aside as Mideast Broker   132

    Mouin Rabbani

An Apocalyptic Air of Approaching Peril: Zionism at the United
Nations   135

    Sherene Seikaly

IV | Representation   139

Roundtable on Palestinian Diaspora and Representation   140

    Naseer Aruri, Sherene Seikaly, Seif Da'na, and Karma Nabulsi

Guy S. Goodwin-Gill Legal Opinion on Palestinian Statehood Bid 167

John Quigley Critique of Goodwin-Gill Legal Opinion on Palestine
Statehood Bid   173

A Note on the Palestinian Diplomatic Initiative at the United
Nations   176

Statement by Palestinian Youth Movement on the September 2011
Declaration of Statehood   179

US Palestinian Community Network's Response to the Palestinian
Authority September Statehood Bid   181

BNC Reiterates Its Position on September   185

Beyond Sterile Negotiations: Looking for a Leadership with a
Strategy   189

    Noura Erakat

V | Back at the UN Again 2012   198

Statehood Bid One Year Later: No State, No Bid, No Freedom   199

    Noura Erakat

Quick Thoughts on the Significance of the November 2012 Palestine
UN Bid   205

    Noura Erakat

More Quick Thoughts on Palestine at the United Nations   207

    Mouin Rabbani

Citizenship and the New "State of Palestine"   210

    Lauren Banko

The Palestinian Authority, UNESCO, and the Illusion of
Triumph   215

    Ryvka Barnard

Palestine at the United Nations?   219

    Mouin Rabbani

Colonial Planning of My Grandfather's Hilltop   222

    Dana Erekat

Conclusion   230

    Nadia Hijab

VI | Appendix   241

Palestinian Statehood at the United Nations: An Information
Resource   242

Report on Palestine's Application for Admission to the United
Nations   244

Text of Obama Address to the United Nations General Assembly 256

Text of Abbas Speech to the United Nations General Assembly   267

Text of Netanyahu Speech to the United Nations General
Assembly   277

Foreword

Richard Falk

It is not clear whether the recognition of Palestinian statehood will shorten the long road to self-determination for the Palestinian people. Nevertheless, scrutinizing the meaning of the bid and its various implications among stakeholders remains a worthwhile endeavor. For example, how should we interpret the Palestinian leadership's initiative for United Nations recognition; does it represent a step forward in the underlying struggle, or is it just one more roll of the dice while the deadly clock of more than forty-five plus years of occupation and annexation continues to tick?

Perhaps these moves at the United Nations during the past two years toward statehood deserve a preliminary vote of confidence, on the basis of a popular pattern of reasoning that posits: "What Israel so vigorously opposes must have merit." After all, the Israelis play their diplomatic cards well, and rarely make foolish mistakes. We can be rather sure Tel Aviv would not waste its breath if the Palestinian statehood bid is indeed inconsequential. Perhaps the Israelis know better than their Palestinian counterparts that they are no longer primarily engaged in a hot war, but are now dangerously enmeshed in what might best be called a "legitimacy war." If this is so, there is no doubt the United Nations is a key symbolic battlefield.

Nevertheless, perhaps Israeli opposition, with the accompanying American support, facilitates Israel's semi-secret strategy of pretending to support "the peace process" while taking steps in the occupied territories to make its implementation increasingly implausible. As such, Palestinians could interpret the pursuit of bare bones statehood within the UN as a diversion from these more substantive concerns. It could, after all, be the case that diplomatic maneuvering to achieve greater recognition represents a far less tangible gain for the Palestinians than continuing to expose and confront the Zionist master plan of settlement expansion and ethnic cleansing.

Ever since the Oslo Agreement was launched with great fanfare on the White House lawn in 1993, international pressure on Israel has greatly diminished, producing an ever-greater imbalance between the two parties. This disparity has permitted Israel to accumulate more "facts on the ground," or as Hilary Clinton more felicitously puts it, taking into account "subsequent developments." Time and delay is not neutral. It helps Israel complete its work of de facto annexation in the West Bank, and puts the Palestinians in an increasingly weakened negotiating position.

What is most disturbing about the Oslo era is the degree to which Israel can flagrantly defy the authority of the United Nations and international law without suffering the slightest adverse consequence. Is it any wonder that the Palestinian people living under occupation or enduring refugee status and in exile have become disillusioned, and look elsewhere to carry on their struggle?

With stunning irony, President Barack Obama in his 2012 General Assembly address had the temerity to piously declare, "We know from painful experience that the path to security and prosperity does not lie outside the boundaries of international law and respect for human rights." In light of the consistent, unabashed, and unembarrassed support shown by Washington for Israel's every defiance of international law, it is nothing short of astonishing that an American president thinks he can make such a statement to the United Nations and not have it derisively dismissed as crass hypocrisy.

The examples of Israeli defiance of United Nations resolutions and international law are legion. Taken together, they offer a continuing narrative of Israeli policy and strategy covering the entire period since Israel's establishment in 1948. Admittedly, however, those violations have become more blatant in recent years as the Israeli electorate has drifted further and further to the right. To select a few recent highlights, the following seem worthy of mention: Israel's refusal to respect the 2004 International Court of Justice Advisory Opinion concluding that the Israeli separation wall constructed on Palestinian territory should be immediately dismantled, and individual Palestinians compensated for whatever harm incurred; repudiating in the harshest language the 2009 Goldstone Report that called for mechanisms to be established for assessing criminal accountability of Israel's alleged responsibility for war crimes and crimes against humanity committed in the course of the Gaza attacks carried out at the end of 2008 and early 2009; and disregard for international maritime law in 2010 by attacking with excessive and lethal force in international waters a flotilla of unarmed ships carrying peace activists bringing medical supplies and challenging the unlawful blockade of the Gaza Strip.

In addition to these and other specific instances there are the persisting patterns of unlawfulness and criminality. Consider, for example, Israel's imposition of massive collective punishment on the entire civilian population of Gaza since 2007 in violation of Article 33 of the Fourth Geneva Convention governing belligerent occupation. Consider also Israel's establishment of an apartheid structure in the course of administering the West Bank; its ongoing settlement construction and expansion in the West Bank and East Jerusalem; and the enactment of policies implementing a gradual yet determined policy of ethnic cleansing in East Jerusalem.

It is worth recalling that decades ago, United Nations Security Council Resolution 242 (1967), despite some marginal ambiguity about the exact demarcation of boundaries, represented the unequivocal assertion by the community of nations in asserting an Israeli obligation to withdraw from all territory occupied during the just-concluded 1967 War. This agreement was much heralded at the time and was clearly understood by everyone (save perhaps the Israelis) as including East Jerusalem in its withdrawal mandate. Yet Israel, from day one, openly defied the will of the international community as reflected in Resolution 242, and immediately enacted legislation that defined the whole of Jerusalem as a unified city under the exclusive, sovereign, and permanent control of Israel. By government fiat, Israel even significantly enlarged the Jerusalem metropolitan area, incorporating contiguous land situated within the Occupied Palestinian Territory (OPT). What should have been disturbing from the outset was the extent to which the organized world community turned a blind eye toward this calculated effort by Israel to proceed with its unilateral plan to encroach upon as much of historic Palestine as it could get away with while lamenting the insecurity it suffered at the hands of Palestinian "terror."

Within this overall setting of Israel's intransigent refusal to respect international law, it still seems important, despite the passage of decades, to underscore what might properly be labeled "the crowning violation" that deserves to head the list of any enumeration of severe Israeli violations. It is helpful to remember what is too often conveniently forgotten or brushed aside: that Resolution 242 made explicit that "a just settlement of the refugee problem" was indispensable if a sustainable peace was to be achieved in the Middle East. Of course, what constitutes a just settlement for Palestinian refugees can be endlessly debated. However, international law and United Nations General Assembly Resolution 194 of 1948 clearly set forth the broad contours of the rights of the Palestinian refugees that Israel's contrarian behavior is incapable of legally, politically, and morally extinguishing.

Surely a just settlement in 2012 cannot be reasonably understood as permitting a blanket denial of refugee rights, although this is precisely what many apologists for Israel's categorical refusal to accommodate Palestinian refugees within its territory seem to suppose. Despite the changes over the years, the refugee issue remains vital and integral to realizing the inalienable Palestinian right of self-determination. It is folly to think that the deep grievances of an estimated 6.5 million Palestinian refugees will vanish into thin air while the official negotiators for the parties implicitly agree that the words "just settlement" can be substantively ignored, provided lip service is paid to refugee claims in some hypothetical future solution of the conflict.

No matter how hard diplomats conspire to pretend that the conflict is purely territorial, as indicated by an acceptance of the "land for peace" formula or through the attainment of "statehood," Palestinian refugee communities continue to make their rightful demand for return, repatriation, and rehabilitation. Those demands serve as a warning to political leaders that such an approach rests on the political fantasy that the refugees will graciously leave the stage with hardly a whimper. In this regard, the overall conflict will never be resolved by some nominal gesture of responsiveness to refugee claims, such as allowing a tiny number of Palestinians to return annually to their original places of residence within the Green Line. It cannot be repeated often enough, especially in the United States, that a just and sustainable peace can, and should, only emerge if, and when, Israel respects the full spectrum of Palestinian rights. This is not as self-evident an observation since Palestinian and Israeli diplomats and the media have been for years wrongly presupposing that the conflict is essentially territorial and can therefore be solved territorially.

Emphasizing the refugee dimension of the conflict also embraces a rights-based approach to resolving the conflict. This departs from the two-decade old bargaining process that treats diplomacy between unequally situated parties as one between equals. It is this deformed bargaining process that should have been discredited long ago. Indeed, its outcome could easily have been anticipated given existing power disparities, the tenets of maximalist Zionist ideology, the colonialist character of the settlement project, and America's utterly inappropriate partisan intermediary role.

Over the years, a superficial effort has been made to obscure this impropriety, most notably by the establishment in 2002 of the Middle East Quartet consisting of the United States, Russia, the European Union, and the United Nations. The Quartet was assigned the mission of presiding over the implementation of the 2003 Roadmap, but in practice has functioned as little more than a transparent fig leaf for continued American monopoly of Middle East diplomacy. This flimsy form of political subterfuge is also producing serious collateral damage. Above all, the co-optation of the United Nations as a member of the Quartet has neutered the organization in relation to the conflict. It has provided the secretary general, and the United Nations generally, with the rationalization that any formal criticism of Israel, however justified and deserved, interferes with the United Nation's role in the Quartet of promoting the resumption of direct negotiations between Israel and the Palestinians—negotiations that seem neither legitimate nor effective.

Beyond this, the Palestinian leadership, as internationally represented by the Palestine Liberation Organization and the Palestinian Authority, has been seriously compromised by its continued willingness to accept a flawed diplomatic framework. Flawed because it includes an acceptance of the negotiating conditions without qualification or objection despite the Israeli refusal to curtail settlement activity even temporarily. Such Palestinian Authority acquiescence to this state of affairs, as many of the contributions to this volume of *Jadaliyya* articles make clear, compromises the legitimacy of such leadership for an increasing number of Palestinians.

This questioning of the Palestinian leadership and its strategy has been expanding and deepening in recent years, and is evident throughout this manuscript. The overarching criticism is directed at the Palestinian Authority's willingness to play along with the peace process, which it justifies by insisting that there is no other diplomatic option, making the inter-governmental negotiations "the only game in town." Such a rationalization sidesteps any proper assessment of the game, including an acknowledgement that this so-called peace process has sustained the occupation since 1993, and has allowed Israel to pursue its expansionist goals without significant resistance.

To make matters clearer, it seems evident that the Boycott, Divestment, and Sanctions campaign is offering the Palestinian people a different "peace process" by which to seek vindication of their rights, including the right of self-determination. To continue on the intergovernmental path fails to acknowledge the deadly effects of the political bargaining approach on the Palestinian people so long as the rules of the process continue to be set by Tel Aviv and Washington. At the very least, such critics contend, the Palestinian leadership in Ramallah should be voicing an acute skepticism that seems long overdue, and repudiate the unacceptable back-room concessions awkwardly revealed in the *Palestine Papers* released by Al Jazeera in early 2011.

As things stand, this official Palestinian leadership has arguably lost symbolic and political control over the Palestinian resistance movement, which has been shifting in recent years to civil society actors, and has been increasingly capturing the imagination and support of the wider public. The growing global solidarity campaign that is aligned with the Boycott, Divestment, and Sanctions movement, and the heroics of the Freedom Flotilla and the Free Gaza movement, have become the centerpieces of Palestinian resistance in the twenty-first century. In a broader sense, Palestinian resistance has shifted tactics in the direction of non-violence, waging a legitimacy war designed to capture from the Israelis the moral and legal high ground, and, with it, world public opinion.

Ever since the collapse of European colonialism, the side in a conflict that controls this moral and legal high ground has generally, although not invariably, prevailed over an opponent with hard power superiority. Palestinian reliance on non-violence has recently been dramatized by an extraordinary series of lengthy hunger strikes by Palestinians incarcerated in Israeli prisons without charge or trial. These have in duration surpassed those of IRA prisoners in 1982, which eventually led London to change its approach to the IRA. This shift thus enabled negotiation of the Good Friday Agreement. While not perfect, the agreement has led to a generally peaceful process of conflict resolution in Northern Ireland, replacing what had been previously regarded as a struggle without a foreseeable end. It is in this regard most unfortunate that the world media has looked the other way during the Palestinian prisoner strikes, and done so despite years of lecturing the Palestinians that if they adopted non-violent tactics their cause would experience an immediate upsurge of sympathetic attention.

Today, most Palestinians are not only disillusioned with the United Nations and international law, but also with their own leadership. The Palestinian leadership works within established inter-governmental channels of traditional diplomacy augmented with awkward periodic shows of deference to American political priorities. Each episode in the peace process constructed on the basis of the Oslo Declaration of Principles has ended in frustration for the Palestinians and is coupled with mutual recriminations that assign blame for the failure, with the Palestinian side represented in the media as mainly responsible for the disappointment and Israel lauded for its supposed generosity. What often follows is a perverse reaffirmation of the confidence of both sides that "the process" forms the only viable option for a peaceful settlement. In turn, this has led to a cycle of raised and shattered expectations associated with the resumption of direct negotiations.

It is here that bewilderment merges with disillusionment. Why give credibility to a structure of negotiation that is so deeply flawed? Can any sane person expect such a negotiation to lead to a just outcome when the intermediary is both the most powerful political actor on the global stage and an explicitly unconditional partisan of the stronger side? The unintentionally candid Dennis Ross in his diplomatic memoir tells it all when he indicates that the central question that tormented him throughout the 2000 Camp David negotiations was "Will the Israelis swallow this?" He never asks, or even considers, the relevance of the complementary issue, "Will the Palestinians swallow this?" Or rather, "Can and should the Palestinians swallow this?" This double standard is so revealing because it discloses the unconscious depths of the American approach: defer to Israeli sovereign consent while providing the Palestinians with a single alternative: accept what is on offer. In his long book, Ross never pauses to reflect on how odd it should seem for an "honest broker" to consider the responses of only one side of the conflict.

This last observation brings us back to the statehood bid. In one respect, as has been ably argued by John Quigley in "The Statehood of Palestine," Palestine is already a state. It has garnered over a hundred diplomatic recognitions by governments since the 1988 PLO Declaration of Independence, and subsequently established a governmental presence within relatively fixed boundaries. Of course, this PLO-proposed resolution of the conflict was the most gigantic territorial concession made by either side since the end of World War II, seemingly accepting a Palestinian state limited to the territories occupied in 1967. These territories constitute only 22 percent of historic Palestine and form less than half the territory allotted to an Arab state pursuant to the partition of Palestine proposed by the United Nations in General Assembly Resolution 181 (1947), rejected at the time as unfair by the Palestinians and the Arab states. With hindsight, it should not be surprising that Israel has offered the Palestinians nothing in response to acknowledge the significance of their willingness to normalize relations with Israel on a basis that evinced a clear intention to resolve the conflict.

Despite this background to the statehood bid of 2011 and 2012, it is correct to appreciate that United Nations certification of Palestinian statehood gives the claim considerable additional political weight. The American effort to defer indefinitely the Palestinian Authority's 2011 bid for United Nations membership bears on whether an acknowledgement of statehood without membership is a step forward for the Palestinian people. It becomes questionable whether General Assembly recognition of Palestine as a state, granting enhanced observer status, is of sufficient practical benefit to offset the earlier, more fundamental, UN rebuff by the Security Council.

There are some potentially helpful tangible effects that if subsequently acted upon could advance the Palestinian struggle. A key context is a possible Palestinian recourse to the International Criminal Court, bearing in mind that the most important achievement of the 2011 initiative was arguably the successful undertaking to become a member in UNESCO, where no veto applies. Yet at this stage the Palestinian leadership seems unlikely to pursue such bold moves, and seems willing to continue playing hide and seek when it comes to representing the Palestinian people on the global stage. Of course, the viability of the Palestinian Authority is under constant stress due to its financial and political dependence on Tel Aviv and Washington.

In the background lies the widespread assumption that whatever the fate of the statehood bid, including the now clearly "impossible" application for full UN membership, it will not relieve the suffering of Palestinians living under occupation, in refugee camps, or in Israeli jails. In fact, the assumption is that Israel would likely intensify these decades-long hardships, a kind of vengeful "price-tag" reflex analogous to extreme settlers violently punishing West Bank residents whenever the Israeli government places restraints on their ambitions. Recognition of Palestinian statehood at the United Nations is not likely to overcome the terrible vulnerability of statelessness that Palestinians have faced since 1948, including living without the benefit of the rule of law or any right to rights. It is humanly lamentable in our state-centric world order to be denied the protection of a state due to the absence of citizenship or recognized permanent resident status. Of course, formal rights are no guarantee. Persons belonging to a persecuted minority are also acutely vulnerable, as the territorial sovereignty of a state serves to insulate it from accountability by acting within sovereign territory, thereby meting out forms of genocidal violence worse than what has been inflicted up to this point on the Palestinian people.

It may very well be possible that Israel did make one of its rare political mistakes by objecting to Palestinian statehood. This is because, in all likelihood, statehood would be widely understood as giving the Palestinian people what they had been striving for, and there would be little wind left to propel the vessel of resistance throughout the world.

Foreword

If Palestinian leadership is to again obtain legitimacy, and it is a long shot, it must begin by using all the instruments at its disposal to expose the criminal abuses of the Palestinian people, including voicing the full agenda of Palestinian grievances and claims. These must include a clear rejection of the Oslo approach as well as the intermediary role played by the United States, and accompanied by a proposal for an alternate framework for negotiations. Beyond this it must actively endorse and support the range of non-violent initiatives by Palestinians living under occupation and throughout the world, and do all that can be done to heal the rifts that have fragmented leadership and strategy among the Palestinians the world over.

It is against this background that I welcome this collection of essays and documents. It provides a major contribution to our understanding of the current stage of the Palestinian struggle, its obstacles and opportunities, and especially its robust challenges at the level of leadership and strategy. These essays exhibit a brilliantly sustained quality of analysis that *Jadaliyya* has achieved in relation to the Israel-Palestine conflict in the short duration of its online lifetime. We have been given an indispensable resource for reflection, stimulation, and study. The *Jadaliyya* editors that have brought this project to fruition deserve our deepest expressions of gratitude.

March 2013

Introduction

Noura Erakat and Mouin Rabbani

As the 1993 Oslo Agreement approaches its twentieth anniversary, two decades of evidence provide a definitive body of proof of its congenital inability to affect Israeli occupation, Palestinian statehood, or Israeli-Palestinian peace. More damningly, Oslo has failed even as an interim arrangement to bring these objectives more clearly into view. Twenty years after the handshake on the White House lawn consecrated this agreement, the prospect of Israel's colonial domination of the Palestinian people being replaced by peaceful co-existence between equals appears exponentially more remote than it did in 1993.

The short explanation is that Oslo was never intended as a process of decolonization. Indeed, terms like "occupation," "statehood," "right of return," and "self-determination" are nowhere to be found in the text of either the original Declaration of Principles or any of the subsidiary agreements negotiated in subsequent years. Rather, Oslo was designed to consolidate and perpetuate Israeli control by reconfiguring it in light of the political transformations ushered by the 1987-1993 Palestinian uprising, the end of the Cold War, and the 1990-1991 Gulf Crisis.

Thus the Palestinian Authority (PA) replaced the civil administration of Israel's military government in the occupied territories without altering the structure of Israeli control. The PA assumed responsibility for policing its people and providing them with services, but exercised jurisdiction over only limited and isolated territorial enclaves. Not less importantly, the international community was replaced by the United States, more often than not in the form of Dennis Ross. Relevant United Nations resolutions and international law were shredded wholesale at the twin altars of American supremacy and the security of Israeli occupation. Meanwhile, and in what many consider the ultimate indictment of the process, Israeli colonial expansion in the form of Jewish settlements accelerated at an exponential pace relative to the years before Oslo.

The entire edifice came crashing down in 2000. The failed Camp David summit demonstrated that the maximum Israel was prepared to countenance on each and every issue of substance fell far short of the minimum any Palestinian leader—no matter how accommodationist—was prepared to accept. As the ensuing 2000-2005 uprising petered to an end and Yasir Arafat was replaced by Mahmoud Abbas, renewed Israeli-Palestinian diplomacy, under the exclusive sponsorship of first the Bush and then Obama administrations, confirmed the view that negotiation had become an end in itself. Its strategic objective: the renewal of process. Rather than transform the status quo, it confirmed it.

By early 2011 the leadership presided over by Mahmoud Abbas was in a situation almost as unenviable as that of the Palestinian people. It had lost not only the 2006 parliamentary election to the Hamas movement, but control of the Gaza Strip to the Islamists as well. Meanwhile, the anticipated promise of Obama's administration came to nothing as the new president's Middle East policy—with Ross still in a pivotal role—was characterized by an almost seamless continuity with that of his neo-conservative predecessor. For its part, Israel was ruled by the world's most radically right-wing elected government.

Added to the gamut of strategic, political, and economic challenges confronting Abbas was the wave of uprisings sweeping across the Arab world and sweeping away decades-old authoritarian rulers. Feeling pressure to act before others acted against him, and equally driven to despair by Israel and the Americans, the Palestinian leader turned to the United Nations. What some denounced as a tactical ploy to revive rather than replace the Oslo process, others lauded for its potential to internationalize the question of Palestine and see off the formula of fruitless bilateralism and destructive US diplomatic hegemony that had prevailed since the early 1990s.

This collection of essays, comprising commentary and analysis published in *Jadaliyya* during 2011-2012 as the Palestinian bid at the United Nations unfolded, examines this initiative from the key perspectives of strategy and leadership; international law and statehood; US foreign policy; and representation. It also includes more recent material from the 2012 sequel to the 2011 initiative, and relevant appendices.

As the contributions to this compendium make clear, the Palestinian initiative at the UN marks a turning point in Palestinian fortunes. Between fears about the status of Palestinian rights and hopes for a definitive rupture with Oslo, most authors agree that this event is more significant for what it signals than what it accomplishes. Like critical junctures before it, the statehood bid marks yet another turning point in the fate of the Palestinian people and their struggle for self-determination. This collection attempts to trace the pulse of political developments leading up to it as well as to highlight the most relevant social, political, and economic elements that will comprise the coming phase.

Part I of this collection, National Liberation Strategies, examines the broader question of national liberation strategy and the Palestinian quest for self-determination. In particular, it explores questions raised by the PLO's bid for statehood at the United Nations, which it announced at the height of the Arab Uprisings. Only months after the ouster of Tunisia's Zine El Abidine Ben Ali and Egypt's Hosni Mubarak, the potential for popular revolt rightfully concerned leaders across the Arab world. Despite its provisional status as an interim government, this was no less true for the PLO/PA, which has struggled to maintain legitimacy in light of the comprehensive failure of its strategy as devastatingly laid bare in Al Jazeera's *Palestine Papers*. The announcement that the Palestinian leadership would shift course and move beyond a US-brokered bilateral process to internationalize the Palestinian struggle was therefore met with both skepticism and relief. While Palestinians were optimistic that its leadership was finally exploring a Plan B, they remained skeptical that the move represented a strategic shift rather than an improvised tactical gesture designed to maintain power and revive the Oslo process.

The Palestinian statehood bid has several dimensions in international law. First there is the perennial question of what constitutes a state under international law. This is defined by the Montevideo Convention, which provides a fairly straightforward set of criteria regarding the elements of statehood. Then there is the related question of what qualifies a state for United Nations membership, which is largely answered in the 1950 International Court of Justice Advisory Opinion, Competence of Assembly regarding admission to the United Nations. But beyond these technical questions are others that examine the political efficacy of statehood in furthering Palestinian self-determination. Part II of this collection, International Law and Statehood, explores these issues. It begins with a roundtable discussion on the utility of Occupation Law in light of the existing one-state reality between the Mediterranean Sea and the Jordan river. The Roundtable also evaluates the prioritization of an end to Israel's occupation of the West Bank and Gaza Strip in view of the multiple dimensions of Palestinian self-determination. This section further explores the intersection of law and politics in other liberation struggles, including an inquiry about accountability in international criminal tribunals. It concludes with a critical challenge to the illusion of progress.

Introduction

The US role in the Israeli-Palestinian conflict is central and cannot be overestimated. A global superpower that compulsively resorts to its power of veto in the UN Security Council, the US has also habitually utilized its capacity to formulate and implement policy in defiance of both international law and the international community. A proper understanding of US Middle East policy, and the interests which underpin it, is therefore essential. Indeed, since the demise of the Republic of Vietnam at the conclusion of the Vietnam War in the mid-1970s, Israel has become the largest recipient of US foreign aid. It has also benefitted diplomatically from forty-three UNSC vetoes since 1972. This strategic alliance notwithstanding, Washington has appointed itself not only an "honest broker" between Israel and its adversaries, but the sole mediator between them to the exclusion of all other parties. Part III of this collection, US Foreign Policy, explores the impact of US Middle East policy on the conflict in general and the UN statehood bid in particular.

The most contentious debates concerning the statehood bid did not play out between global powers or even Israel and the Palestinians, but rather amongst Palestinians themselves. Well before the intention to launch the initiative was proclaimed in Ramallah in 2011, Palestinians from across the political and geographic spectrum had begun to organize themselves in an effort to rehabilitate the national movement and overcome the various dimensions of fragmentation. Several developments precipitated this nascent movement. These included growing frustration with a dead-end "peace process," a similarly moribund effort to overcome the schism between Fateh and Hamas, and the seeming abandonment of Palestinian refugee rights by the national leadership. The contributions to Part IV, Representation, trace debates surrounding this theme as they unfolded within the context of the UN initiative. It includes a roundtable discussion on diaspora and representation among Palestinian scholars that preceded the bid's announcement, as well as a legal memo and a rejoinder regarding the impact of statehood on inclusion and exclusion from the Palestinian body politic. Finally, it features three Palestinian statements expressing discontent with, and even outright rejection of, the statehood bid.

Just as it seemed that the statehood initiative had been allowed to lapse and die a quiet death within the UN Security Council, it reemerged in the wake of Israel's late 2012 assault on the Gaza Strip at the UN General Assembly's 67th session. By this time, the Palestinian leadership had made clear that it would not confront the US within the Security Council. However, the extent to which it would indeed internationalize the Palestinian quest for self-determination remained open to question. In this context, the Palestinian leadership returned to the UN, this time to upgrade Palestine's UN status to that of Non-Member Observer State. This would afford the PLO greater opportunities to challenge Israel in international forums, most notably at the International Criminal Court. Part V, Back at the UN Again: 2012, discusses these developments, the horizons for change, and the challenges ahead.

The documents included in the Appendix are intended as a resource. They include a commentary, a resource compendium, and the speeches of President Barack Obama, President Mahmoud Abbas, and Prime Minister Benjamin Netanyahu during the first statehood bid in 2011.

I | National Liberation Struggles

On the Possible Recognition of a Palestinian State at the United Nations

Rashid Khalidi

There is much interest in what will happen regarding Palestine at the United Nations in September. Contrary to much of what has been written on this subject, this is not a matter of "declaring" Palestinian statehood. The Palestine Liberation Organization (PLO) already declared the independence of Palestine in 1988. Like many things in life, this is something you can only do once. Moreover, this already-proclaimed state of Palestine did not and does not enjoy sovereignty, jurisdiction, or control over the territory it claims. Neither does the PLO, which proclaimed this state, or the Palestinian Authority. The latter is an interim self-governing authority (whose legal existence technically lapsed in 1999 in accordance with the terms of the Oslo Accords) that in practice is fully under the authority of Israel.

Israel is the only entity with any of the attributes of sovereignty in any part of the territory of former Mandatory Palestine, although it has no internationally recognized sovereign rights in the occupied territories or in any part of Jerusalem, east or west. Israel has de facto military jurisdiction and control over the occupied territories, subject to the Fourth Geneva Convention (which it constantly flouts). This jurisdiction and control is subject only to the provisions of accords with the PLO, which Israel has routinely violated, such that in practice they do not constitute serious constraints on its freedom of action. It is vital to stress these points, because they mean that, irrespective of what happens at the UN in September, the state of Palestine is not now and will not soon become a real state in any meaningful sense of that word.

If this is true, what then are the actual possible outcomes of the diplomatic maneuvers the PLO/PA are currently engaged in? Palestine would presumably be applying for UN membership as a state under occupation within certain boundaries, specifically the 1949 armistice lines that were in force until 5 June

25

1967. Although it is still denied sovereignty by the occupying power, in the intervening years since 1988 the putative state of Palestine has come to fulfill more of the requirements of statehood under international law as set down in the 1933 Montevideo Convention. Specifically, it has a permanent population; a defined territory within the 1967 lines; a government in the form of the Palestinian Authority; and the capacity to enter into relations with other states, notably the 120 states that already recognize the state of Palestine, and fifteen others that have diplomatic relations with the PLO.

However, before an application for full membership of a state in the United Nations can be voted on by the General Assembly, where it must obtain a two-thirds majority vote by member states (there are currently 192), it has to pass through the Security Council. That avenue seems blocked, with the Obama administration guaranteed to veto such an application less than fourteen months from a presidential election, irrespective of the merits of the case (where Palestine is concerned, the merits of the case have mattered little to US policy-makers since 1947). There has been mention of using the "Uniting for Peace" mechanism developed around the time of the Korean War, whereby a resolution can be sent to the General Assembly to get around an obstruction that threatens world peace in the Security Council. Another idea has been to treat the membership of Palestine as a procedural matter (on which there is no veto). Neither of these seems to be a serious alternative. No state has ever been admitted to the UN in these ways, and there may not be a Security Council majority (nine votes are required irrespective of the veto) in any case.

So presumably, even if the PLO follows this course, it will fail to obtain full UN membership because of the obstruction in the Security Council of the United States, and perhaps of its British and French allies. The PLO will thereafter have to do something else once the application of the state of Palestine for full UN membership has been vetoed, if it ever comes to a vote. This brings us to the question of what the objective of this exercise is in the first place. If it is simply intended to produce another inoperative and unenforceable General Assembly resolution on the desirability of the independence of a Palestinian state, and of its membership in the United Nations, that can certainly be achieved. It might even be possible for a Palestinian state to be accepted as an "observer state" in the United Nations, which only requires a simple majority in the General Assembly.

However, at least equally urgent issues for consideration as General Assembly resolutions are the unceasing expansion of Israeli settlements in the occupied territories and the dangerous and deteriorating situation in Jerusalem. The Holy City is the scene of menacing and accelerating settlement activity in the Arab neighborhoods of Shaykh Jarrah, Silwan, and Abu Dis; disturbing underground excavations and new construction in the Old City in the vicinity of the Haram al-Sharif, including at the Bab al-Maghariba gate to the Haram; and further encroachments on the oldest Muslim burial-ground in the city, the Mamilla Cemetery, where permission has just been granted for the building of a massive Center for Human Dignity/Museum of Tolerance on the site of graves going back to at least the eleventh century, and where Jerusalem Municipality bulldozers were destroying yet more ancient gravestones on 25-26 June 2011.

Obtaining General Assembly resolutions on all of these issues with large majorities, including European and other countries that normally back Israel, would certainly be a worthy objective. However, if the objective is to do more than that, then membership of Palestine in the United Nations and the other two issues should be suggested for consideration not just by the General Assembly but also by the Security Council, notwithstanding the fact that they will face an inevitable US veto. This should be the case, if the aim is to finally declare independence of a bankrupt American-Israeli dominated "peace process" that is grotesquely misnamed. Far from bringing about peace, it has brought about a twenty-year process of deepening occupation and colonization and postponing resolution of the core issues of Jerusalem and refugees, while enabling Israel to do everything possible to establish a status quo that obviates their just resolution.

If this kind of declaration of independence is the basic objective, then winning a Security Council majority on carefully worded resolutions, and forcing US vetoes on them makes a great deal of sense. It is certain that such vetoes will do the US considerable harm in the Arab world, even with some close American allies (in this regard it is worth noting the opinion editorial by Saudi prince Turki al-Faisal that was highly critical of US policy over Palestine). The United States is sure to bring all its considerable influence to bear to avoid such resolutions being brought before the council for just this reason. But the fact that such a course would clarify the situation, and finally extract a small price for the United States' shameless pandering to Israel, is precisely the reason why this is a course to be seriously considered.

There will certainly be disadvantages to such a strategy. The Obama administration is sure to retaliate against both Palestinians and Arabs for having the temerity to follow an independent course. Congress will undoubtedly outbid the administration in its expression of outrage and demands for retribution.

Israel will extract its usual vengeance for any measure not to its liking with more "facts on the ground" and the imposition of penalties on the Palestinian Authority. Instead of this punishment giving rise to lamentation and despair, it could be the occasion for greater Palestinian and Arab solidarity and further sacrifice in response to the material sanctions sure to be imposed.

This might even constitute the occasion for the beginning of the first serious attempt since the Balfour Declaration to explain the Palestinian cause fully and properly to the entire world. This must take place not in terms of the arcane and incomprehensible legal minutiae of the so-called "peace process," but by laying out the basic components of the Palestine cause, buttressed by international law, that this process was ingeniously designed to obscure. These include the necessity to seek justice for the victims of ethnic cleansing sixty-three years ago through guaranteeing inalienable refugee rights; the need for Jerusalem to be free of the discriminatory, exclusive control of a domineering Israeli state, and for the city to belong to all those who live and worship there and see it as their capital; the need for a definitive end to occupation and colonization in the occupied territories that have now entered their forty-fifth year; and achieving long-delayed self-determination for the Palestinian people.

28 June 2011

Can the Palestinian Leadership Pave the Way from Statehood to Independence?

Noura Erakat

Middle Eastern analysts concerned with the Palestinian statehood bid have rightly highlighted the benefits conferred by such status. They assume, however, that the current Palestinian leadership is willing to take the necessary steps in order to lead Palestinians from statehood on paper to independence in practice. In the early 1990s, the Palestinian leadership supplanted its struggle for self-determination with a state-building project. In its narrow pursuit of a mandate to govern, it placed undue faith in the United States' willingness, and arguably its ability, to pressure Israel to end its prolonged occupation thus shunning a resistance platform. In its bid for statehood, the Palestinian leadership must resume its self-determination struggle. Doing so requires that it abandon any faith that US benevolence will deliver independence. Consequently, such a resumption means resisting the United States' unequivocal support for Israel as well as a willingness to take the lead from Palestinian civil society, which has successfully led a global Boycott, Divestment, and Sanctions (BDS) campaign aimed at pressuring Israel to comply with international law and human rights norms.

From Statehood to Independence

The Palestinian Liberation Organization (PLO) has held observer status in the United Nations since 1974. To achieve recognition as a state, the PLO needs to garner the vote of two-thirds of the 192 member states. To be admitted as a member state in the UN, the UN Security Council must first make a recommendation to the General Assembly. According to the International Court of Justice, statehood is impossible without a Security Council recommendation. The 1950 Advisory Opinion on Article 4, paragraph 2 of the UN Charter holds that "recommendation of the Security Council is the condition precedent to the decision of the assembly by which the admission is effected."[1] It is clear that the United States, a permanent member of the Security Council, will veto such a recommendation.

In all likelihood, the majority of UN member states will recognize Palestine within the General Assembly thereby granting Palestine statehood but not UN membership. In the unlikely scenario that the United States does not block a Security Council recommendation and Palestine also achieves membership, Israel will still prevent Palestinians from exercising control over their natural resources, ports of entry, movement, security, education, and economy. Therefore, with or without statehood, Palestinians will still need to wage a robust, multi-dimensional, and global campaign to achieve self-determination. Such a scenario is not unique, as demonstrated by the Namibian precedent, which achieved UN recognition in 1962 but did not achieve independence from South Africa until 1988.

Therefore, while analysts sympathetic to Palestinian self-determination are debating the benefits of statehood and how best to achieve it, the better question to ask is whether such a bid is part of a broader reorientation in goals and strategies on the part of the current Palestinian leadership. The Palestinian Authority (PA), no longer distinct from the PLO, which I will refer to as the PA/PLO, is marred by a dismal track record in the past two decades, making such a reorientation highly unlikely, but not impossible.

Protect Palestinians, not the Occupation

Within the current status quo, Palestinians neither benefit from their status as a dispossessed nation entitled to self-determination nor as citizens of a sovereign state adorned with all the duties and responsibilities of a sovereign entity. Instead, the US-brokered peace process has made the Palestinian people appear like equal counterparts to the Israeli state while their lived realities reflect no such parity. Worse, in its futile attempt to demonstrate its capacity to govern and maintain order, the PA/PLO has arguably relieved Israel of at least a portion of its military burden as an occupying power.

In the West Bank, the PA/PLO has not demanded a peacekeeping force to protect Palestinian civilians from Israeli military forces patrolling their lives and homes. Instead the PA/PLO has steadily built a security apparatus popularly known as the Dayton Forces to police Palestinians. Lieutenant-General Keith Dayton, in his description of his forces' role in the West Bank during Israel's twenty-two day offensive against Gaza, clearly articulates the seemingly seamless alliance with the PA/PLO:

> The IDF also felt—after the first week or so—that the Palestinians were there and they could trust them. As a matter of fact, a good portion of the Israeli army went off to Gaza from the West Bank—think about that for a minute—and the commander was absent for eight straight days. That shows the kind of trust they were putting in these people now.[2]

As Palestinian security forces earned the trust of the Israeli military, Palestinian civilians continued to be subject to the violent brunt of Israel's military occupation. A short survey of this ongoing violence would include the forced population transfer of Palestinians from their homes in East Jerusalem, the rise in Israeli settler violence against Palestinians, and the incarceration of Palestinian children in Israeli military prisons.

Resistance, not Compliance

For the length of Oslo's two decades, the PA/PLO has appeased the US in the delusional hope that Israel's staunchest ally would deliver some palatable version of freedom to appease their constituencies and serve their interests. Palestinian statehood may be in the United States' best interest, however, rather than broker peace, the United States has served as Israel's advocate, by shielding it from accountability, and its benefactor, by subsidizing its colonial expansionist enterprise.

The US has insisted that the only resolution to the conflict will be through political negotiations. In doing so, they continue an all too familiar pattern of the disavowal of Israel as an occupying power, the bold disregard for human rights and international law, the circumvention of the illegality of settlements, and the denial of the refugees' individual and collective rights. This pattern has been central to the Oslo process. Rather than establish peace on a rights-based framework, as has been the case in Ireland, Bosnia-Herzegovina, and South Africa, the United States treats the case of the Palestinian-Israeli conflict as if there are no terms of reference. Each new peace process cycle resumes from a new point of departure that deems Israel's creeping annexation of the West Bank as the new basis for pragmatism.

For example, drafters of the Oslo Accords deliberately omitted reference to Article 49 of the Fourth Geneva Convention prohibiting the transfer of an occupying power's population into the territory it occupies, and relegated the settlements to final status negotiations. Consequently, Palestinian negotiators today must contend with nearly 500,000 settlers, whereas only 250,000 colonized the West Bank at the advent of the peace process in 1991. The United States accepts these developments, which constitute the basis of ongoing conflict, without contest. President Barack Obama said so himself when he explained, "The basis for negotiations will involve looking at the 1967 border, recognizing that conditions on the ground have changed, and there are going to need to be swaps to accommodate the interests of both sides."

Rather than resist the United States' unequivocal support for Israel, the PA/PLO has fully complied with its prerogatives. The Palestinian leadership should have either demanded clear terms of reference or walked away from the counterproductive peace process long ago but it pursued neither option as the *Palestine Papers* illustrated with devastating clarity.

The statehood bid is the PA/PLO's first direct confrontation of the Israeli occupation and US support for it since the peace process. However, unless the PA/PLO considers the bid the first step on a new strategic course, the diplomatic maneuver is little more than a bluff, a slight diversion before resuming the status quo of US-brokered bilateral negotiations.

Charting a New Course

In a lucid policy memo, legal scholar Victor Kattan lists the many benefits of statehood. These include immunity from suit for acts of terrorism in US courts, jurisdiction in the International Criminal Court, as well as status for Palestinian militants as soldiers entitled to protections of the Second Geneva Convention as opposed to their current status as "terrorists."[3] However, reading Kattan's memo one would think that but for the lack of statehood, the PA/PLO would have made significant strides in protecting Palestinian rights. Yet, as demonstrated by the missed opportunities of the 2009 Goldstone Report and the 2004 International Court of Justice (ICJ) Advisory Opinion, that is not the case. Instead, failure to further the cause for Palestinian self-determination reflects a strategic choice on the part of current Palestinian leadership and not a lack of capacity.

The PA/PLO did not use the Goldstone Report to hold Israel to account for its alleged war crimes during Operation Cast Lead. Instead the PA/PLO delayed its review by the Human Rights Council for the sake of attaining the United States' offer of a better negotiating position. While the Palestinian leadership waited for the United States to deliver on its empty promises, international civil society worked furiously to sue alleged Israeli war criminals in European courts under universal jurisdiction. While no trials have ensued, their efforts have deterred Israelis from traveling to Europe. Moreover, Israel has now developed a legal fund to challenge such attempts, which counter the Zionist narrative of a courageous David facing the menacing Arab Goliath.

Similarly, the 2004 ICJ Advisory Opinion held the route of Israel's separation barrier illegal for being built inside the occupied West Bank as opposed to on the 1949 Armistice Line and affirmed the illegality of Israel's settlements. Accordingly, the world's highest judicial tribunal recommended that all state parties to the Fourth Geneva Convention cease to, or refrain from, aiding in Israel's expansion of the wall. The PA/PLO had the perfect opportunity to run a diplomatic marathon and encourage the signatories of the Geneva Conventions to either impose sanctions on Israel for its ongoing constructions, cease the sale of any materials intended for the development of the wall, or refuse to purchase Israeli goods produced in the illegal settlements.

The PA/PLO did nothing of the sort and exactly one year later, a broad swath of Palestinian civil society organizations launched the BDS campaign against Israel. To date, the scarcely funded international BDS movement has made tremendous strides in fulfilling the ICJ's recommendations. Most notably, it has encouraged several European banks to sell their holdings in Veolia, a French multinational company set to build Jerusalem's light rail to connect illegal Israeli settlements. Their gains have been so impactful that last week, the Israeli Knesset passed a new law prohibiting Israeli individuals and organizations from boycotting settlement products and Israeli enterprises.

Statehood may afford the PA/PLO with more meaningful means to challenge Israel's occupation and apartheid. However, the lack of such status was not the sole obstacle containing the PA/PLO's resistance to injustice. In the meantime, Palestinian and global civil society have made strident gains. The missing link is not statehood, it is a commitment to resist rather than appease Israeli occupation and US prerogatives.

The statehood bid will be yet another test of this commitment. Both houses of the US Congress have overwhelmingly voted to cut aid to Palestinians if the PA/PLO pursues its statehood ambitions. In striking resemblance to its choice for a better negotiation position in lieu of accountability for war crimes committed during Operation Cast Lead, the PA/PLO ambassador to the United States responded by proclaiming the indeterminacy of the statehood bid "if negotiations resume."[4]

Failure to pass this threshold will signal the irrelevance of the PA/PLO all together.

But ultimately statehood is not the panacea for independence. It is one step of many that the Palestinian leadership has failed to take for the past two decades. These missed, but still necessary, steps must focus on applying pressure upon Israel to abandon its colonial practices, dismantle its apartheid system, and come into compliance with international law and human rights norms. The PA/PLO need not look very far for useful strategies as its own Palestinian grassroots leaders, organizers, and activists, have steadily and successfully stayed the course towards meaningful self-determination.

For the statehood bid to be significant, for Israel, for the United States, and for the Palestinian people, it must be part of a much larger reorientation in strategy and aims. At the center of such a shift, the PA/PLO must be ready to take its lead from the bottom.

28 July 2011

[Originally published on Al Jazeera English]

---

[1] "Competence of Assembly Regarding Admission to the United Nations, Advisory Opinion," (ICJ Reports, 1950), http://www.icj-cij.org/docket/files/9/1883.pdf.

[2] Quoted in: Jim Zanotti, "US Security Assistance to the Palestinian Authority" (Congressional Research Service, 8 January 2010), http://www.fas.org/sgp/crs/mideast/R40664.pdf.

[3] Victor Kattan, "A State of Palestine: The Case for UN Recognition and Membership" (Al-Shabaka, May 2011), http://al-shabaka.org/sites/default/files/policybrief/en/state-palestine-case-un-recognition-and-membership/state-palestine-case-un-recognition-and-membership.pdf.

[4] Josh Rogin, "House Leaders to Palestine: Seek U.N. Recognition, Forget Foreign Aid," *Foreign Policy Blogs*, 15 July 2011, http://thecable.foreignpolicy.com/posts/2011/07/15/house_leaders_to_palestine_seek_un_recognition_forget_foreign_aid.

Palestinian Options at the United Nations

Camille Mansour

What could be called the September "Wende" is fast approaching, and interpretations put forward by Palestinian officials abound as to what will be possible and impossible to attain at the United Nations (UN). This has engendered a certain confusion in Palestinian, Arab, and international public opinion, as it is not clear which of these interpretations stem from a priori political considerations, which are based on an adequate understanding of UN procedures, and which are grounded on expectations of how member states will vote, or even on external pressures. In this article I intend to present the options that could be considered by the Palestinian leadership as it looks to the UN for a way out of the present impasse in negotiations with the United States and Israel. Two avenues will be considered: direct approaches to the General Assembly (option 1); direct approaches to the Security Council (option 2 and rejoinders, and option 3).

Option 1.A: Directly approaching the UNGA to adopt a resolution recommending that member states that have not yet done so, recognize the State of Palestine on the 1967 borders.

It seems to me that such a resolution would be easily attainable, since it requires a simple majority vote of present and voting General Assembly (GA) members (abstentions do not count). Indeed, many of the resolutions in the long list of GA resolutions on Palestine passed since 1974 are far stronger in the principles they contain than this option. At its sixty-fifth session, which opened in September 2010, for example, the GA adopted seventeen resolutions in support of Palestinian rights, including the right to self-determination, right of return in accordance with Resolution 194, the right to an independent state, non-recognition of the annexation of Jerusalem and the changes effected by the occupation, condemnation of Israeli settlement activity, and so on.

Option 1.B: Directly approaching the GA to obtain the status of non-member observer state at the United Nations.

The UN Blue Book, issued each year by the Secretariat's Protocol and Liaison Service, categorizes Palestine, since 1998, under the heading: "Entities Having Received a Standing Invitation to Participate as Observers in the Sessions and the Work of the General Assembly and Maintaining Permanent Observer Missions at Headquarters." No other entity figures under this heading. A simple majority in the GA could, at any ordinary future session, decide to grant Palestine the status of non-member observer state, replacing the term "entity" with the term "state." In this event, Palestine would be placed on the list of observer states, which currently comprises only the Holy See, the other fourteen countries once on this list having since become full members. It should be noted that such a status is not provided for in the UN Charter, but is the cumulative result of customary practice of the GA since its establishment. We should also recall that in December 1988 the GA resolved that it "acknowledges the proclamation of the State of Palestine by the Palestine National Council on 15 November 1988" and that more than 100 countries recognized the State of Palestine at the time.

Option 1.C: Directly approaching the GA to issue a resolution incorporating options 1.A and 1.B with additions.

It seems to me that the Palestinian leadership's decision on 26 June 2011 "to approach the UN this coming September to obtain recognition of the State of Palestine on the 1967 borders and Palestinian membership in the international community" was ambiguous in two respects, perhaps intentionally. UN recognition of a given country is virtually meaningless, there is no manifest effect that such recognition per se would have. However, what the GA could do is adopt a single resolution that would include the following: welcoming (in addition to acknowledging) the 1988 proclamation of the State of Palestine together with Palestinian achievements since 1993 with regard to the establishment of state institutions; merging options 1.A and 1.B (i.e., calling on GA members to recognize the State of Palestine and granting it non-member observer state status); and giving some additional privileges to Palestine's UN mission in terms of protocol or its ability to contribute to GA debates, but without a right to vote. Secondly, the Palestinian leadership's declared intention to gain "Palestinian membership in the international community" is also vague. The term "international community" could not be more general, to such an extent that one could say that Palestine has been a member of this community for the past three decades because of its status at the UN and the number of countries that have recognized it, as well as the near-consensus it has enjoyed among peoples across the globe. If, however, the leadership's goal is to obtain membership in the UN, the procedures governing such an application are of a different order, more difficult and with greater political and diplomatic implications. Such a process requires a positive recommendation from the UNSC, to which we now turn.

Option 2: Approaching the Security Council for Palestinian membership in the United Nations.

The positive recommendation from the Security Council (SC) needed for membership in the United Nations must be followed by a two-thirds majority of the UNGA's present and voting members. It can be assumed that a SC resolution recommending Palestine membership would easily be approved by the GA; the difficulty, clearly, would be obtaining the required nine-vote majority of the SC, or, in the event that this majority were obtained, avoiding a veto by one or more of the SC's permanent members. The question, then, becomes whether the GA can find ways to circumvent possible opposition in the SC. In such cases, the Palestinian delegation might approach the GA to adopt one or more of the following procedures.

Option 2.A: The GA could respond by inviting the SC to reconsider its position.

There are several precedents for such an action, dating back to the late 1940s and early 1950s. In addition to expressing the GA's support for Palestine, such an action would reflect its desire to keep the Palestinian membership application alive in the UN system until suitable conditions arise that allow for the approval of the application. However, the preferred course of action in the past seems to have been to resubmit the request once such conditions were met (as with Japan in 1952, then in 1956).

Option 2.B: The GA could respond by inviting the SC to reconsider its position, while recognizing Palestine's status as a non-member UN observer state until such time as the SC reconsiders its objection.

This option means merging options 2.A and 1.B.

Option 2.C: In the event that the Palestinian request enjoys a majority of SC votes, but is denied as a result of a veto by one of the SC's permanent members, the GA could respond by requesting that the International Court of Justice (ICJ) give an advisory opinion on the following question of principle: "Is a negative vote by a permanent member of the SC to be treated as a veto in voting on membership applications?"

Although the permanent members of the SC will not welcome such an action, which clearly impinges on their prerogatives, a number of major regional

37

powers (e.g., India, Brazil, Argentina, South Africa) that are at the forefront of those calling for SC reform may see such an option as serving their interests. It is worth mentioning that in a March 1950 ICJ advisory opinion declaring that the GA could not go against a negative recommendation by the SC on a membership application, the minority opinion added that the court should have distinguished between two scenarios. The first scenario would be the one in which the application failed to receive majority support in the SC—the negative recommendation. The second would be where the application received the majority approval, but was opposed by a permanent member. In this latter case, it would not have been permissible, according to the minority opinion, for a permanent member of the SC to obstruct the acceptance of a membership request that received majority approval by the SC, and two-thirds majority support from the voting members of the GA.

Option 2.D: In the event that the Palestinian request enjoys a majority of SC votes, but is denied as a result of a veto by one of the SC permanent members, the GA could overcome the veto on the basis of Resolution 377, known as the Uniting for Peace Resolution.

The GA adopted resolution 377 in November 1950 during the Korean crisis, and expressed its readiness to take the initiative by recommending the collective action necessary for the maintenance of international peace and security if the SC was unable to carry out this responsibility because a permanent member exercised its veto power. This option would be based on the argument that obstructing Palestine's admission as a member of the United Nations threatened regional security, while Palestine's acceptance would further the goals of international peace and security. This option, as I see it, would require two consecutive steps: the first would be a recommendation by the GA that its members accept the State of Palestine's application for membership, as if the GA substituted for a SC incapacitated by the veto of one of its permanent members. The second step would be another GA vote within its usual mandate, giving the final approval of the recommendation for Palestine's membership. The required majority vote in each of the steps is a two-thirds majority of present and voting states, i.e. that only "yes" and "no" votes count, abstentions being considered a non-vote.

Option 3: Approaching the SC with a request to accede to the Statute of the ICJ.

Article 93 of the UN Charter stipulates that a non-member state may become a party to the Statute of the International Court of Justice under conditions to be determined in each case by the GA on recommendation of the

SC. In every case in which this procedure has been followed (for example, for Switzerland and Japan, when they were not UN members), the GA, upon the recommendation of the SC, approved the conditions in which the applying state must comply in order to become a party to the ICJ Statute. The GA's conditions were the same in each case, namely: the applicant's acceptance of the provisions of the statute of the court; acceptance of all the obligations of a member of the UN under article 94 of the charter, which calls on states to accept the court's decisions in cases to which the state is party; and undertaking to contribute to the expenses of the court within the fair limits determined by the GA. Among the benefits of this option—assuming the SC veto obstacle can be overcome—is that it would provide Palestine with the same judicial tools offered by membership in the UN. This would include the ability to resort to the ICJ as a full-fledged state, and accession to the International Criminal Court.

Conclusion

It is not easy to prioritize the options listed here. On one level, it must be stressed that it is not appropriate to set priorities according to the various options' chances of success at the UN, since the measure of success must be held to the standards of progress towards achieving Palestinian national goals, and not necessarily in terms of bringing about the issuance of a given resolution. Moreover, a short term procedural failure at the UN (as a result of a US veto, for example) could contribute political gains in the medium term, while passing a GA measure to Palestinian advantage may constitute little more than a marginal gain in real terms.

On another level, the Palestinian leadership is currently facing a dangerous political and diplomatic battle following an obstructed negotiations process, increasingly brutal Israeli practices, the retreat of the United States, and the destabilization of the Arab system as a result of the Arab revolutions. Despite the great risks and mounting pressures marking this critical period, it is up to the Palestinian leadership to navigate the difficult waters ahead: approaching the UN, and, at the same time, moving the intra-Palestinian reconciliation process towards a successful resolution, and preparing to counter possible Israeli provocations through popular mobilization.

On a third level, the adoption of any option will depend on Palestinian success in marshaling the support of friendly and neutral countries, as well as mobilizing international opinion, on the cohesion and credibility of Palestinian proclaimed positions, and on the skill of the Palestinian diplomatic corps in assessing which states can be rallied and at what stage. In this area, there are no closed doors that are either preordained as such or that result from set-in-stone legal rules (e.g., the notion that it is impossible for the GA to surmount a possible US veto with regard to the Palestinian request for full UN membership). It is states that develop—or indeed create—UN legal procedures, in accordance with their interests, the values to which their societies are attached, and the compromises they negotiate with each other.

Given these considerations—and also to demonstrate the seriousness of our position on the conditions for resuming negotiations; to manifest our lost confidence in the ability of the United States to serve as honest broker for the Palestinian–Israeli peace settlement; to ensure that the coming September is indeed a real landmark; and provided the effective support of the Palestinian people is mobilized at home and abroad—I think it necessary for the Palestinian leadership to confront the great powers and other influential states in the international system with their political diplomatic responsibilities through its submission of a formal request for full membership in the UN, namely through the SC, as outlined in option 2 above. In terms of the other options, I suggest that we not deal with them until the SC meets to vote on the formal Palestinian request, and that preference be given to the options (not just those mentioned here) that involve approaching the SC as a first step. It is also necessary to emphasize that even if a great and course-changing victory is won at the UN, such an achievement can hardly be more than a modest step forward on the long road toward achieving the Palestinian national project.

2 September 2011

Going to the United Nations, Sanctions, and the Tick-Tock of the Palestinian Spring

Raja Khalidi

Now it is official: if the Palestine Liberation Organization (PLO) pursues recognition of the Palestinian people's claim to statehood in the United Nations this month, financial sanctions will follow. Such a response can be expected not only from Israel, which channels around one billion dollars of Palestinian public revenue to the Palestinian Authority (PA) per annum, but also from major donors whose collective aid has averaged around 1.5 billion dollars in recent years.

Unfortunately, we have been here before and the history of a century of settler colonialism tells us that the economic damage such a move will inflict is considerable. The resilience of a battered people, dispersed between occupation and exile, will be again put to the test as a risky diplomatic strategy unfolds amidst considerable international controversy and internal dissent and skepticism.

Proponents, mainly PLO officials and some scholars, argue that recognition of statehood at the UN is a natural, inevitable outcome of a struggle to end occupation and exercise self-determination; there is no turning back now, indeed no alternative. Detractors include pro-Israeli voices that are hostile to Palestinian rights in any form; for them, the only effective response is one that squeezes the Palestinians, especially financially.

Meanwhile, a wide swath of Palestinian activists consider the statehood initiative problematic from legal and representational angles, because of its primary focus on statehood rather than the panoply of denied Palestinian rights. For them the bid for state recognition is better abandoned or possibly reformulated, as it might lead to either an even more complex situation or hollow diplomatic victory.

Two major encounters are on the horizon. The first, and of greater significance, is how the PLO will address concerns expressed within a national movement fractured along factional, geographic, and, increasingly, generational lines. In the second, the PLO and its allies at the UN are confronted with efforts to derail or defuse this initiative. Paradoxically, both of these dynamics are pushing the PLO in the same direction, strengthening its resolve to pursue its strategy come what may. Battle lines are already being drawn, and it is difficult for advocates of any position to escape being perceived as serving one or the other agenda.

If the Palestinians succeed in closing ranks behind the statehood strategy, something that is not apparently imminent, there are ready alternatives to violent resistance. New strategies should aim to strengthen Palestinian economic steadfastness (*sumud*) and development in a context of national reconciliation, confronting occupation and establishing Palestinian sovereignty, incrementally if need be.

***

If financial sanctions do take hold, this would not be the first time that the reigning powers have deployed them in the century-old struggle over territory and resources between Palestinian Arabs and Zionist (then Israeli) Jews. An eye to history is essential for understanding this conflict's dynamics as they unfold today. From the British Mandatory authorities' response to the earliest Palestinian anti-colonial uprising in the 1930s, to military rule over Palestinian Arab minority citizens in Israel from 1948-1966, to the annexation of eastern Jerusalem in 1967, to the civil administration of the Israeli military government in the occupied territory, each era had its instruments and purposes.

Nor would it be the first time that finance has impinged on PLO strategies. Beginning with the aftermath of the 1982 Lebanon War, a battered, exiled, and isolated PLO had to operate on a tight budget and struggle to maintain its relevance. After 1988, during the first Palestinian intifada, economic sanctions were deployed by Israel throughout the occupied territory to counter popular protests and the PLO's resurgence. Following the first Gulf War, Arab aid was halted for many years, adding pressure on a reluctant PLO to acquiesce to the terms of the Oslo Accords.

Needless to say, for any national liberation movement, especially one with a major part of its constituency in exile, the support of allied states significantly affects its room for maneuver. This has not been any less the case for the PLO. And when, after the establishment of the PA in 1994, the primary source of funding shifted from external to local revenues largely under Israeli control, this dynamic became even more critical.

Soon after the second intifada erupted in September 2000, Israel withheld import taxes it collected on behalf of the PA, helping to promote a "reformed" PLO which foreswore armed resistance by 2005 and returned to negotiations soon after. And then again, in the wake of the 2006 PA legislative elections, Israeli revenue clearance to the PA was halted, along with direct donor aid. It was only with the Fateh-Hamas schism between the West Bank and Gaza Strip in 2007 that Israeli clearance of revenues was resumed and aid channeled to support the PA budget through consolidated accounts in Ramallah under Prime Minister Salam Fayyad.

By 2010, the PA payroll had become aid and clearance dependent to an extent that interruption of these flows implies a collapse of the PA similar to that experienced in 2002-2004. It is ironic that the fate of the PA, the principal *institutional* manifestation within Palestine of the PLO, is today dependent on uninterrupted flow of "conditional aid" for its very existence.

From this perspective, the real economic miracle of the post-2005 Palestinian regime is not the middle-class urban boom epitomized by Ramallah, much less the institutional achievements of the PA program of the past two years. Rather, what is impressive is that the Palestinian people, at least half of whom live in poverty, continue to resist settlement, occupation, fragmentation, and deprivation. The resilience and ingenuity of this core human resource and social capital spread throughout Palestine and beyond should be the lynchpin of a new Palestinian strategy to confront economic and financial sanctions under all and any conditions.

Since the collapse of Palestinian-Israeli negotiations last year, pundits, politicians, and the Palestinian public have been debating with increasing intensity the pros and cons of "going to the United Nations" this September. Confusion remains rife as to the exact strategy and purpose of such an initiative, or what shape going to the UN will take after 23 September when PLO Chairman Abbas is due to address the General Assembly. A range of options has been suggested, based on different assumptions as to *exactly where* in the UN the PLO is going (Security Council and/or General Assembly) and with *what outcomes* in mind (full member or observer state).

But process can easily trump everything in the UN. Small words here and there, choosing this or that rule of procedure, and making this or that alliance, counts for everything in such a diplomatic push fraught with risks. By simply depositing an application for admission as the 194th state member, the PLO will have "gone to the UN" and could conceivably leave it pending. An alternative route could go further, namely requesting the General Assembly to "recognize" the State of Palestine on the 1967 borders and accord it the status of observer state (instead of the PLO's status since 1974 as observer national liberation movement). However, following the law of unintended consequences, drawn out negotiations coupled with the looming threat of sanctions could produce a resolution with new language. This would have to be reconciled with the historic consensus positions set forth in key UN resolutions since 1947, which constitute the legal framework for any resolution of the "Question of Palestine," an item on its agenda for sixty-five years.

Regardless of the procedural and legal pitfalls, for those states opposed to this initiative, the Palestinians are damned if they do and damned if they don't. The Palestinian national liberation movement has tried everything: a failed armed struggle for forty-five years; two popular uprisings ignited by deprived youth; two decades of fruitless bilateral negotiations; and, in the PA, a proto-state —a security and service-delivery apparatus devoid of sovereign powers and split between two (already separated) regions.

Now, friends and foes alike are telling the PLO that recourse to the legal framework of the UN, the international custodian of the Palestine question, may have dire economic and political consequences. And if the PLO does not go to the UN, then it will be held accountable one way another. The vocal Palestinian "patriotic" public opinion concerned about the initiative, either in principle or in its formulation, should not be underestimated.

The PLO is facing diplomatic pressure because this initiative is perceived as an attempt to redefine an otherwise moribund bilateral "peace process" within a broader multilateral setting. But General Assembly Resolutions 181 and 194, and Security Council Resolutions 242 (1967), 338 (1973), and 1397 (2002) are not just historical footnotes to today's conflicts. The UN has been the indispensable venue for setting the basic parameters of a just (and therefore durable) resolution to the "Question of Palestine." And Palestine is ingrained in the UN agenda not out of inertia, but rather owing to its inherent staying power as a festering heritage of twentieth-century colonialism. So bringing it back to the UN could indeed be an important first step in applying the lessons learned from twenty years of failed diplomacy.

Efforts to try to neutralize this initiative can be expected through creative language and generic formulations of goals, desired actions, and outcomes. Other potential traps could be endorsement of yet another interim period, the most recent version of which was the PA Homestretch to Freedom of 2009-2011. In such an eventuality, major economic consequences and a popular backlash against the status quo are well within the realm of the possible, given the history of failed Palestinian expectations.

From the PLO's vantage point, retreat is not an option. And while vibrant internal debate is a healthy sign of a pluralist political culture, it has yet to influence existing plans. For better or worse, a Palestinian initiative is imminent, and millions of Palestinians, and others, will be watching closely to see how it unfolds.

For all intents and purposes, the "Question of Palestine" is going back to the UN this September. And when the financial heat is likely turned up, the Palestinian economic situation basically goes south. Hence, my concern as a development economist is to examine what I can claim, with some confidence, to know something about.

***

Little of the flood of political, legal, and media analysis of this story has touched on what might happen—including economically—after the dust of the diplomatic battle has settled. What impact might the face-off of the coming months and its diplomatic fallout have on the livelihoods of Palestinians living under Israeli occupation in the West Bank and Gaza Strip? Will life just go on under the economic union between six million Israeli Jews and five million Palestinian Arabs, living under the same fiscal, monetary, trade, and security regime (geared to the interests of the Israeli Jewish economy) since 1967? And how might this affect the fate of over one million Palestinian Arab citizens of Israel and millions of Palestine refugees?

For most donors, the PLO initiative might not warrant reconsideration of their 1.5 billion dollar annual aid commitments, which comprises around a fifth of Palestinian national income. But for Israel, which clears to the PA, or captures through external trade flows, an even greater proportion of Palestinian public revenue, the Palestinian economy has always been a captive market. For the PLO and PA, which has no contingencies or savings for a rainy day to deal with what might happen after September, any reduction in budget support is a matter of immediate and vital concern. Its 170,000 public sector employees constitute a major source of grievance if the government can no longer honor its obligations.

The fractured Palestinian economy is vulnerable to yet another shock to its enfeebled structure, which renders its viability a moot point.[1] This is despite a much-vaunted recent recovery that included "building the institutions of the state" and a decade of Washington consensus-style reform and "good governance."[2]

One way or the other, after September the Palestinian economy will pay a price.

Whatever the outcome, insistence on recognition of the Palestinian state in the West Bank and Gaza implies, for the PLO, *living up to that claim* through starting to *act as a sovereign entity* where possible. This is not only a matter of protocol and diplomatic relations, but equally should be manifested in a major shift on the ground, differentially in the West Bank than in the Gaza Strip. In 1988 we witnessed the PLO's Declaration of Independence of the State of Palestine, and in 2011 we might yet see belated international recognition. Yet after all that has been learned (or not), might the current juncture provide a chance to actually begin *establishing* that state in 2012?

In Gaza for example, the occupying power's control over economic policy (fiscal, trade, industrial, investment, banking) is already less than in the West Bank, a crack in the matrix of economic control that implies a policy space begging to be expanded. And if an overdue Palestinian reconciliation enabled a return of the PLO to Gaza, enormous economic implications would ensue from re-establishing the Palestinian financial center of gravity in Gaza where it was based from 1994-2001. Though this would call for new Palestinian power-sharing arrangements, there should be no doubt that the Palestinian economy will pay dearly without national unity and sustained efforts to combat geographic fragmentation. The risk of ending up with little more than bantustans, ruled through differential levels of occupation and local authorities, cannot be overemphasized in considering any statehood strategy. The economic dimensions of such an outcome would be no less devastating than the process in South Africa where settler colonialism morphed into apartheid.

In response to expected sanctions, the putative state of Palestine, headquartered perhaps in the beachhead afforded by Gaza, would need to plan for alternative arrangements for public finances and external trade. It would have to move away from the failed neoliberal prescriptions of recent PA economic policy.[3] The Gaza Strip has a potentially open border with Egypt, and since 2007 Israel has effectively abandoned application of the customs union, which remains in effect in the West Bank. In Gaza, at least, the direct financial lever of Israeli control of tax revenues need no longer be a sword held over the Palestinian public purse.

Even with continued Israeli control of the Palestinian coast and airspace, Gaza's trade with the rest of the world could be re-routed to transit through Egypt and Jordan. Arab financial aid for reconstruction and development could also flow freely and employ a capable but forcibly idled workforce. New proactive monetary arrangements could be considered consistent with a national development vision. Aid could be focused on the most pressing social welfare, infrastructure, and productive sector rehabilitation needs.

A resurgent Gaza, cushioned by some degree of economic predictability in the West Bank, could serve as the nucleus of a *developmental* state of Palestine, economically integrated with its Arab hinterland and enjoying a tentative degree of real sovereignty. While a state of Palestine might be able to carve out some independent security, political, and economic policy space in the Gaza Strip, the fate of the occupied West Bank cannot be dealt with in isolation, as colonial policy might have it.

It would be wholly consistent with the principle of going to the UN that the administration of Palestinian public finances, security, and other services currently delivered by the PA in the West Bank territory still controlled by Israel, be assumed by an international trusteeship, in close consultation with the PLO, until it was freed of occupation. In such an eventuality, the Protocol on Economic Relations, in place since 1994, could be administered by the international trustees along with technical departments run by current PA staff. The same local authorities and bureaucracy could provide social services and public utilities.

This would constitute a transformed landscape. It is wishful thinking perhaps. Yet, this vision allows for peaceful progress towards achieving Palestinian rights while minimizing reversal of Palestinian institutional and diplomatic achievements of the past decades.

As elsewhere in the region, Palestinian youth are losing trust in the PLO and its aging leaders. The recent rumblings of a Palestinian social movement indicate that many have also lost respect for the judgment and wisdom of governing elites. Combined with the tensions arising from the growing nonviolent popular struggle against prolonged Israeli occupation, and its latest stage of boycott, disinvestment, and sanctions, this makes for a potent brew indeed.

A reformed and accountable PLO, freed of the burden of directly administering the occupied West Bank, would have to be prepared for long-term, peaceful, mass mobilization. It should be inspired by a new model of growth with equity emanating from Gaza and echoing the changes ongoing in the region. Building a Palestinian developmental state calls for more than technical solutions and indeed foresees a societal transformation no less significant than that of the Arab Spring.

If the state-recognition bid at the UN is considered to be such a threat to the "peace process," then it is time for the international community to offer something new instead of donor-driven economic prosperity within West Bank bubbles. This will require an end to diehard habits of blindly supporting occupation while simultaneously throwing aid at the Palestinians to keep them quiescent—economic peace indeed! Regrettably, the most enduring accomplishment of the peace process, launched twenty years ago in Madrid, has been expanded Israeli settlement and prolonged occupation. Those opposed to peaceful diplomatic and legal initiatives should offer a meaningful and effective vision for Palestinian freedom and sovereignty that delivers an end to occupation and not yet another road map to nowhere.

Assuming this sea change does not occur, the Palestinian people should be prepared to respond proactively to sanctions through a sustained campaign to achieve self-determination. Its contentious legal and political implications aside, the state-recognition bid at its core is a cry for help from a people who have for too long been wandering through a Kafkaesque landscape of broken promises, fragmented leadership, and seemingly eternal statelessness. The Palestinian national movement has tried everything, and yet has not been able to fulfill its promise of liberating the land and the people, neither for Palestinians living as "citizens" without citizenship under Israeli rule nor for those refugees awaiting return from their diasporas.

So let the process of national liberation resume, and may a thousand Palestinian flowers bloom, maybe even into a Palestinian Spring.

12 September 2011

---

[1] "Report on UNCTAD Assistance to the Palestinian People: Developments in the Economy of the Occupied Palestinian Territory" (United Nations Conference of Trade and Development, July 2011), http://unctad.org/en/docs/tdb58d4_en.pdf.

[2] Raja Khalidi, "Reshaping Palestinian Economic Policy Discourse: Putting the Development Horse before the Governance Cart," *Journal of Palestine Studies* 34, no. 3 (2005): 77–87.

[3] Raja Khalidi and Sobhi Samour, "Neoliberalism as Liberation: The Statehood Program and the Remaking of the Palestinian National Movement," *Journal of Palestine Studies* 40, no. 2 (2011): 6–25.

Palestine at the UN . . . Again

O.I.L. Editors (Noura Erakat, Lisa Hajjar, Mouin Rabbani, Sherene Seikaly, Max Ajl)

Just about ninety minutes ago, Mahmoud Abbas, president of the Palestine Liberation Organization and the Palestinian Authority, posed the perennial Palestinian question to the delegations assembled in New York: Is there one people too many or one state too few?

For the past two decades, bilateral negotiations have quarantined a matter of broad international concern and consequence. Under the veneer of the "peace process," Israel has consolidated its occupation and escalated its colonial settlement expansion. The forced population-transfer of Palestinian civilians has continued unabated under the weight of the Israeli imperative of creating facts on the ground. Rather than challenge those policies on behalf of the Palestinians it purports to represent, for the past twenty years the Palestinian leadership has succumbed to US pressure. The PA has muted its public protest and international advocacy against Israeli policies in exchange for the promise of a better negotiation position.

Abbas's speech today signaled that that policy has proven ineffective and must come to an end. It was an attempt to move the conflict out of the dark and hushed corners of bilateralism to the stage of multilateral strategies.

Several days ago President Obama gave as clear a response as any American president has ever provided to this question: The Palestinians will remain an occupied, dispossessed, and stateless people unless and until Israel chooses otherwise, and the United States will use all of its resources, and any means necessary, at any cost, to ensure that Israel remains in perennial control of the Palestinian people.

Today, the General Assembly, with its repeated applause and standing ovations during Abbas's address, gave a very different answer to this question. More importantly, it gave the definitive lie to the proposition that Washington's views on the Israeli-Palestinian conflict are in any way representative of the international community. For today it was the international community itself, in the most visible manner possible, expressing its views. These comprise a vision of

Israeli-Palestinian peace on the basis of Palestinian statehood and self-determination that is for all intents and purposes diametrically opposite to the agenda emanating from Washington. Indeed, the international community demonstrated that it claps and cheers to a rather different tune than does the US Congress.

The Palestinian priority must now be to work systematically and ceaselessly toward the internationalization of the Palestine question, in all of its dimensions, and end the American monopoly on Middle East diplomacy once and for all. Because the American role is hopelessly compromised to the point of being politically and morally bankrupt, and its record is one of systematic failure.

For Palestinians, this is the only meaningful path towards self-determination.

Words of course do not amount to deeds and it is yet to be seen whether the Palestinian leadership intends to pursue the internationalization of the Palestinian struggle beyond the proceedings of the General Assembly's 66th session. If so, next steps will include the inclusion of the Palestinian national body in representative elections, meaningful reconciliation with Hamas, and a diplomatic marathon intended to encourage compliance with the ICJ's 2004 Advisory Opinion on the wall and making actionable the recommendations enumerated by the fact-finding mission to Gaza.

In the meantime, in drawing on the words of Mahmoud Darwish and the legacy of the PLO's liberation struggle, Abbas's words of "Enough, Enough, Enough" reminded us of a pre-Oslo moment.

On Netanyahu's Speech

Israeli Prime Minister Benjamin Netanyahu's speech demonstrated precisely why Palestinians need to internationalize their cause and definitively break away from bilateral negotiations under unilateral American custodianship.

Consider Netanyahu's call for negotiations without pre-conditions. In practice this means not a single right accorded to the Palestinian people by the United Nations and international law forms a relevant basis for the resolution of the conflict. At the same time, Israel—several decades after negotiations have commenced—is free to raise entirely new and outrageous demands, in this case recognition of Israel as a Jewish state, as pre-requisites for agreement. If the only thing he has to offer in 2011 is negotiations without preconditions, we can reasonably assume his successor will be making a similar plea in 3050.

Rather than endorse or even acknowledge the will of the international community as repeatedly proclaimed in United Nations resolutions, Netanyahu attacked the international consensus in a pitiful display of demagoguery: the Gaza Strip enjoys total freedom, settlements are so irrelevant they form not even a nuisance, and Palestine is and has always been the exclusive preserve of his people. And to prove it all, he found a ring with his name on it. As might be expected, those who even slightly demur from this patently nonsensical narrative were denounced as Nazis determined to exterminate the Jews.

Once again proclaiming the theory that attempts to delegitimize either Israel or its occupation form the leading threat to international peace and security, Netanyahu lost no opportunity to delegitimize the Palestinians, their rights and aspirations, and did so with a characteristic display of vulgarity. Netanyahu lecturing and hectoring about Israel's right to forever control the destiny of the Palestinian people admittedly produces ecstatic responses in the US Congress. As we saw today, however, the international community is much less impressed by such rhetoric.

23 September 2011

Abbas's Next Move

Mouin Rabbani

Mahmoud Abbas's address to the United Nations General Assembly on 23 September 2011 fell considerably short of Yasser Arafat's electrifying 1974 speech from the same podium. Nor did it compare with Haidar Abdul Shafi's dignified—and unanswerable—call for justice at the 1991 Madrid Peace Conference. Yet it may come to be seen as a historic turning point in the fortunes of the Palestinian people.

Abbas's agenda was transparent. He was sending the Americans a message: grow a spine, stop appeasing Israel, and launch credible negotiations—because if you do not, my next failure will be my last. There are several problems with his approach. For one, the so-called peace process is working precisely as designed, to give political cover to Israeli colonization and maintain America's diplomatic monopoly. Second, the United States has become even more extreme than Israel. Obama's speech delighted Avigdor Lieberman but was denounced by American politicians as a betrayal of Israel. Third, there is nothing to negotiate about with Israel's current rulers, who refuse even to acknowledge the occupation, let alone commit to ending it.

That the Palestinian application for full membership of the UN is certain to fail, thanks to the US, is neither here nor there. The point, rather, is that the Palestinians have taken the essential first step towards internationalizing their struggle and reviving the rights codified in UN resolutions and international law as the framework for resolving the conflict. With Washington so out of step with the rest of the world, it is imperative for the Palestinians to break free of the American orbit.

In its most recent maneuver, Washington sank the Quartet's attempts to devise a framework for renewed negotiations by insisting that they begin without preconditions (such as a settlement freeze) and that the Palestinians submit to Netanyahu's demand that they recognize Israel as a Jewish state. With countries such as Holland blocking an EU consensus that deviates from Israel's position, Europe, too, is in no position to offer Abbas a dignified path back to negotiations.

If Abbas cannot backtrack and survive, he also cannot remain still for long and remain in place. There are growing signs that Palestinians will not tolerate

Oslo for much longer. In practice this means that Abbas—or, should he prove unable or unwilling, his successor—has no choice but further initiatives toward the internationalization of the Palestine question.

Internationalization can only be part of a new Palestinian strategy, however. There is a need, too, for real inter-Palestinian reconciliation, leading to a rejuvenated national movement in which all constituencies are properly represented. Palestinians must also break free of the notion that inalienable rights have somehow to be earned or negotiated, or obtained through collaboration with an occupier. And while it would be foolish for the Palestinians to renounce their right to defend themselves with armed force, they should unambiguously commit to the principles of warfare laid down in international law. Perhaps more to the point, present circumstances suggest Palestinians can achieve more, and more rapidly, through a combination of popular mobilization, legal and political advocacy, and formal and popular international solidarity than through armed struggle.

Apart from the almost complete absence of preparatory dialogue and consensus, many of the objections Palestinians have raised to the UN initiative do not make much sense: fears that UN membership would somehow dilute either the representational claims of the PLO or refugee rights were misplaced for the simple reason that the application never had a chance of success to begin with. Such criticisms made even less sense when the posited alternatives were to remain mired in Oslo or participate in the Boycott, Divestment and Sanctions movement (BDS). BDS is a tactic rather than a national program, and its sponsors and activists are no substitute for a national movement in urgent need of rejuvenation.

More coherent are the objections raised by advocates of a one-state solution, for the simple reason that the international consensus and recognized rights of the Palestinian people point inevitably towards a two-state approach. In this respect, those promoting a one-state framework in response to Israel's deepening colonization of the occupied territories have yet to explain how failure to overcome the lesser challenge of ending the 1967 occupation justifies the exponentially more ambitious objective of a secular democratic state throughout historic Palestine. For the moment, however, arguments about the relative merits of a one or two-state solution bring to mind a convict the night before his execution agonizing over which pension plan to join.

27 September 2011

[Originally published in the London Review of Books*]*

Is There a Palestinian Strategy?

Salim Tamari

A frequently asked question following the Arab Spring rebellions was why were the Palestinians left out? Why did they not join their Tunisian, Egyptian, Yemeni compatriots, and other Arab youth in seeking regime change? Why were there no reenactments of the actions of the first intifada of 1987, or of the second intifada of 2000?

The short answer is that there was indeed a rebellion that went substantially unnoticed in the midst of neighboring Arab uprisings. Palestinian youth throughout the early spring of 2011 moved collectively in two directions. They occupied public squares in Nablus, Ramallah, Hebron, Jenin, and Gaza demanding an end to the division between Gaza and the West Bank, and demanding the reconciliation of the two parts of the national movement, Fateh and Hamas. They also moved in successive waves to confront settlers and soldiers in key areas throughout the cities of the West Bank and in the heart of Jerusalem.

But the major question remains unanswered because these protest groups do not, and did not then, amount to a mass movement and have in fact occurred in the context of a relative quietism, if not complacency, among the majority of Palestinians. Nor did they put forth any demand to bring down the government (*isqat al-nizam*) or even a regime change. It seems to me most Palestinians realize that both Haniyeh and Abbas (as well as Hamas and Fateh) are themselves hostages of the Israeli regime of occupation, which they see as their main protagonist and tormentor.

There were, in fact, several proposals voiced in the local press. Some of them were coming from within the ranks of the Fateh Revolutionary Council calling for the dissolution of the PNA, and the transfer of power to the Israelis—thus "unmasking the colonial nature of Israeli control" as many delegates put it, as well as highlighting the emasculated capacities of the Palestinian Authority, and its ability to govern. What undermined this proposal were two factors—one was the fear that some local potentate, including some figures from within the national movement, would step forward and fill in the vacuum on behalf of the

Israelis leading to a process of Somalization of the Palestinian territories. This concern echoed similar events in 1988-1990 when the Village Leagues became local surrogates of Israeli power prior to the Oslo Agreement. Within the ranks of Fateh, secondly, fears were expressed that the Hamas leadership might see the proposal for dismantling the authority as a failure, not of the PNA but of the Fateh leadership, and therefore an invitation for them to govern, as the "legitimately elected" party.

At the heart of this dilemma, and the failure of a resistant strategy, lies a major consequence of the Oslo Accords—namely, the successful redeployment of the Israeli military government and the Israeli army and their relocation from inside the urban centers of Palestine, to peripheral nodes of control—creating at the seams a formidable network of bypass roads, checkpoints, and the wall of separation. Within this network of control emerged the Palestinian Authority in 1996, as the visible but non-sovereign surrogate power. Thus, unlike the situation during the first intifada, where civil disobedience was successfully directed at the occupation regime and its infrastructure, the new system of control—ushered in since 1994—is insular and hidden. It is circumvented by a continued regime of indirect occupation and masked by the security apparatus of the PNA. The hands of Israel shall be felt, but not seen, as Moshe Dayan was fond of saying when he was defense minister.

Having realized these constraints and limitations, Palestinians living in the OPT also understand that a frontal confrontation with the army and the settlers would result in massive losses, without achieving any tangible results, thus leading to a situation where their resources have been depleted. This explains how the demands for regime change in Palestine were paralyzed by the absence of a meaningful alternative. And that is why many people, outside the PA and within it, came to expect deliverance from external factors rather than from popular action.

But the external elements which the PLO and the PA (and in a different setting, within the Hamas government in Gaza) had depended on have proven to be problematic. Both the Quartet and the United States have demonstrated time and again that they are unwilling and/or unable to break the political stalemate by insisting on "continued negotiations" between Palestinians and Israelis as a key platform for ending the deadlock. Continued and sustained negotiations became a hollow formula, now an American mantra, even when it was clear that Israel used the negotiations as a cover for consolidating the building and extension of settlements.

An astonishing, and little noticed, news item appeared in mid-October just before the UNESCO vote in which the United States warned Israel against the continuation of building a new settlement extension, Gilo, south of Jerusalem. Such a move, the US ambassador asserted, "would harm US efforts to thwart the Palestinian bid for statehood at the United Nations." This line was enunciated in a meeting a week earlier between US Envoy to Israel Dan Shapiro and Interior Minister Eli Yishai. (Note that the message of the US administration is communicated between the US ambassador and the Israeli ministry of interior—not between the American envoy and the PM or the foreign minister, as is normal in state to state relations).

The Jerusalem District Planning Committee, according to *Haaretz*, announced at the end of September that it would approve the construction of 1,100 new housing units in Gilo, despite US objections concerning any work that would expand the neighborhood further beyond the Green Line. The purpose of these expansions was to seal the last remaining gap which connects greater Jerusalem to the Arab areas in the West Bank.

What is striking about this statement is not US objection to the construction, but the rationale it brought against it. Namely, that it would undermine US efforts to thwart the bid for statehood at the UN Security Council. Thus, under the Obama administration the United States has culminated a progressive shift in its Middle East policy, from one of mediating the Arab-Israeli conflict (at the Madrid Peace Conference), beginning with a call of return to the 1967 borders (UNSC Resolution 242); to calling settlement activity as being contrary to a peaceful resolution of the conflict; to settlements being "unhelpful," and now to settlement expansion as undermining the strategy to stop the Palestinian bid for statehood, in favor of "direct negotiations between the two parties."

On the Israeli side the objective has been rather consistent. It was, in effect, to create irreversible facts on the ground through re-drawing boundaries, zoning laws, categories of residency, and the physical movement of (Jewish) communities from Israel and abroad in order to create and buttress new settlements. The idea was to make any return to the 1967 boundaries physically impossible and politically unfeasible. This is a strategy of preemption that has been eminently successful and was able to impose a fait accompli on the Palestinian people, with faint verbal protestations from the Europeans and the United States. What is worse is that it succeeded in producing a colluding connivance from the Clinton administration and all successive US administrations since "it is no longer practical to go back to the June 1967 borders."

It was this (belated) realization that the American position is a de facto endorsement of Israeli preemptive strategies that drove the Palestinian leadership, this September, to seek international redress at the UN in its bid for statehood admission. The move was seen as necessary to signal a shift from a strategy of dependence on American and European mediation, even though the chance of success for this bid is very slim. This is due to Palestine's inability to muster the essential nine nation support and because of the inevitable American veto if such support is garnered. It is also supplemented by the fact that the European relative autonomy from American policy is not leading anywhere. The reasons stem from the inability of the EU to present a united foreign policy and the subordination of the Quartet, and its mediator Tony Blair—in Palestinian eyes—to US and Israeli diktat.

Against these conditions we witness new regional conditions that accompanied the Arab rebellions of this spring. Those include:

- A new energized, but yet not stabilized Egyptian regime that is bound to lift the embargo against Gaza, and most likely to bring to an end the isolation of the Hamas Government. This is offset by the decline of Syria as a logistic asset and patron of the Hamas leadership in Damascus.

- The emergence of Turkey as a new regional economic power and political arbiter, drawing on its Ottoman heritage, who openly talks about a new Middle East that does not tolerate Israel's continued intransigence. Despite the Mavi Marmara incident, we should not discount Turkey's ability to continue as a mediating force in future negotiations with Israel. The AKP, and Recep Tayyip Erdogan himself, managed to placate the nationalist groups and anger the Muslim Brothers at the same time by referring to the congruence of Islam and secularism, during Erdogan's October visit to Cairo.

- We should add to this the continued and significant differentiation within the European community on the need for intervention; with France, Spain, and Belgium (but not Sweden anymore) leading the pro-Palestinian forces, and Holland, Britain, and the Eastern Europeans veering towards the Israelis. Significantly, Germany and Italy have been vacillating on which role to play.

- Finally the UNESCO vote, in early November, which brought in the UN as a significant arena in the struggle for Palestine, one which can play a crucial factor in mobilizing regional, European, and international actors (some of whom possess critical clout with Israel) for intervention, and for creating an alternative to the hegemonic role of the UN and the paralyzed role of the Quartet.

These are the elements of the new regional forces, signifying the need for a new Palestinian strategy that is not dependent on the Quartet—or at least not dependent on the American-European initiatives within the Quartet.

But what would be an alternative strategy—if there is one—in the face of these overwhelming odds?

It is clear that Palestinians cannot produce miracles, and that the objective situation in the world today is lopsided against Palestinian aspirations. There are built-in structural factors that mitigate against bringing in an early Israeli withdrawal. Most critical assessments have been referring to the crisis of leadership—one that is rooted in factionalist politics, suffering from endemic corruption, and unaware of its own impotence. Yet, even though we are witnessing a crisis of leadership in Palestine, it is important to realize that the weakness of the leadership is the product, not the cause of, these structural impediments.

To the extent that the Arab rebellions have triggered critical thinking about alternate strategies, both inside the country and in exile, this reflection is creating a new momentum with several trajectories. These trajectories, listed here at random, are obviously being led by various Palestinian groups, sometimes at odd with each other, and encompassing the PNA and its adversaries:

- The need for reconciliation and unity between Gaza and the West Bank, and between Fateh and Hamas—as a condition to resolve the issue of representation—either through elections or through a coalition government.

- There is a consensus on the futility of continued dependence on American mediation of the conflict, and the need to pursue their case within an international context that includes formal UN institutions, as well as seeking strategic alliances with key European states such as Spain, Belgium, and France.

- There is an emergent strategy of confrontation with the settlements and settlers, against the building of the wall and for a sustained struggle against the land grab policies of the Israeli government. These struggles are taking place on a daily basis in Bil'in, in Qalandia, in Budrus, in Sheikh Jarrah, in Nabi Saleh, and in several other nodes of defiance. They belong to a movement that has been non-violent, focused, and sustained. Its success, despite the campaign of vilification against the International Solidarity Movement and other international and Jewish participants in it, has been largely due to its non-violent tactics. It effectively contains community activists, villagers, and international supporters. It brought international attention to the predicament of Palestinians under occupation and highlighted the centrality of the land question in this struggle. This confrontational strategy, and its significant political results, should be compared to the futile and counter productive use of unguided rockets in Gaza against Israeli targets.

- A significant dimension in this new strategy is the international campaign for boycott and divestment, which highlights the colonial nature of the Israeli regime and draws on a comparison with the apartheid system in South Africa. So far this campaign has had limited success. This is partly because Israel and its allies are able to muster a much more powerful machinery of opposition than apartheid South Africa possessed—and also because the boycott campaign has failed to gain popular support inside Palestine, where the Palestinian economy is heavily dependent on, and is penetrated by, the Israeli market and Israeli commodities.

Finally, Palestinians realize that their protagonists are powerful and the system of occupation is formidable, but not invincible. Their political objectives require a policy of protracted struggle in which survival, resilience, and the building of local institutions of sustenance are crucial. In many ways this period recalls the conditions that sustained the first intifada, both in tactics and objectives, despite the changed circumstances.

The problem today is that these types of struggles, diplomatic and activist-based, are undertaken by various segments of political currents and are often (falsely) portrayed as exclusive of each other. For example, there is a tendency to portray the international campaign for UN recognition in terms of an outdated negotiations strategy, and that the boycott campaign is predicated on seeking the creation of a single electoral solution for the Palestinian-Israeli conflict. Either you negotiate or your fight has been a recent posture. Either you struggle for a single all-encompassing state in Palestine, or you succumb to a mini-state equivalent to a bantustan status.

These are false alternatives—partly because they are not based on political options that the Palestinians can choose from. If the struggle for statehood within the 1967 borders is becoming increasingly elusive, we need to realize that the elusiveness is due to the manner in which Israeli expropriation of land and building of settlements have eroded territorial contiguity in a future Palestinian entity, and because it undermines the possibility of territorial sovereignty. If this is the case, then the struggle for a single state in historical Palestine is doubly out of reach because it is predicated on the liquidation of the Israeli state and the creation of a new constitutional entity with a supranational character.

We should ultimately learn to combine modes of struggle that are realizable and have international legitimacy. These twin considerations are pivotal, and necessary for the long struggle ahead.

16 January 2012

[This article was originally a transcript for a lecture given at the Palestine Center in Washington, DC on 4 November 2011]

II | International Law and Statehood

Occupation Law and the One-State Reality

Darryl Li

For decades, the international law of occupation—a branch of the laws of war (or "international humanitarian law")—has played a major role in structuring debates around Israel/Palestine. As applied to the West Bank and Gaza Strip, the law of occupation has provided a useful and globally shared set of criteria for analyzing Israel's discriminatory and repressive policies, as well as certain Palestinian actions.

There is perhaps no legal document cited more frequently in debates on Israel/Palestine than the Fourth Geneva Convention, held up by many as a sacred pact of civilization enshrining basic standards of humanity in wartime. But as the impossibility of partition (the so-called "two-state solution") as a viable way to end the conflict becomes ever-clearer, it is long past the time to grapple with how the law of occupation can also hamper collective thinking and action.

For over forty years, ten million people between the Jordan River and the Mediterranean Sea have lived under a single segregated political regime—the State of Israel. Occupation law is not merely an inadequate tool for analyzing this regime; it can also help legitimize the very spatial arrangements upon which it depends.

A Law of Otherness

Since 1967, the international community has demanded that Israel apply the law of occupation to the West Bank and Gaza Strip and has condemned its many violations of that law. The law of occupation—as embodied primarily in the Fourth Geneva Convention (1949) and the Hague Regulations (1907)—provides a set of standards governing a state's conduct when, due to an armed conflict, it finds itself in control of territory other than its own. These standards are generally more detailed and theoretically more robust in enforcement than similar provisions in international human rights conventions. Designed to balance the security of the occupying power against the rights of the occupied population, they shape public debates by enunciating basic ground rules, such as the well-known prohibitions on torture, collective punishment, and destruction of property without military necessity. These rules impose duties on states; some of them also impose responsibility on individuals when violated (such violations are known as war crimes).

Since the eruption of the first intifada in 1987 placed the West Bank and Gaza Strip at the center of the Palestinian struggle, much of the diplomacy, activism, and scholarship related to the conflict has revolved around three questions: to what extent should the law of occupation apply? Do the acts of Israel or others comply with this framework? And how can this framework be implemented or enforced? Instead of revisiting these old debates, let us re-examine the assumptions behind the consensus position of the international community upon which Palestinians and their allies have relied.

Seizing territories in wartime is not illegal in itself, but modern international law forbids their unilateral annexation. Accordingly, the modern law of occupation treats these situations as temporary and seeks to preserve the status quo ante pending a conflict's final resolution through a peace treaty or other political agreement. Consistent with this logic is the Fourth Geneva Convention's absolute ban on colonizing occupied territories ("settlements"). This assumption of "temporariness" obviously falls apart in the Israel/Palestine case: not only because the occupation has continued for so long, but because it involves a state committed to the demographic transformation of these territories.

It is no secret that respect for occupation law in Israel/Palestine is in short supply. But it is important to draw attention to two crucial assumptions implicitly embedded in the *demand* to apply occupation law in this case, assumptions that themselves perform political work even when the demand itself is not heeded; assumptions whose consequences we must reckon with.

The first assumption is that the State of Israel is an international legal entity delineated by the Green Line boundary that existed until 1967, distinct from the West Bank and Gaza Strip.[1] The second is that Israel at most owes the inhabitants of these territories a kind of basic normality: providing for their humanitarian needs and allowing normal commerce to the extent possible, but without any specific *political* relationship or responsibility to them. Unilateral annexation, and therefore citizenship, is off the table. Let us call these assumptions of otherness: otherness of the land, otherness of the people. Together, they reproduce the idea that the West Bank and Gaza Strip and their inhabitants are outside of, distinct from, and not part of Israel.

Occupation law does not require either of these two propositions, but its widespread use as an analytical framework and normative model undeniably helps normalize them. The demand that Israel stop settlements or the separation barrier *because occupation law says so* cannot be easily separated from occupation law's framing principles of temporariness and its assumptions of otherness. One reason why occupation law enjoys widespread appeal—why it can provide a shared language that Palestinian nationalists, liberal Zionists, and the "international community" alike can employ—is because its implementation would be consistent with the so-called "two-state solution" to the conflict. Indeed, in light of occupation law's ban on colonization, one can argue that its implementation is crucial for ensuring the viability of any Palestinian state in the West Bank and Gaza Strip.

Partitioning the Imagination

Occupation law's assumptions of otherness, premised on a simple dichotomy between occupied territory and occupying states, are not particularly helpful in grasping a basic fact: since the 1967 War, the territory of the British Mandate of Palestine has been ruled by a single supreme authority. The Green Line has defined the state of Israel for less than one-third of its lifetime (1949-1967). Meanwhile, it has constructed a complex set of political, legal, economic, and social relationships that have essentially dissolved the West Bank as a coherent entity and converted the Gaza Strip into a large-scale holding pen for a quarter of the country's indigenous population.

That this regime discriminates between its inhabitants is well-known, favoring Jews, whether they live inside the Green Line or outside of it, whether they are from the country or not. But equally important to maintaining this privilege is segregation amongst non-Jews, who are divided into various categories according to a spatial logic.[2] Those inside the Green Line may, at most, hold Israeli citizenship (*ezrahut*) with some formal rights, while lacking the true inclusion that comes with possessing Jewish nationality (*leom*). Next come residents of occupied Jerusalem, who have mobility without citizenship, followed by West Bank residents who have neither, and then finally Gazans at the bottom of the ladder. Refugees outside the state, of course, enjoy no share in this polity at all.

While the law of occupation does not require partition as a political solution, it does contribute to a partitioned understanding and analysis of this regime. Occupation law's assumption of the otherness of the occupied territory encourages us to treat pre-1967 Israel as a given while limiting attention to settlements and various repressive practices only as so many different "violations." Even when such violations are treated as systematic, they are detached from the larger context. They focus solely on only the twenty-two percent of the country comprised of the West Bank and Gaza Strip, leaving parallel situations inside the Green Line to be analyzed separately as "domestic" problems under international human rights law.

At the same time, the otherness of the occupied population is not only unquestioned and left to the realm of "political negotiations," it is also a crucial feature of this regime. Israel persists in the notion that there is a Jewish and democratic majority inside the state, even as the state's refusal to define its boundaries renders the very idea of "insideness" inherently unstable. Annexing the territories and their populations would destroy this illusion. Thus, occupation law, with its concomitant strictures against annexation, is a useful legal placeholder once divested of any real ability to constrain colonization. Contrary to what some may believe, Israel has never rejected occupation law wholesale; right-wing ideologues may assail it as some kind of security threat, but Israel's military lawyers and courts continue to selectively rely on occupation law when it suits their purposes.

This is also why partisans of Israel display incredible bad faith when they rhetorically demand to know why Tibet, Kashmir, or Chechnya are not considered occupied territories. China, India, and Russia may be just as or even more repressive than Israel, but they at least extend citizenship to the populations involved and pretend to accept their equality. And that is the *last* thing Israel wants to do. Occupation law may make many demands on a state to respect certain basic rights of civilians. But the one thing that it does not demand—and that it never could demand—is the extension of equal citizenship to occupied populations.

Sovereign Voids and Native Administration

The segregated regime described above is constantly evolving through "facts on the ground" that reshape lived space, such as the separation barrier, checkpoints and roadblocks, and new roads and colonies. In order to clarify how occupation law's basic assumptions can facilitate this process, let us compare Israel's policies towards native self-administration with the South African bantustan experiment.

For the better part of the last two decades, Israel has relied for native management in significant part on the Palestinian National Authority (PNA), a self-rule body that exists in dozens of disconnected enclaves run by Fateh in the West Bank and Hamas in the Gaza Strip. The PNA has been widely criticized for legitimizing and extending the occupation: it assumes the burden of caring for natives, while Israel maintains the ultimate ability to dictate their conditions of life while colonizing as it wishes. Israel maximizes its control while minimizing its responsibility. At the same time, the Palestinians are stuck with maximum responsibility and minimum control: they are expected to "crack down on terrorism" in the absence of any political solution or sufficient rudiments of statehood.

Many critics have compared the PNA to the bantustans in South Africa. The apartheid regime sought to deflect international criticism of white minority rule by concentrating much of the native population into disconnected patches of territory, and then declaring some of them to be independent sovereign states. Derisively called "bantustans," these enclaves were tiny, often non-contiguous, and entirely dependent on the apartheid regime, much like the PNA. However, the bantustans largely failed to gain international recognition as states—although Israel and Taiwan supported them through security, political, and trade ties.

The scattered areas of PNA jurisdiction and the bantustans may share many similarities, but there is a crucial difference from the standpoint of international law (to say nothing of their contrasting approaches to the problem of native labor). In South Africa, the state was attempting to alienate parts of its own sovereign territory and, more egregiously, to denationalize its own subjects. International law has spent so much time dealing with states *claiming* territory that it was unclear how it should even approach states trying to unilaterally *rid themselves* of territory, as South Africa attempted to do. It became apparent that the regime could not simply create "sovereign voids" in its own territory; it had to convince other states to step forward and affirmatively recognize the bantustans as independent. Otherwise, the default option was that South Africa maintained its responsibility for those areas and their inhabitants, which is exactly what happened.

Israel/Palestine is different from the South Africa case. Thanks to occupation law's assumption of otherness, classifying the Gaza Strip and West Bank as occupied territories means that by definition they were not part of Israel to begin with. Moreover, they have the unique status of *already* being "sovereign voids" in the sense that they did not transition from their status as colonial territories to belonging to any recognized nation-state.

From this starting point, it is far easier to relieve oneself of responsibility for resolving the political status of natives. South Africa faced widespread criticism for attempting to denationalize its own citizens. In contrast, Israel is not legally required to confer citizenship to occupied populations in the first place, or provide them with any political status whatsoever.

Territorially, South Africa needed states to recognize the bantustans, and none did so. But in Israel/Palestine, we instead face the more ambiguous legal question of whether a territory is occupied, a question that turns on factual analysis instead of formal declarations. Israel's 2005 "disengagement" from the Gaza Strip gave rise to a set of debates as to the status of the territory, even though it continued to exercise authority there through regular ground incursions, management of crucial infrastructure and administrative tasks, and control over borders and airspace. Although Israel did not convince the world that the occupation had ended, it created sufficient doubt and confusion to provide political cover for portraying its new relationship with the Gaza Strip as one of parity, between two neighboring states trading rocket and artillery fire. Israel reclassified the Gaza Strip from something like an occupied territory to a "hostile territory" with an even lower level of legal restraint.[3] This helped legitimize a massive escalation of repression, including the tightening of the siege and the 2008-2009 onslaught.

In terms of legitimizing discrimination and conferring discretion to the state, Israel has achieved far more than the apartheid regime could have hoped to accomplish. But all of these rearrangements in the structure of the occupation have distracted from a much more important question. That is the question of why the people of Beit Hanoun in the northern Gaza Strip and Sderot in southern Israel should live as neighbors under the same supreme authority for over four decades, but with entirely different sets of rights.

Conclusion: At the Frontiers of Law

The purpose of this essay is not to attack occupation law, nor those who have devoted efforts to understanding and upholding it. The benefits and importance of this body of law are undeniable, and as someone who has worked over the past decade for various human rights groups on this issue I have no interest in repudiating it. But serious questions remain as to whether occupation law—historically developed and applied mainly around Europe (including parts of the Ottoman Empire such as Bosnia-Herzegovina and Egypt)—is an appropriate tool for facing the challenge of contemporary settler colonialism.

And this challenge is not merely a theoretical one. After decades of fruitless negotiations and unceasing colonization, there is a growing awareness of the limitations of partition in addressing the Israel/Palestine conflict. Some celebrate this as a step towards building a single non-colonial state for all of its citizens. Others mourn this development, either because they wish to preserve the Zionist project or because they fear that the demise of the partition option will only herald more bloodshed and suffering without respite. My point here is not to argue that the end of partition is a good thing or a bad thing. My point is that as partition recedes as a viable option, the evolving situation on the ground raises difficult legal questions that require sustained consideration.

Israel has skillfully deployed multiple juridical categories while physically reshaping the territories and populations under its control. Grappling with this situation requires more than reliance on static categories such as those of occupation law, or other approaches described as "apolitical" or technocratic. Instead, jurists, legal scholars, and activists would be well-served to also engage core questions of political belonging, responsibility, and equality in a manner that creatively engages the evolving spatial dynamics of this regime. In exploring the limitations and problems of occupation law, this essay is an attempt to join this difficult but necessary conversation.

2 August 2011

[This essay is based on a lecture delivered at the University of Palestine Law Faculty in Gaza, 2 July 2011]

---

[1] There are of course problems with treating the Green Line as an international boundary, but I think this is a reasonable statement of mainstream assumptions, for better or worse.

[2] Discrimination between Jews is also important but beyond the scope of this essay, as are the rights of foreigners inside the Green Line.

[3] Avi Issacharoff, Barak Ravid, and Shlomo Shamir, "Cabinet Declares Gaza 'Hostile Territory'," *Haaretz*, http://www.haaretz.com/print-edition/news/cabinet-declares-gaza-hostile-territory-1.229665.

Roundtable on Occupation Law: Part of the Conflict or Part of the Solution?

Noura Erakat, Lisa Hajjar, Dena Qaddumi, Ahmad Barclay, Aslı Bâli, Nimer Sultany, and Darryl Li

Introduction by Noura Erakat

September 2011 marks a historic juncture in the struggle for Palestinian self-determination, as the Palestinian leadership approaches the United Nations with an application for membership into the community of nations as a state. This move is rife with potential implications, including a shift from bilateralism to multilateralism and an insistence on the applicability of international law. At its best, this would signal a welcome move away from the past two decades of bilateral negotiations, which have subjected non-negotiable rights as well as provisions of occupation law to political contestation. However, even this best-case scenario is neither guaranteed, as indicated by the lack of a more robust strategy on the part of the Palestinian leadership, nor necessarily optimal.

In his provocative and lucid piece, "Occupation Law and the One-State Reality," Darryl Li illustrates how occupation law fails to grasp the legal and geographical realities of the Israel-Palestinian conflict and may actually threaten to legitimize the racially segregated and oppressive regime that it currently masks. Li argues that whereas the laws of occupation underscore the possibility of partition and the illusion of separateness, in fact, "for over forty years, ten million people between the Jordan River and the Mediterranean Sea have a single segregated political regime—the State of Israel." Rather than challenge its political dominance and racially-driven policies, occupation law reinforces elusive possibilities of partition at the expense of challenging a legal regime of systemic inequality and domination.

In this roundtable, five scholars respond to Li's article and Li responds in turn. In her contribution, Lisa Hajjar arrives at the same conclusions regarding Israel's singular authority over the lands between the river and the sea as well as occupation law's inefficacy. By using a sociological approach, she argues that the current reality is not a function of law explaining politics but rather that politics explains law. Hajjar scrutinizes the impact of Israeli politics upon the interpretation and applicability of occupation law to the OPT and, more broadly, the conflict. She focuses on the influence of Meir Shamgar, Israel's former military advocate general and chief justice of its supreme court, who shaped Israel's positions on the laws of occupation. Shamgar's work challenged conventional interpretations of the laws of occupation and, as Hajjar puts it, "pioneered the interpretive disconnect between human beings and humanitarian law."

Dena Qaddumi and Ahmad Barclay approach Li's proposition by focusing on geography and spatial realities. They affirm Li's thesis that like occupation discourse, maps of the land also reify and enhance partition's potential. By depicting the Gaza Strip and the West Bank as discrete entitles, maps fail to illustrate the inseparability of settlements from Tel Aviv and Jerusalem. The maps also create a false distinction between Israel's Judaization policies inside the Green Line and outside it. Qaddumi and Barclay offer innovative ways of reading the conflict by subjecting it to what they describe as the "arena of speculation."

Asli Bali takes Li's thesis about the impact of prolonged occupation and proffers a legal equation about the relationship between human rights and humanitarian law. There are two sets of legal regimes that govern the conduct of states and non-state actors: human rights law and humanitarian law. Human rights law is applicable during peacetime and humanitarian law is applicable during wartime—there exists ample scholarly argument that they also coexist. Whereas human rights create a social contract between a state and its inhabitants, humanitarian law is meant to balance an occupier's military needs and an occupied population's humanitarian ones. Humanitarian law regulating occupation is meant to be temporary in nature. So what happens when the occupation is prolonged, as has been in the case of the Palestinian territory? Bali argues that in this case, the occupier's military needs are no longer tenuous because the occupation has become durable. Thus, the "occupied Palestinian population's welfare is insufficiently protected because [the Fourth Geneva

Convention] does not provide for a social contract between them and their de facto government." Accordingly, as an occupation becomes more durable, human rights should be incrementally applied. Ultimately, when the occupation is in fact durable, an occupier's duty under a human rights framework will require the full enfranchisement of the occupied population.

Unlike Li, Hajjar, and Bali, who grapple with legal challenges within a legal framework, Nimer Sultany insists that occupation law's deficiencies are not unintended consequences of the law but rather its predictable outcome. Sultany builds on the work of critical legal scholars who have "long pointed out the dark side of law" as he, in his own words, pleads for disenchantment. By unpacking several categories related to law more broadly, including law and justice, legalism, and legitimation, Sultany demonstrates the incapacity of the law-only approach to adequately treat injustice. He insists that law cannot be separated from politics, nor uncritically associated with justice. Indeed, because "law is not a closed, autonomous system with its own inner morality," Sultany warns that "one should be careful not to conflate the application of law with the approximation of justice." He does not disavow the law altogether but insists that for law to be an effective tool for the oppressed, it must be part of a well-thought out political strategy.

Part I by Lisa Hajjar

The West Bank and the Gaza Strip are the quintessential "hard case" in international humanitarian law (IHL). With the benefit of hindsight, we know that the authors of the 1949 Geneva Conventions were not very good at predicting the future when they promulgated the Fourth Geneva Convention (GCIV) to regulate the governance of territory and populations occupied in war. Rather, they were responding to the treatment—often horrific—of occupied populations and territories during World War II. When that war ended, so did the *military* occupations of foreign countries (as distinguished from continuing colonial occupations which were not addressed by IHL until the 1970s). Recent past experience guided the authors of GCIV, who deemed that military occupations are temporary, that territories conquered during a war cannot be lawfully annexed by the captors, and that wars end.

Yet the West Bank and Gaza have been occupied by Israel since 1967, and the state of (regional) war that contributes to the sustenance of that situation, although only intermittently "hot," is not ending any time soon. Darryl Li's "Occupation Law and the One-State Reality" addresses this situation:

> For over forty years, ten million people between the Jordan River and the Mediterranean Sea have lived under a single segregated political regime—the State of Israel. Occupation law is not merely an inadequate tool for analyzing this regime; it can also help legitimize the very spatial arrangements upon which it depends.

Li's argument, as I understand it, is threefold. First, the longevity of this occupation and the extreme transformations that have occurred since 1967 diminish the utility of GCIV as a framework to resolve the status of the West Bank and Gaza. Second, the Israeli government's disregard for its rules and norms—and the international community's failure or inability to enforce its provisions—has created a de facto "one-state reality." Therefore, third, the attachment to GCIV by scholars and critics of the occupation, which hinges on the dichotomy between "occupied" (West Bank/Gaza) and "unoccupied" (Israel inside the 1949 Green Line) territory, has come to "partition the imagination." His point is that the one-state *reality* begs for an approach that is not contingent on the presumptive temporariness of occupation or the kind of dichotomous "otherness" that undergirds "the law of occupation."

I concur with Li's assessment about the one-state reality and the inadequacy of dichotomous thinking to address the empirical (politico-legal-demographic) complexities among the various categories of people who reside between the Jordan River and the Mediterranean Sea in a structurally unequal relationship (i.e., Jews, Arabs, Druze; citizens, occupied populations; West Bankers, Gazans, East Jerusalemites; settlers, refugees, and so on). There *is* only one state in Israel/Palestine, and that state is Israel.

However, I think that Li, in his effort to think outside of the partitioned-imagination box, attributes to "occupation law" a greater explanatory power for contemporary politics than it merits. He writes:

> Thanks to occupation law's assumption of otherness, classifying the Gaza Strip and West Bank as occupied territories means that by definition they were not part of Israel to begin with. Moreover, they have the unique status of *already* being "sovereign voids" in the

sense that they did not transition from their status as colonial territories to belonging to any recognized nation-state.

I would urge a shift from a law-explains-politics emphasis to the reverse: politics-explains-law. This would provide a different (more sociological) route to get to the same conclusion about the one-state reality and the inefficacy of GCIV in protecting the rights of an occupied Palestinian population, let alone actually bringing about an end to the occupation. (Legally, as Li correctly points out, IHL is entirely silent about the status and rights of Palestinian citizens of Israel). Take, for example, the quote above. I would argue that laws do not assume anything; people do. And what people—that is, empowered people like government officials, lawmakers, and judges—do with those assumptions constitutes "law in action."

Israeli officials have not ignored IHL. On the contrary, the history of Israel's control over the West Bank and Gaza involves a great deal of law in action. These actions are marked by prodigious, decades-long efforts to interpret the meaning and applicability—or, rather, the ostensible inapplicability—of GCIV to Israel's rule in the territories seized in 1967 in order to "legalize" practices like Jewish settlements and collective punishments that defy international consensus. "The law" did not make this happen (nor did law predetermine the outcome of particular and odious Israeli interpretations), people did.

I will illustrate my politics-explains-law point by drawing on the example of Israel's historic engagement with IHL generally and GCIV specifically. This engagement began before the 1967 war and, indeed, anticipated the occupation. The power of the Israeli state, the determination of influential officials, the novelty of the politico-legal status of the West Bank and Gaza, and the incapacity of the international community to head off, let alone reverse, consensus-defying interpretations all contributed to the vast gap between "law in the books" and law in action. The manifestation of this gap is, as Li notes, the one-state reality. But how did we get there?

The fact that the Israeli military court system was established on the third day of the 1967 War illustrates the state's preparedness for occupation. This was one of the first official acts of the new military administration in the conquered West Bank and Gaza. These preparations began in earnest in the early 1960s, spurred by political instability in Jordan in 1963. The planning was informed by Israel's brief occupation of Gaza during the 1956 Suez War, which ended when the United States and the Soviet Union uncharacteristically allied themselves to force a withdrawal back to the 1949 armistice border (i.e., the Green Line).

Meir Shamgar, who served from 1961 to 1968 as Israel's Military Advocate General (MAG, the army's top lawyer), played a leading role in these preparations. He developed courses for officers to train them for the challenges of governing a foreign population, and he created a *Manual for the Military Advocate in Military Government* "a long time before hostilities began." According to Shamgar, this manual included:

> ...a large set of precedents of military government proclamations and orders, vital at the initial stages of military government, as well as detailed legal and organizational instructions and guide-lines. These facilitated, from the outset, the legal and administrative activity of the sections, according to a previously planned scheme.[1]

What kind of reasoning informed this "previously planned scheme?" Long before 1967, Shamgar had conceived that the extension of Israeli control over any additional part of *Eretz Israel* (i.e., the West Bank and Gaza) would not constitute a "foreign occupation" (territorially, that is) because Jews had historic rights in these areas. This was the core of the Revisionist Zionist ideology to which he subscribed. In the *yishuv* era, Shamgar was a member of the Irgun, a radical right-wing Jewish paramilitary organization headed by Menachem Begin. Irgun (like the even more extremist breakaway LEHI/Stern gang) was distinguished from mainstream Zionist organizations by the unwillingness of its members to brook any territorial concession on future Jewish sovereignty over all of *Eretz Israel* and rejection of the policy of (armed) restraint. They used armed violence and terrorism (e.g., the bombing of the King David Hotel in Jerusalem and the massacre of Deir Yassin) to advance their Iron Wall agenda. Shamgar was arrested in 1944 for anti-British activity. The British detained him and other members of the Irgun and LEHI without trial. They then rendered the men to detention in East Africa where they remained until after the establishment of the State of Israel in 1948. The Irgun of the *yishuv* became the core of the Herut Party after independence, which later evolved into the Likud.

Shamgar's record of involvement in a Jewish terrorist organization and his right-wing politics—in a country dominated for decades by the more liberal-Zionist Labor Party—did not inhibit his rise to power. On the contrary, after 1967, Shamgar used his position as a high-ranking policymaker to institute his

Revisionist Zionist views. These became the cornerstone of Israeli doctrine on the legal status of the territories and the Israeli state's rights within them. In 1968, Shamgar became attorney general, then a justice on the Israeli Supreme Court, and finally its chief justice. He played an enormously important and political role in establishing Israel's positions on the "law of occupation."

What were the premises of Shamgar's-cum-Israel's positions on the law of occupation? First, Shamgar reasoned, Israeli control of the West Bank and Gaza would not constitute "an occupation" because the displaced rulers, Jordan and Egypt, were themselves occupiers since the 1948 War. This was premised on the claim that a territory is occupied *only* if it had been part of the sovereign domain of the defeated and expelled state. According to Shamgar's formulation, Israel would not be occupying but "administering" these "disputed" territories whose status was sui generis.[2]

Second, Shamgar contended, GCIV was not applicable to Israel's control of these territories on a de jure basis. The politics of this position was explicit: If Israel were to regard itself as bound by the GCIV, the government would be acknowledging its own status as an "occupant" which would give Jordan and Egypt ex post facto status as displaced sovereigns which they did not have, and would compromise Israel's prospects to claim permanent control to all or part of these areas in the future. The obligations and restrictions of GCIV could be sidestepped by interpreting the Geneva Conventions as applicable *only and exclusively* to High Contracting Parties (i.e., state signatories to this body of IHL). While Jordan, Egypt, and Israel were all parties to the Geneva Conventions, the former two were not sovereign in the areas from which they had been expelled in 1967 and, therefore, GCIV was not binding on the latter, Israel, *in this context*.

Third, Shamgar maintained that while IHL did not apply de jure, the state would abide on a de facto basis with its "humanitarian provisions." Neither Shamgar nor any other Israeli officials ever specified which provisions they regard as humanitarian. Again, the politics of legal interpretation is explicit: the International Committee of the Red Cross (ICRC), official guardian of the Geneva Conventions, regards them—correctly—as humanitarian in their entirety. Shamgar noted but dismissed the ICRC's position:

> This difference of views [between him/Israel and the ICRC] was mainly and primarily of a theoretical nature, because the Israeli Governmental [sic] authorities [i.e., himself] had decided to distinguish a

priori between the formal legal conclusions arising from its approach and the actual observance of the humanitarian provisions of the Convention.[3]

The fourth premise is a particularly vivid example of the kind of hyper-sovereigntist politics that Shamgar-cum-Israel embodies. It is the claim that GCIV could not be binding on Israel even if there was no dispute over the status of the West Bank and Gaza because at least part of the convention constituted "conventional" rather than "customary" international law (the former binding only on signatories, the latter universally applicable). In the Israeli legal system (as in many others), conventional law does not supersede "local" law unless the Israeli Knesset were to enact the convention as domestic legislation or until *the state* recognized that it had ripened into custom. However, this particular position actively (proactively, I would suggest) disregards the fact that there is an international consensus that the Geneva Conventions are customary international law, demonstrated by the fact that every state in the world has signed or acceded to them.

A particular brand of right-wing politics instigated these interpretations of IHL. Similarly, in the aftermath of 9/11, the right-wing politics of officials and lawyers in the Bush administration instigated a pattern of legal interpretation to assert the inapplicability of the Geneva Conventions to the "war on terror." Israeli officials, and more recently American officials, asserted that the statelessness of enemies was a legitimate and valid reason for the state to disregard—that is, to feel unbound by—the rules and norms of IHL.

Israeli officials like Shamgar pioneered the interpretative disconnect between human beings and humanitarian law. Asserting that IHL pertains exclusively to the rights and duties of sovereign states (the High Contracting Party-only position) made it possible to argue that stateless people in militarily conquered areas were not their intended beneficiaries. The politics of interpretation on the legal significance of Palestinian statelessness went like this: Because there never had been an independent, sovereign state of "Palestine," the Palestinian people *could not be* the lawful sovereigns of the West Bank and Gaza because nothing in international law prescribes the recognition of sovereignty to a "non-state," and nothing in law demands the creation of a heretofore nonexistent state in territories seized in war.

It is true, as noted above, that the authors of GCIV did not anticipate a situation like Israel's occupation of the West Bank and Gaza. However, I would stress that it was not "the law of occupation" but the Israeli interpreters (and military, political, and judicial enforcers of their interpretations) that created the rights-violating, highly discriminatory, and unequal one-state reality that prevails today.

Li is absolutely correct that homage to GCIV will not alter the facts on the ground. I agree with his concluding point "that as partition recedes as a viable option, the evolving situation on the ground raises difficult legal questions that require sustained consideration." However, I believe that the rules and norms enshrined in this international law continue to provide an important *tool* (and not just an abstract point of reference) to press an international agenda to try to force the Israeli state to alter the way it rules on both sides of the Green Line.

For it is IHL, above all, that allows us to reject spurious claims that the occupation of Gaza has "ended." It is IHL that allows us to reject the massive use of armed force as a legitimate and legal option in either Gaza or the West Bank *because* they remain occupied territories and therefore Palestinians residing there are, legally, "protected persons." Serious violations of IHL are war crimes which are legally, albeit very imperfectly, prosecutable in foreign court systems. The use of courts and legal processes to punish or restrain state agents and other powerful actors who engage in serious violations of IHL should continue to be the negative/non-violent side of the struggle for Palestinians' rights.

Part II by Ahmad Barclay and Dena Qaddumi

As Darryl Li argues, occupation law has effectively masked the settler colonial origins of the Israeli state as well as encouraging a "partitioning of the imagination" whereby the Green Line divides "Israel" and "Palestine." Allied with notions of a "temporary" occupation, this not only legitimizes an ongoing colonization but also stifles creative, provocative action. As architects and urbanists, our approach is not only to critique the dominant spatial perceptions of Israel/Palestine but also to engage with modes of activism centered on a notion of "spatial resistance."

While the production of spatial perceptions is significant in any context, it is in Israel/Palestine where the transformation of physical space, the consolidation of territory through maps and the translation of space into imagery have been particularly consequential. Further, perceptions are also shaped by a selective absence of information. In 2000, Edward Said described a "censorship of geography"—particularly in the US media—arguing that a lack of territorial context in "the most geographical of conflicts" had allowed the nature of the power relations to be distorted.

However, a sphere of advocacy has emerged in the last decade aiming to challenge this "censorship." Specifically, it seeks to document Israel's spatial control over the West Bank and Gaza Strip. Architect Eyal Weizman's work with B'Tselem has been instrumental in this regard, as they began a process of mapping settlements, checkpoints, restricted roads, and the separation wall.[4] This work has been subsequently developed and reified in the publications of UN-OCHA, which expanded the scope and detail of this mapping work.[5]

While these maps offer a powerful image of Israel's unilateral control over the West Bank and Gaza they also embed and perpetuate the trappings of occupation discourse. They present the West Bank and Gaza as discrete entities, whereby Israel is grayed out or omitted. Such a conceptualization disembodies the spatial logic of the settlements—which function as suburbs of Tel-Aviv and Jerusalem—and separates them from "Judaization" policies within Israel. Crucially, it also reinforces the notion of a Palestinian "national space" confined to the "occupied territories."

Another problem these images create is the perceived solidity of Israel's "matrix of control." A line on a map can emote a permanence that is not indicative of reality. The contours of Areas A, B, and C in the West Bank are an example. These temporary lines—purportedly outlining a defunct Israeli withdrawal plan from the era of the Oslo Accords—have been etched into the Palestinian collective consciousness. Yet these lines have no legal validity or sanctity. The Israeli government operates within a much more fluid reality, continually shaped and re-shaped by "facts on the ground," in which these lines are only one among many pseudo-legal mechanisms for legitimating continued colonization.

Combined, these preconceptions help to reinforce the idea of a truncated Palestinian geography and the perceived "absoluteness" of Israeli power. In reality, the physical manifestations of this power are more crude and ad-hoc than the map would have us believe. In actuality, they are sustained through the continued threat of further dispossession and violence. Yet, as cleverly encapsulated in Suad Amiry's *Nothing to Lose But Your Life*, it is possible to circumvent such physical and psychological obstacles, even if just as a means of survival.

The potentials for transformative agency are perhaps better revealed through an analysis which elevates human geography, rather than one which fetishizes territory, borders, and mechanisms of control. Consider, for instance that more than a million Palestinians remain to the "west" of the Green Line and that the majority of Palestinian refugees—even those in Jordan, Lebanon, and Syria—live within tens of kilometers of their historic sites of dispossession. From this perspective the obsession with drawing neat lines between a future Israel and Palestine is not only irreconcilable but irrelevant. Increasingly, initiatives throughout Israel-Palestine and beyond have attempted to break with this trajectory, expanding the scale of the struggle and shattering dominant spatial perceptions.

The organizers of TEDxRamallah, a cultural initiative that attempted to bridge this fragmented geography, describe how the notion of "Palestine" acted as a key "common denominator." They described the event as "a platform that brings forward the realization that Palestine is a topic that goes beyond a country occupied, and beyond a refugee stranded. It is one that starts apprehending the very essence of Palestinians and Palestine . . . since being Palestinian has no border or nationality."[6] Such a narrative underlines the possibility for Palestinian national aspirations to be defined in "universalist" terms of equality, rights, and shared humanity, rather than simply mirroring the Zionist model of ethnic nationalism. It is also a means to re-energize a geographically fragmented Palestinian diaspora as a stakeholder and a strategic asset in the struggle for justice and self-determination.

On the ground, projects such as Riwaq's 50 Villages transform the built environment to reconstitute a Palestinian civic space. Their strategy is one of collective participation, which harnesses the rehabilitation of historic village centers as a means for socio-economic development, and at the same time challenges the spatial restrictions of Oslo. This strengthens the notion of collective agency and reframes sites of occupation as potential sites of liberation.

In a different vein, DAAR (Decolonizing Architecture Art Residency) adopts the tools of architectural inquiry as a means to challenge and subvert the current spatial reality. In their early projects, DAAR posed the question, "How can Israeli settlements and military bases (the architecture of Israel's colonization in Palestine) be reused, recycled, or re-inhabited by Palestinians, at the moment that it is unplugged from the military/political powers that charge it?"[7] Such a line of questioning explicitly undermines the notion of "facts on the ground," as our conception of permanence is not just physical, but rather is informed by social and political meaning. Moreover, visually articulating the spatial possibilities for reappropriating such material structures opens space for critical debate (what DAAR describe as an "arena of speculation"), neither constrained by nor entirely removed from present realities.

Following a collaboration with DAAR, Zochrot, an Israeli NGO, organized a workshop bringing together Palestinian and Jewish citizens of Israel with the aim of confronting the practical and pragmatic implications of planning the return of refugees. The processes, methodologies, and assumptions in this exploratory initiative are explained in a segment of their periodical *Sedek, A Journal on the Ongoing Nakba,* entitled "Counter-Mapping Return." Through the production of counter-maps, as a means to articulate shared space and alternative realities from those presented in the "official" maps, the workshop represents the beginnings of transforming imagined geographies into reality.

At the time, such a workshop may have seemed fanciful, yet the events of 15 May 2011 seem to have dramatically shifted the horizon of possibility. As Palestinian refugees in Lebanon, Syria, Jordan, Gaza, and the West Bank marched toward their villages of origin, we witnessed a collective agency, which directly challenged the notion of borders, the perceived solidity of maps, and the purported geographical scale of the struggle. It broke through longstanding psychological barriers and asserted the possibility for mass grassroots actions to transcend existing political processes.

We argue that it is in these forms of strategic activism—where weaknesses in the present power structures are exposed, and the lines between spatial intervention and critical imagining are blurred—that alternative spatial futures for Israel-Palestine will emerge.

Part III by Asli Bâli

Darryl Li has made a valuable contribution to debates concerning the application of international humanitarian law in the Israeli-Palestinian context. One of the most vexing aspects of the occupation from the perspective of international law is the tension between two widely held views. One view maintains that the appropriate international framework for understanding the obligations of the Israeli government as the belligerent occupant of the territories it gained control of in 1967 is the Fourth Geneva Convention (GCIV). The other maintains that GCIV was not written to address long-term belligerent occupation on the scale and duration undertaken by Israel and therefore does not provide an adequate legal framework for this context.

The first view, commitment to the applicability of GCIV, has long been an article of faith among international lawyers, particularly those who would resist official Israeli efforts to treat the status of the West Bank and Gaza as "disputed" and who reject Israeli claims that the Geneva Conventions do not apply. (In its advisory opinion on the legality of Israel's West Bank wall, the International Court of Justice rejected the "missing reversioner" theory that undergirds Israel's claim that the status of the territories is sui generis and affirmed the applicability of the Geneva Conventions.) This approach was deemed a necessary international legal protection against any attempt by Israel to claim the *legal* right to either annex or colonize (that is, settle its own population in) the occupied territories. In short, GCIV was deemed not only the appropriate legal framework but also the most *attractive* option for protecting the rights of the Palestinian occupied population.

The second view incorporates a critique of the idea that humanitarian welfare can be adequately protected through the laws of war when long-term occupation would leave millions of civilians subject to foreign military, political, and administrative control. On this account, the occupied Palestinian population's welfare is insufficiently protected because GCIV does not provide for a social contract between them and their de facto government. The tension, then, arises from the fact that the protections afforded to civilians under international humanitarian law may become an obstacle to the meaningful realization of their human rights under conditions of prolonged occupation.

Because occupation was understood by the authors of the 1949 Geneva Conventions to be of a provisional nature (with de jure sovereignty over the territory remaining with its civilian population), the law of occupation was understood as an arrangement to meet temporary needs through a balance of the security interests of the occupier and the basic rights of the occupied. Should occupation become durable, however, that balance may no longer be sufficient to meet even minimum human rights standards. In this sense, the law preserving the de jure sovereignty rights of Palestinians has enabled the de facto quotidian denial of the human rights of that same community. The suffering of Palestinians living under the yoke of Israeli occupation for over forty years bears eloquent (and deeply troubling) witness to the urgent need to resolve this tension.

One set of proposed solutions advocated by some international lawyers relies on the introduction of standards drawn from human rights law into a more demanding and comprehensive law of *long-term* occupation. Under such proposals, the belligerent occupant would assume a greater role in the governance of local affairs than contemplated by GCIV. That role would entail obligations drawn from the (peacetime) human rights regime, such as those related to the protection of human dignity and the rights to education, welfare, health, family, privacy, work, property ownership, freedom of religion, and so on. In other words, a separate and higher standard of obligations would be imposed on belligerents that deliberately prolong their occupation of territories seized in war. The balance between the security interests of the occupier and the human rights of the occupied would shift further and further in the direction of the latter with every additional year of occupation. Taken to its logical conclusion, this solution would eventually result in Li's proposition that the full human rights of the population under occupation in the long-run will require their full enfranchisement.

But this logical conclusion has rarely been articulated, for reasons that are readily apparent. If belligerent occupation becomes permanent and if arguments in defense of human rights eventually require the enfranchisement of the occupied population in the state of the occupier, occupation devolves into annexation. For decades, Palestinians have resisted precisely this outcome—the annexation of the Palestinian territories (or perhaps, more accurately, the West Bank including Jerusalem) to Israel—because they identify such annexation as coterminous with the extinction of their national rights of self-determination and sovereignty and the abandonment of the cause of a Palestinian state. For instance, those on the Palestinian side who argue for a "one-state solution" (reuniting all of the territories of Mandate Palestine under a single sovereign) typically frame their arguments in terms of a united Palestine (albeit democratic and secular) rather than an enlarged Israel. Li's article is refreshing precisely because, through careful analysis of the status quo, he offers an explicit argument for pursuing Palestinian enfranchisement *in Israel* as an alternative to the two-state solution or the conventional framing of the one-state solution.

Li's argument centers on one core insight: The full enfranchisement of Palestinians through the annexation of the Palestinian territories to Israel may represent the only viable means for the realization of Palestinian rights of self-determination, sovereignty, and self-governance. In other words, under present circumstances only through the creation of a democratic social contract between the state of Israel and all Palestinians subject to its administrative, political, and military control (on both sides of the Green Line) are Palestinians likely to achieve meaningful participation in any self-governing polity.

Understanding self-determination (and sovereignty) in terms of a right to direct representation in the political institutions of governance (rather than secession or partition) is broadly familiar in the realm of international human rights. By shifting the focus away from the law of occupation to the question of how Palestinians might achieve the right to participate in the government that controls their territory, Li highlights the fundamental injustice that durable occupation has wrought: maximizing Israeli discretion in its treatment of Palestinians under occupation while legitimizing de jure discrimination against them. As he puts it, the law of occupation has diverted attention from the core question: "Why the people of Beit Hanoun in the northern Gaza Strip and Sderot in southern Israel should live as neighbors under the same supreme authority for over four decades, but with entirely different sets of rights."

An honest and realistic accounting of any one-state scenario will have two logical corollaries at the current historical juncture: the annexation of the occupied Palestinian territories to Israel; and the transfer of the long struggle for Palestinian rights from the inter-state arena—expressed through the language of the laws of war and sovereignty—to the intra-state arena, in the idiom of human rights and anti-discrimination. However, it would be a mistake to interpret this shift as extinguishing Palestinian rights of self-determination and sovereignty. To the contrary, Li suggests that this reconceptualization of the question will enable Palestinians in the here-and-now to make cognizable legal demands for equal status, rights, and political self-representation on the territory they inhabit. In other words, Palestinians will enjoy a legal right of political belonging, backstopped by the full spectrum of international human rights law, through a social contract that entitles them to political representation in, and equal rights under, the polity that governs their territory. Enfranchisement would, in this sense, be a realization of the right of self-governance which is at the core of demands for self-determination and the meaning of sovereignty.

Considered in light of the historical record of the relentless expropriation and colonization of the Palestinian territories and the disenfranchisement of the residents of those lands, the law of occupation has facilitated massive repression without affording Palestinians any opportunity to realize their rights. The reversal of the decades-long settlement policies that have enabled half a million Israelis to inhabit Palestinian lands is, as a practical matter, unattainable. The goal of the present Israeli government appears to be maximizing control over the lands and resources of the occupied Palestinian territories (particularly of the West Bank, including Jerusalem) while minimizing Israeli obligations to protect the humanitarian welfare of the Palestinian population. As Li suggests, one logical means of accomplishing this goal would be to adapt the South African bantustan model.

Arguably, this is what the forms of "autonomy" afforded to the Palestinians under the Oslo Accords have accomplished. The Israelis relieved themselves of their duties toward the Palestinian population while herding them into smaller and smaller enclaves ("Areas A" in Oslo parlance) of putative self-rule in a sea of Israeli-controlled lands which their Palestinian inhabitants and owners may no longer access (in "Areas B and C"). By contrast, requiring Israel to confer citizenship rights on the occupied populations would reverse this trend. Palestinian citizenship would either generate far greater obligations on the State of Israel to secure the welfare of *all* of the inhabitants of the territories (and limit government discretion in the discriminatory disposition of land) or it would result in democratic reversal, with Israel openly embracing a system of de jure discrimination in its constitutional order.

The latter scenario might not result in an immediate improvement in the conditions and rights of Palestinians in the occupied territories, but it would certainly deprive Israel of any claim to international legality or legitimacy in the continuation of its current policies. Such a scenario would at least have the benefit of laying bare the reality of the discrimination underlying Israeli administration of the territories. Further, it would likely provoke a crisis of identity in Israel's self-understanding as a democracy and galvanize a broader international movement in defense of Palestinian rights.

The Palestinian Authority (PA) is, at present, pursuing a statehood bid at the United Nations. The meaning of this initiative, its scope and implications, have yet to be clarified by the leadership of the PA (as of the time of this writing). Without knowing more about the details of the proposal, some have argued that it may run the risk of ratifying the view that self-government in the Area A enclaves is sufficient to meet the requirements of Palestinian self-determination and sovereignty. Others worry that the statehood bid runs the risk of undermining the right of return of Palestinian refugees, by reducing the rights of the Palestinian community to those living in the West Bank and Gaza. Whether or not these risks are realized, they reflect the severe constraints that four decades of belligerent occupation have placed on a conception of Palestinian self-determination through a "two state solution."

The most important implication of Li's analysis, to my mind, is shifting the framing of the self-determination question away from the law of occupation in a way that recognizes (and averts) these risks. Li has put in relief the most important implication of the spatial configuration—resulting from ever-accelerating colonization—that today characterizes the occupied Palestinian territories. Nearly half a century of settlement policy in violation of the law of occupation has resulted in the (territorial and political) diminution of any two-state arrangement at the expense of the Palestinians. Under present conditions, then, enfranchisement as citizens of Israel may be *closer* to a realization of the rights of self-determination and sovereignty for the Palestinian community than preserving a conception of Palestinian rights grounded in the law of occupation.

Part IV by Nimer Sultany

Darryl Li is correct in pointing out some of the shortcomings of occupation law. I would like to use this limited space to commend such critical reflection on the role of law in the plight and/or empowerment of the oppressed in order to call for disenchantment with the law. Let us face it: It is not only that the reality of power often trumps humanist and universal moral codes like those expressed in the law of nations (e.g., international humanitarian law); it is also that these universal codes are often too abstract, contradictory and ineffective to be instrumental in advancing concrete outcomes. The question of Palestine is no exception.

While no one denies that the law plays a role in the reality of political conflict, the question remains, however, the precise nature of that role and the scope of its impact. Indeed, critical scholars (whether legal realism, the Critical Legal Studies Movement, the Law and Society Movement, or third world approaches to international law) have long pointed out the dark side of the law. These scholars do not deny the occasional utility of adjudication and the deployment of legal means for the purpose of advancing the interests of the weak in specific issues. They are, however, concerned with those aspects that go unnoticed when the weak deploy the law as a means to advance their ends. They are concerned with the mystification of the role of law. These aspects, and this required demystification, can be briefly summarized as follows:

Law and Justice: There is a gap between law and justice and therefore one should be careful not to conflate the application of the law with the approximation of justice. The latter does not necessarily follow from the former. There are many reasons for this. To begin with, law is not a closed, autonomous system with its own inner morality; rather it is deeply influenced by politics and ideology and these cannot be cleansed by merely using legal nomenclature and reasoning. Secondly, law often addresses the symptoms of the conflict and offers ad hoc solutions and it rarely addresses the root cause of the conflict. It follows that even if the law were fully applied that would not necessarily lead to meeting the demands of justice.

Legalism: "The law" includes gaps, contradictions and ambiguities. Therefore, it does not necessarily produce the results at which one aims in the deployment of legal action. Rights are abstract and indeterminate and can be deployed by competing parties to advance conflicting interests. This condition of the law makes it a medium for manipulation and political conflict, especially when studied diachronically rather than synchronically. There is nothing inherent in the law that makes it favorable to the Palestinians and immune from Israeli or pro-Israeli manipulation. (Of course, the opposite is also true: there is nothing inherent in the law that makes it an enemy of the oppressed.)

Law in the books and law in action: Even if the law produced the results that are congenial to the causes championed by the oppressed, it remains to be seen whether legal stipulations have any bite in real life. The ICJ's Advisory Opinion on the separation wall is a sad testimony to the fact that highly publicized judicial proclamations by the highest possible authorities may produce little change in the reality of the oppressed. That does not mean that the opinion is valueless (it is rhetorically useful for the sake of argumentation), but it does mean that it has been, thus far, ineffective.

Legitimation: Using the legal means despite their uncertain results and quite limited effect is not without a price. First, when one uses the law, one is acknowledging the overall legitimacy of the legal system. Thus, bad legal opinions or decisions may make the situation of conflict look more natural or necessary than it is. One would have to explain the selectivity in accepting the good decisions and rejecting the bad ones when they originate from the same power structure. Moreover, even good rulings/legal opinions have bad effects. Indeed, representing the conflict from the legal perspective (or the human rights perspective) may distort the reality of conflict by depoliticizing it. The alleged power of the human rights rhetoric (its professionalism, its apolitical posture) is —simultaneously—its greatest weakness. Furthermore, by focusing on the legal venue one may marginalize other venues that may be available to the oppressed.

Let me explain some of these points through a recent example. The Goldstone Report, which has been uncritically celebrated by human rights advocates, may demonstrate the limits of legal and human rights discourse. First, the report accepts the Israeli claim that Israel was entitled to and acted in self-defense. Second, the exclusive focus on *jus in bello* (conduct during war) rather than *jus ad bellum* (the justifications for launching a war) is disturbing. By focusing on questions of excessive use of force and indiscriminate attacks, i.e., proportionality and distinction between civilians and combatants, human rights discourse seeks to shy away from political controversy surrounding justifications for wars. Yet, the focus on proportionality means that the debate revolves around the number of Palestinians Israel may be justified in killing. Third, the UN formed the committee in reaction to what is seen as an exceptional episode in the life of the conflict or the Palestinians. The report by its very nature and mandate singles out a limited set of facts and a limited period of time both as the primary locus for investigation and for the purpose of recommendations for action.

The consequences of the self-imposed limits of the legal and human rights discourse as exemplified by the Goldstone Report, in order to present a professional image and avoid larger political and moral contexts, are not insignificant. First, it distorts reality by presenting Israelis and Palestinians as equally culpable, identically situated agents of violence, despite the fact that Israel is the occupying power and the Palestinians are the occupied party and despite the gross asymmetry of power. Second, it distorts reality by focusing on and recommending actions against the "exceptional" outburst of violence while Israel is consistently pursuing the colonization of the West Bank and Jerusalem by creating facts on the ground and thus providing the breeding ground for violence. The focus on what is seen as "exceptional" implicitly renders other periods normal. But the occupation is no less oppressive during normal times. Third, it distorts reality by focusing on symptoms (the resistance) rather than the root cause of the conflict (the occupation and ongoing colonization), by focusing on Palestinian violence instead of the siege, and by focusing on one Israeli soldier rather than the thousands of Palestinian prisoners.

In addition to the aforementioned, the Palestinian case gives rise to two other questions of particular importance:

Compartmentalization: International law allows us to understand and analyze reality through categories. However, these categories may actually blind us from seeing the reality of the conflict clearly. Categories and distinctions that have bad normative effects should be collapsed. Law fragments reality into different legal compartments. It is akin to focusing on the trees while concealing the forest. In other words, the general questions are marginalized and obscured. Concretely, the Palestinians are divided into three main categories: citizens inside Israel, refugees, and residents of the occupied territories ("protected persons" in the jargon of international law). These categories are a codification of the results of naked power and violence (i.e., the outcome of war). But these categories do not overlap with the complex reality and thus work to create distortion and representational issues. The "refugee" exists inside the category "citizen" (we call them "internally displaced persons") and inside the category resident of the occupied territories. It is not only the refugee in Lebanon who cannot return, it is the same with the refugees in Nazareth, Haifa, and Tira who happen to be citizens. Additionally, the difference between the resident and the citizen is a question of degree rather than kind (this, I think, will become more apparent as the oppression of the Palestinians inside Israel increases and their life conditions keep deteriorating). Indeed, the hollow citizenship granted to the Palestinians is separated from the benefits of nationality. Furthermore, segregation, colonization, and killings with impunity exist on both sides of the Green Line. As the repression of political activists increases, poverty levels go up, and organized crime "flourishes" inside the Palestinian communities in Israel—the more the Palestinian minority will look like an occupied community.

One state/two state solutions: This compartmentalization is consequential for political visions of resolving the question of Palestine. There is an obvious tension between adopting the language of international law and the call for a one-state solution (e.g., many supporters of BDS, on the one hand, conceive of BDS as a means to force Israel "to abide by international law" and, on the other hand, call for a one-state resolution of the question of Palestine). Indeed, as Nathaniel Berman has illustrated in an article published in 1992 by the Harvard Law Review, international law is first based on the Westphalian model of the nation-state as the cornerstone for the international order. Additionally, it is based on the partition view of resolving "national" conflicts, a view that dominated the international legal discussions between the two world wars.[8] The partition of Palestine is a primary example of this approach.

This is, then, a plea for disenchantment. It is not a call for abandoning the legal venue altogether. But it is a call for a greater degree of critical reflection on the usage of the law. And, to the extent one decides to use it, to approach the legal venue with a greater degree of skepticism. Investing in the legal venue cannot be a substitute for direct political action and tools. Law is not free of politics and thus it cannot be an escape route from politics. While it may be part of a larger and well-thought political strategy, it is obvious that such strategy is lacking in the Palestinian case. In the absence of credible Palestinian political leadership and well-functioning, representative institutions equipped with an overarching political strategy, legal tools will remain sporadic, disorganized, and ineffective; indeed, futile. As such, they cannot challenge the status quo and the existing structure of power relations in fundamental ways. It is a mistake to think that in the absence of political advancement the legal venue can or should become a major venue and that it can get the Palestinians any closer to their goals. Like Kafka's man before the law, Palestinians may risk waiting for a legal promise that may never materialize.

Part V by Darryl Li

A reckoning is upon us—not simply a tallying of votes over the campaign for Palestinian membership in the United Nations, but of the dilemmas facing both the Palestinian leadership and the Zionist project. In both cases, there are lessons to be learned for the relationship between politics and law in the question of Israel/Palestine.

Unequal Dilemmas

Mahmoud Abbas's campaign to upgrade the legal status of "Palestine" at the UN has sparked widespread and indeed helpful debate among Palestinians and their allies, directing public attention to some fundamental but rarely discussed issues. For decades, the Palestine Liberation Organization (PLO) has purported to be the sole, legitimate representative of Palestinians worldwide, but has faced a basic contradiction: it led a nation whose members were mostly located outside of the homeland it sought to liberate. Although a minority of the Palestinian people remained domiciled in the country—some holding Israeli citizenship, a larger number residing in the occupied West Bank and Gaza Strip—they were seen by many as a defeated remnant, not the engine of the national liberation movement. It has only been since the eruption of the first intifada in 1987 that the shorthand phrase "the Palestinians" has referred to that minority of the Palestinian people living under belligerent occupation in the West Bank and Gaza Strip.

The first intifada led to a renegotiation of the relationship between Palestinians inside and outside the country, but not necessarily a positive one.

The Oslo Accords allowed the PLO's leadership in exile to move to the occupied territories in order to run the native self-administration body that grandly calls itself the Palestinian National Authority (PNA). In doing so, Israel disconnected the leadership from the diaspora and gained a new, valuable, and ultimately dependent partner in managing the unruly denizens of the 1967 territories.

The potentialities of this process have now played themselves out to their farcical extremes in the possibility of the PNA gaining widespread international recognition as a state. For the Palestinian majority in the diaspora, it is the danger of ratifying and reifying their decades-long marginalization. For Palestinians inside the West Bank and Gaza Strip, it may legitimize the state of indirect and dysfunctional rule under which they live. Indeed, if somehow the statehood bid were to "succeed" in terms of convincing the international community to treat the PNA legally as a sovereign entity, this would only exacerbate the disconnect between the responsibilities it shoulders and the powers it actually possesses. In particular, this would dovetail with a scenario in which Israel "Gaza-fies" the West Bank—completing the shift from a direct model of repression befitting an occupying power (house raids, mass arrests) to one of a belligerent attacking a foreign state (air strikes, blockades). And how long will it be until Israel and the United States demand that, as a sovereign state, Palestine's aid from the World Bank and IMF should come as loans rather than grants? In a broad sense, we can say that Palestinian "statehood" carries the danger of sovereign debt without the sovereignty.

In contrast, Israel's dilemmas are more tactical than strategic. If a state of Palestine is allowed to join the International Criminal Court, this would raise the costs to Israel of preventing the prosecution of any of its officials for war crimes. At the current moment, the possibility does not exist due to lack of jurisdiction, so future attempts to forestall accountability in this forum will require more direct interference from Israel's allies. Down the road, however, statehood does represent one significant—but not fatal—threat to Israel's demographic policies. Critics have compared the PNA to the bantustans in South Africa, and there is merit to this. But there is an important difference at play here: The apartheid regime wanted to create *multiple* bantustans as a means to keep the native population divided. Insofar as the PNA purports to be sole international representative of Palestinians across the West Bank and Gaza (or even simply the West Bank), it remains an obstacle to long-term Israeli goals. Israel's policies on the ground, especially the fragmentation of Palestinian lands, are heading in the direction of rendering the PNA incapable of representing even the West Bankers. If it is successful, Israel may still get something like the localized autonomy plan of the "Village Leagues" that it failed to achieve in the 1970s. Elevating the PNA's international status to full statehood would thus be an obstacle to its eventual disposal after it has outlasted the point of usefulness to Israel.

What Israel is discovering is that even puppet rulers can sometimes act out in ways that cause headaches. South Africa learned this painful lesson when some of its own bantustan leaders either turned against it or were themselves threatened by coup attempts and uprisings. Recognition of statehood is therefore suboptimal from the current Israeli standpoint, but not a serious obstacle that would fundamentally alter the strategic calculus on the ground to its detriment. The same can be said of recognition of the PLO—once considered taboo, but after facts on the ground weakened the PLO's position to the point where it had to accommodate the Zionist project, the costs of recognition to Israel were outweighed by the benefits.

Tools or Cages?

The dilemma facing the Palestinian leadership over the UN is only one example of a broad problem that I outlined in my remarks on occupation law— the challenge of how to take on the law as a tool while not allowing it to become a cage that overly constrains one's actions. That is the challenge I raised in questioning the utility of occupation law in dealing with a settler-colonial power, insofar as it brackets questions of equality and political belonging. The same is true, even more vividly so, with cartography, as Ahmad Barclay and Dena Qaddumi demonstrate in their essay. One useful role for scholars and critics to play in struggles for justice is to help provide warning labels for some of the hazards that come with the tools used by movements.

Aslı Bâli's contribution thoroughly explores this dilemma and then poses the question of what other legal tools might be useful in realizing the right of self-determination under such unusual circumstances. Her analysis shows how a second body of law—international human rights law—intersects with the law of occupation and carries its own potentialities. Simply put, international human rights law, for all of its problems, at least does not presume the denial of shared citizenship that is at work in the law of occupation.

This contrast can be illustrated in the context of West Bank settlements. When Israel builds a Jews-only city in the West Bank, such as Ma'ale Adumim, this is roundly condemned because the Fourth Geneva Convention prohibits an occupying power from transferring its own civilians into an occupied territory. The problem, essentially, is state action directed at bringing the settlers, prompting the absurd charge from some extreme right-wing Zionists that the Palestinian demand for evacuating settlements is tantamount to ethnic cleansing (or, in their colorful language, a "Judenrein Palestine"). From the perspective of human rights law, the problem isn't the importation of settlers per se, but the discriminatory regime they bring with them: not only the water and land expropriation, but the problem of segregated roads and movement restrictions for natives and, most importantly, discrimination in deciding who gets to live there.

From one perspective, adopting a human rights perspective may seem less "radical" in two respects: First, it would not necessarily require evacuating the colony. Second, under the laws of occupation, such colonization is generally considered a war crime, whereas the human rights framework would not carry an international criminal sanction (although, notwithstanding the concerns expressed by Lisa Hajjar, most other provisions on war crimes, as well as international humanitarian law generally, could continue to apply even in the absence of occupation law). On the other hand, human rights law would be useful here in drawing attention to *why* these colonies are problematic: discrimination, both in the micro and macro senses. And, crucially, this framework for critique could be applied across the entire country and not simply the 1967 territories. Moreover, because international human rights law does not assume, as occupation law does, that Israel and the territories are two separate entities, it can be more easily attached to different kinds of political claims and struggles than the limited ones we have seen in recent decades.

While Bâli expands our conversation about the legal tools one can resort to, it is also important to keep in mind that one's ability to use tools is shaped very much on context. As I mentioned in the earlier piece, Israel has maintained a balance between holding occupation law's ability to impede colonization at bay, while relying on it at times to justify its actions and to win legitimacy in the eyes of the international community. It is powerful enough to treat the law more as a tool than a cage. Hajjar provides a useful starting point by reminding us of Meir Shamgar's arguments in the early years of the occupation denying the applicability of the Fourth Geneva Convention to the occupied territories. In the decades since, Israel's approach towards occupation law has evolved to one of selective incorporation, with careful efforts to avoid the ban on colonization. In the 1979 Elon Moreh case, the Israeli Supreme Court recognized the 1907 Hague Regulations as customary international law and therefore binding on Israel. It has even relied upon some occupation-related provisions of the Fourth Geneva Convention in some of its few timid attempts to regulate the occupation when not otherwise rubber-stamping it.[9] Israel has skillfully managed to adopt a sort of à la carte approach to occupation law: There are some provisions it argues do not apply, and then there are others whose applicability it concedes but then violates anyway.

Endurance and Expertise

While Israel can afford to play all sorts of games with international law, Palestinians are in a situation of relative demobilization, despite all of the momentous events in the region this past year. Space for maneuver also comes from a society's ability to absorb the costs of repression. Palestinians in the West Bank and Gaza are, unfortunately, even more dependent on international aid than ever, severely sapping mobilizing energies.

The provocative kinds of urban planning and architectural projects that Barclay and Qaddumi point to have been very useful in shaping my analysis of how law in its various forms reshapes and is reshaped by the situation on the ground in Israel/Palestine. But both law and architecture, as "expert" forms of knowledge, share a similar dilemma of how to propose bold ideas that actually resonate with popular movements, a problem that is only compounded by the overall state of demobilization.

One kind of spatial practice that I would like to add to our conversation is the persistent, indeed heroic, rebuilding of the Bedouin village of al-'Araqib, demolished by Israeli authorities over a dozen times despite multiple protests and lawsuits. This campaign signals an assertion of rights, engenders solidarity between dissident settlers and indigenes, and forces the state to openly reenact its violence on a regular basis, almost farcically so. Al-'Araqib is a site where spatial acts and claims to citizenship are one and the same. While lawyers and architects may be poorly situated to start or lead social movements themselves, it would seem that cases such as al-'Araqib may provide lessons they can help put into practice when future conditions shift.

Troubling the Waters

Finally, Nimer Sultany's contribution reminds us that no matter how cleverly or doggedly law is used as a tool, one should maintain a healthy attitude of skepticism, or as he wonderfully puts it, disenchantment. The crucial duty of a lawyer to tell the client what the law cannot do sometimes seems to have been forgotten in discussions of Israel/Palestine. The Palestinian struggle has become so suffused with legal discourse in recent decades that we have sometimes lost the ability to distinguish what is legal from what is right.

An excellent example of this has been the fallout over the Gaza flotillas. There is a general international law problem with the policies of economic and social suffocation imposed by Israel on the Gaza Strip. On the one hand, there are various rules encouraging occupying powers to allow in aid and prohibiting collective punishment. On the other hand, occupying powers have the right to regulate and control movement (whether they have the power to impose a maritime blockade, i.e., stopping and searching ships in international waters, is a slightly different issue that hinges in large part on how the legal situation is classified). Unlike a specific violent act such as the bombing of a home that can be readily criminalized, however, the closure is an entire system, and international law—whether occupation law or human rights law—seems to have little to say about that system other than to vaguely encourage its humane application.

In this sense, the power and the promise of the flotilla for me has never been about the illegality of the siege of Gaza in itself. Rather, the flotilla's significance was as an act of civil disobedience, in a context—the high seas—where Israel was forced to assume responsibility for its actions and defend them in a more dramatic fashion than, say, repelling protesters at a land crossing. Civil disobedience is precisely about exposing the gap between legality and legitimacy. Individuals signal their willingness to face the coercive power of the state in order to demonstrate that it is precisely that: coercion and nothing more. Even if one accepts that Israel's actions on that fateful day in May 2010 were criminal and that Israel's siege policies violate international law, it is still very difficult to deny that as an occupying power Israel would not have had the technical right to stop and search those ships if they had crossed into Israel's or Gaza's territorial waters. But that is exactly the point. Israel's "right" to stop the flotilla was about as worthwhile as South Africa's "right" to imprison Nelson Mandela for sabotage or treason—valid in the technical sense, but utterly worthless in light of the greater monstrosity those measures were meant to protect. In this sense, disenchantment with the law does not necessarily mean despair in the world; it can also be a basis for changing it.

22 September 2011

[1] Meir Shamgar, "Legal Concepts and Problems of the Israeli Military Government: The Initial Stage," in *Military Government in the Territories Administered by Israel, 1967-1980: The Legal Aspects* (Hebrew University of Jerusalem, 1982), 25.

[2] Meir Shamgar, "The Observance of International Law in the Administered Territories," in *Israel Yearbook on Human Rights* (Martinus Nijhoff Publishers, 1971).

[3] Shamgar, "Legal Concepts."

[4] "Land Grab: Israel's Settlement Policy in the West Bank," *B'Tselem*, May 2002, http://www.btselem.org/publications/summaries/200205_land_grab.

[5] "OCHA oPt. UN Office for the Coordination of Humanitarian Affairs," http://www.ochaopt.org/generalmaps.aspx?id=96.

[6] "TEDxRamallah: Voices from Free Palestine," *Arena of Speculation*, http://arenaofspeculation.org/2011/04/14/tedxramallah-voices-from-free-palestine/#02.

[7] "UNGROUNDING: Decolonizing Architecture," *Theory Kit*, March 2007, http://kit.kein.org/node/438.

[8] Nathaniel Berman, "But the Alternative Is Despair: European Nationalism and the Modernist Renewal of International Law," *Harvard Law Review* 106 (1992).

[9] See paragraphs 12, 18, and 20 of *Physicians for Human Rights v. IDF Commander in Gaza*.

The Palestinian Statehood Strategy in the United Nations: Lessons From Namibia

Susan Akram

Palestine's pending request for recognition in the United Nations has generated great international interest, both in what recognition will mean for Palestine and the Palestinians, and in whether anything will really change in the absence of territorial independence. I will address this question by way of a comparison between Palestine and South West Africa (Namibia), and what legal strategies were followed in both cases at the UN. I would like to particularly recognize the work done by Stephanie Koury, Victor Kattan, and John Quigley in the book, *The Statehood of Palestine: International Law in the Middle East Conflict* (Cambridge University Press, 2010). I have drawn from their insights in this discussion.

It might seem strange to compare the Palestine and South West Africa/ Namibia cases, but the comparison provides useful insight into the risks and benefits of the present Palestinian bid at the UN. Namibia and Palestine have parallel histories in terms of the way they began their campaigns towards self-determination and independence, and in the way their status was addressed at the League of Nations, and eventually in the UN. Comparing these histories helps to understand two issues: 1) the different ways in which law provides a framework for attaining statehood; and 2) whether independence is a necessary precondition to statehood. This discussion will illustrate the critical role legal strategies in the UN and elsewhere played in the Namibian bid for statehood in the absence of independence. It will also illustrate how the absence of a clear and sustained legal strategy on the part of the Palestinians has affected the bid for statehood in the absence of independence. Put simply, can Palestine achieve what Namibia achieved through the UN?

Strategies & Developments in the UN

At the end of World War I, the Allies adopted the Covenant of the League of Nations. Article 22 of the League Covenant created the mandate system, whereby the colonies of the defeated powers—Germany, the Austrian-Hungarian Empire, and the Ottoman Empire—were to be re-constituted as mandates of the League of Nations, and awarded to specific European countries. The plan created three classes of territories—claimed to be at different stages of development—and established that they would be under the mandate, or supervision, of one of the great powers. The League of Nations Covenant placed Palestine, Iraq, Lebanon, Syria, and Transjordan among the "Class A" mandates, or those most prepared for independence. The Covenant gave Great Britain mandatory power over Palestine. South West Africa (now Namibia), placed under South African mandate, was among the "Class C" countries, or those considered farthest from independence under the League of Nations Covenant. In fact, the League did not contemplate independence at all for the "Class C" territories.

On April 18, 1946, the League dissolved. The mandate countries that had not yet become independent came under trusteeship of the UN. South Africa had sought to fully incorporate Namibia as South African territory, but the UN refused, and the General Assembly voted to put Namibia in trusteeship under Chapter XII of the UN Charter. South Africa however, refused, initiating a lengthy battle in the United Nations. Almost immediately, the General Assembly filed the first of three requests for advisory opinions from the International Court of Justice (ICJ) on various questions relating to the status of Namibia; the Security Council later filed another advisory opinion with the ICJ, and Liberia and Ethiopia filed a contentious case challenging South Africa's apartheid policies and failure to comply with UN requirements towards South West Africa.[1]

In October of 1962, the UN terminated South Africa's mandate, placed Namibia under direct UN responsibility, and set up an ad hoc committee for South West Africa to enable Namibia to gain independence. The ad hoc committee was succeeded by the UN Council for Namibia, entrusted to administering the area until it achieved independence. Although South Africa did not recognize Namibian independence and did not withdraw from its territory until 1988, the world community, following the actions taken at the UN and at the ICJ, had created a defined legal framework for Namibia's status. This framework enabled the UN to declare Namibia's right to independence, impose sanctions on South Africa, and create the mechanisms to implement independence twenty years before independence was actually achieved. Through these mechanisms, Namibia was able to lay the foundation for independence, despite the fact that the Security Council never invoked Chapter VII authority to force South African withdrawal from South West Africa. Much of these developments occurred through a robust legal strategy consisting of early work within the UN General Assembly framework and multiple ICJ submissions.

In contrast, Palestine was the only "Class A" mandate territory *not* to achieve independence by the time the League terminated in 1946. In 1946, the Arab states objected to continuing Palestine's UN trusteeship territory status. Similar to South Africa's mandate over Namibia, the UN accepted Britain's commitment to its mandate obligations rather than putting Palestine under direct UN trusteeship. It is important to note the inconsistencies in Great Britain's own role as mandatory power: Great Britain had, on the one hand, committed to bringing Palestine to independence, while simultaneously committing to securing a national home for the Jewish people in Palestine through the Balfour Declaration. In comparison to Namibia, however, the General Assembly and the Security Council have neither jointly developed the actual foundation for recognition, nor the legal framework for Palestinian independence. Moreover, in the Palestinian case, there has been very limited effort to obtain rulings from the ICJ in support of self-determination.

The General Assembly's ad hoc committee to study proposals on the future government of Palestine rejected the Arab and other states' initial proposals to seek an ICJ Advisory Opinion and, instead, recommended partition. The General Assembly then passed UNGA Resolution 181 in November 1947, recommending partition of Palestine into two states, which the Jewish Agency accepted and the Arab High Committee rejected [UNGA Res 181 29 Nov. 1947]. Israel declared its state in May 1948, gaining control of 77 percent of historic Palestine, beyond the borders demarcated in Resolution 181. The General Assembly passed Resolution 194 [UNGA Res 194 (III), 11 Dec. 1948] a year later. This key resolution incorporated the individual rights of refugee return, restitution and compensation, and conditionally accepted Israel into the UN in 1949 pending compliance. Israel did not comply after admission. Surprisingly, after Resolution 181 passed, the Security Council first asked the General Assembly members to study partition of Israel, but then backed away, subsequently requesting the General Assembly to reconsider alternatives, including a possible trusteeship for Palestine.

However, soon after the passage of Resolution 181, the General Assembly and Security Council began to act in very different and inconsistent ways toward Palestine. The General Assembly developed a significant body of Resolutions affirming both individual rights—such as refugee return, property restitution, and compensation—and collective rights such as those of self-determination, statehood, and independence. It has since insisted on this framework as the one for peace negotiations. In contrast, the Security Council's framework has almost exclusively focused on UN Resolutions 242 and 338 as the basis of a negotiated solution.[2] These two Resolutions create the "land for peace" formula that suggests that the only legal framework necessary to resolve the conflict is some exchange of territory for a permanent peace.

Most critically, the Security Council has failed to affirm the inalienable Palestinian rights—self-determination and statehood, right of refugee return, and Israeli withdrawal from the 1967 territories—that have been the focus of the General Assembly's framework for resolution of the conflict. The Security Council has also blocked UN-sponsored conferences by vetoes or by refusing to consider General Assembly recommendations. The Security Council's approach has been framed by the "land for peace" political formula as a basis for negotiations, with almost no reference to legal rights. Moreover, in marked contrast to Namibia, there has been only one submission to the ICJ over a sixty-year period, the advisory opinion on the wall of 2004.[3] It is my contention that it is the absence of ICJ and other legal law-making of the sort that allowed Namibia to achieve statehood in the absence of independence that may prevent Palestine from achieving the benefits of full statehood in the absence of independence after it obtains formal recognition in the UN.

Comparing Namibian and Palestinian Legal Strategies

In the mid-1960s, in response to the decolonization efforts within the UN of the African states, the Palestinian Liberation Organization (PLO) made a very deliberate change in its UN strategy. By 1969, the resolutions proposed and passed at the UN on the Palestine question had changed their language from that of individual rights to calling for rights of the Palestinian people—collective rights. This may have seemed like an appropriate strategy at the time, but by failing to merge the individual rights with the collective, the PLO has been forced at the negotiating table to exchange one set of rights for another. The Palestinian strategy has focused on ending occupation and effecting international humanitarian law protections rather than a combined strategy of demanding fulfillment of both individual rights and the collective rights of self-determination and independence. Moreover, the Security Council's position has been consistent in reaffirming only Resolutions 242 and 338 as the basis for a negotiated peace. In turn, the negotiation framework from the Oslo Accords onward has referenced only Resolutions 242 and 338 and none of the General Assembly's individual rights resolutions. This has resulted in a deliberate omission of law in favor of a purely political solution.

Unlike in Namibia, the General Assembly and Security Council approaches have been in conflict over Palestine, with the Security Council disregarding the legal framework articulated by the General Assembly. In the Namibia case, the General Assembly and Security Council ended up with an agreement on the underlying legal framework. Though the Security Council came to an agreement reluctantly and late because of the actions of several of the permanent members, it ended up having no choice because the ICJ's four advisory opinions (one in response to the Security Council itself) consistently articulated what the law required. Namibia's relationship to the Security Council was similar to the Palestinians' in the sense that the Security Council did not enforce the sanctions demanded by the General Assembly or call for intervention due to French, US, and United Kingdom vetoes. Yet, because of the ICJ's endorsement of sanctions against South Africa, and the court's insistence on member state obligations to bring about Namibian independence, the sanctions regime was "legalized" to support individual states' actions. In other words, while Palestine's efforts appear to have been defeated by the veto of permanent members of the Security Council, in Namibia's case, the legal strategies were not defeated by similar permanent member vetoes at the Security Council.

Prior to and following the request for the advisory opinion on the Wall issued in 2004, there has been little or no effort by the Palestinian delegation at the UN to work on additional advisory opinions as a distinct strategy. This is surprising, given the PLO's solid support in the General Assembly, especially with the group of non-aligned states. In contrast to the four advisory opinions and the contentious case litigated over decades for Namibia, Palestine has obtained only one advisory opinion, with very little follow-up to use it as an effective tool. Additionally, the PLO and Palestinian Authority appear not to have aggressively worked within the European Union, utilized regional and other mechanisms, or facilitated the filing of lawsuits in domestic courts similar to those filed by the Namibian Council to protect its resources and interests. The Palestinian leadership appears to have failed to incorporate careful legal strategies in its negotiations frameworks. For example, it has failed to insist that Resolution 194, in addition to Resolutions 242 and 338, be incorporated in all negotiation frameworks. It has also failed to insist on inclusion of the West Bank, Gaza Strip, and East Jerusalem as a single territorial entity in all negotiation proposals.

In fact, the Palestinians have taken an almost entirely political, rather than a law-based, approach to the UN. A few key events are important to appreciate the level of support that exists within the UN towards the Palestinian cause, support that has been underutilized by the Palestinian leadership in achieving its goals. On 22 November 1974, the General Assembly adopted Resolution 3237, which granted the PLO "observer" status within the UN, allowing it to participate in all the sessions and the work of the UN, effectively as a "quasi-state." In 1975, the General Assembly passed Resolution 3376, establishing the Committee on the Exercise of the Inalienable Rights of the Palestinian People, entrusted to work toward Palestinian independence and sovereignty, and implement the individual rights spelled out in prior General Assembly resolutions. The committee was also tasked to work with civil society organizations to accomplish its goals. Subsequently, on 2 December 1977, the Division for Palestinian Rights was set up by General Assembly Resolution 32/40B, to support and assist the committee in its work, and to be a liaison with civil society organizations working on Palestinian issues. Over the years, a wide network of well over a thousand such organizations have cooperated in various ways with the committee to help pursue these goals. Despite this broad support within and outside the UN, it can safely be said that the Palestinian leadership has not been committed to using these entities to pursue a legal strategy in the UN. This is most evidenced by a lack of collaboration between the PA and the civil society groups working with the Palestine committee and the division to expand and build on the roles of these UN institutions. On the contrary, the PA has frequently been at odds with these organizations and with civil society activists engaged with the UN, preventing the kind of deep collaboration necessary to put a multi-pronged, solid legal strategy in place. At the negotiations level, too, there has been a critical lack of a robust legal approach. No legal department advised the PLO-PA until after the Oslo Accords, when the Adam Smith Institute established the first legal affairs department for the PLO. Even since, it appears that the PA has not incorporated much of the legal affairs unit's work at the international level. One can safely conclude that the Palestinian leadership has failed to see the importance that legal strategies have alongside political, negotiation, media, civil society collaborations, and the armed struggle.

Defining the Issue: The Scope of the Statehood Question and UN Membership

Statehood

The Palestinian leadership will be raising two issues at the UN: 1) recognition of Palestine as a state, and 2) a request for membership in the UN. These two issues must be defined and understood differently, as they are independent of one another.

There are two views of exactly when a territory or people become a "state" as a matter of international law, and states themselves have not acted consistently on the issue. One position is that statehood is a function of declaration and recognition by other states; the other is that statehood is a function of recognition plus other factors, which may or may not include independence. So far, over one hundred countries have recognized Palestine as a state, and that number may reach 150. Is this enough to designate Palestine a state? The common arguments against Palestinian statehood are that 1) it was not historically a state; 2) it does not meet modern-day statehood criteria; and 3) Palestine has not been recognized as a state by the international community. John Quigley, in his book *The Statehood of Palestine,* argues that there are four errors in these claims. First, as to historical statehood, facts show that Palestine was a state from the mandate period onwards. Second, Palestine is being asked to meet criteria for statehood more extreme than those required by other states in the world. Third and closely related, these criteria do not take into account the effects of prolonged occupation. Fourth, Palestine has already been recognized as a state both explicitly and implicitly for several decades.

The most commonly accepted standard for the elements of statehood is the Montevideo Convention on the Rights and Duties of States (1933, Uruguay). This convention defines the criteria for "a state" as a permanent population, with a defined territory, government, and the capacity to enter into relations with other states. Since Montevideo, it has been widely claimed that an additional element is required for statehood, that of independence. Quigley advances the case for Palestinian statehood with a sharp critique of the criteria set out in the Montevideo Convention. He argues that the convention was intended to clarify that independence was *not* a prerequisite to statehood, and that state practice has not changed to require this. He then makes the case that Palestine presently satisfies all the conditions in that convention—a permanent population, defined territory, government, and the capacity to enter into relations with other states, and that Palestine does not have to be territorially independent to be a state.

As cited in Quigley's book, there are many examples of states that have been recognized without having territorial independence, our primary illustration, Namibia, being just one example. Other examples are the previous Soviet satellite states Belorussia (now Belarus) and the Ukraine; Bosnia, admitted as UN member without having control over territory or independence; Monaco, a mini-state widely recognized as a state even though France controls its domestic and foreign policy; and the US-Marshall Islands, which are UN members even though its defense and security are controlled by the United States.

Under the framework that was established in April 2002 by the Quartet— comprising the Russian Federation, the United States, the European Union, and the UN—a Palestinian state could be established prior to the conclusion of final status negotiations with Israel. The Quartet's framework is that, based on negotiated agreements, the PA can assert its claim to statehood with provisional borders and attributes of sovereignty even before a full Israeli withdrawal. This framework was also the basis of the Oslo Accords. Aside from the 100-plus countries exercising diplomatic relations with Palestine, Palestine has a functioning government in the West Bank and Gaza Strip with a president, prime minister, cabinet, legislative council, and ministers, voted by open elections held in 1966. It has a civil service comprised of thousands of employees. There is an established court system, with first impression and appellate courts as well as a high court. Perhaps there will be a unified government following the recent Hamas-Fateh accord, but even a divided government does not defeat statehood. Most notably, Korea, Vietnam, and Yemen have been divided states for decades, yet are still recognized as states. Thus, if Palestine gains formal recognition by a majority of states in the UN, it will fit the requirements for statehood with the exception of territorial independence.

UN Membership

Statehood and membership in international organizations are entirely separate matters. Article 4(2) of the UN Charter says that a state may be admitted to membership by a decision of the General Assembly upon receiving a recommendation from the Security Council. In its *Admissions* case, the ICJ made it clear that the UN Charter places the responsibility for admission of state membership in the UN squarely on the Security Council, and that the General Assembly cannot act on state admission without Security Council recommendation.[4] US opposition to Palestine's membership in the UN would not necessarily affect Palestine's statehood if a majority of states recognized Palestine at the UN. If the United States vetoes Palestine's application for membership, then Palestine will not become a UN member. Instead its position will be similar to that of Kosovo (whose membership is being blocked by Russia) and Taiwan (whose membership is being blocked by China).

Implications of Statehood

Assuming that the 120 or so states which the Palestinians believe will vote for statehood do recognize Palestine as a state, does the Namibia case tell us that Palestine can effectively become a full-fledged state even without independence? If so, what are the ramifications of such a situation?

First, a great deal depends on what those states do with their recognition. Will they vote for full recognition or agree only on representative status? Will they establish full ambassadorial relations? Where will the recognizing countries' embassies be, in Ramallah, or Jerusalem? Israel is likely to block the establishment of embassies to the State of Palestine in East Jerusalem. Will all recognizing states accept Palestinian passports, issue visas, allow full freedom of movement, and allow consular intervention when Palestinians require it?

Second, what will be the recognized population? Will it only be Palestinians in the occupied territories, or could it include Palestinians within Israel and the diaspora? What about Palestinian refugees? If they become Palestinian citizens, do they cease being refugees? And if so, do they lose their rights as refugees to insist on return and other rights attached to refugee status? How will the PA implement the rights of refugees as citizens of Palestine? These questions have not been addressed through UN resolutions, legal decisions, or opinions from relevant international fora. There are, for example, no definitive legal decisions resolving the highly contested question of who constitutes a Palestinian refugee, when the status of "Palestine refugee" ceases for international protection purposes, or who may hold a Palestinian passport. Yet, the consequences of such decisions are enormous for the global Palestinian population of roughly 10 million persons.

Third, even if we assume that Palestine will be treated as a state among equals on the diplomatic front and enjoy full relations with the states that recognize it, those who do not recognize it, like Israel and the United States, will not treat it as a state. What will that mean for recognition at the ICJ or other international organizations if the US and Israel oppose? This will be determined on a case-by-case basis, but at each venue where Palestine takes its place as a "state" Israel and the United States could object and block admission.

Fourth, and again on questions of consequences: What can Palestine do to enforce the territorial integrity of the West Bank and Gaza Strip in the absence of a withdrawal by Israel? What can Palestine do to enforce withdrawal of settlements? Can it even implement a uniform legal system in its territory in the absence of an Israeli withdrawal and US backing? Answers to these questions could help the community of states define a legal framework to respond to future problems, but none of these issues have been addressed through resolutions, ICJ opinions, or other law.

New avenues will surely become available to Palestine, enabling it to pursue legal remedies against Israel in various international fora. The question pending at the International Criminal Court of whether Palestine can be treated as a state for purposes of acceding to the Rome Statute and the ICC will be resolved through recognition of statehood. But with Israel refusing to be a party and the United States certain to veto any attempt by the Security Council to refer a case against Israeli defendants, what are the practical advantages of such a determination? On another front, in domestic courts where Palestine and Palestinian leaders face criminal prosecutions or other lawsuits, Palestine will be able to assert sovereign immunity, but if the US does not recognize Palestinian statehood, US courts will not recognize sovereign immunity for Palestinian defendants such as those being charged on terrorist-related grounds.

Of course, Palestine's statehood should also mean its security forces would become a legitimate military force, with all the attendant benefits that entails. However, if Israel controls the ability to receive arms and military equipment, army and police may be unequipped and ineffective. Additionally, if Israel refuses to recognize Palestinian soldiers as part of a duly constituted state army, it will continue the status quo of designating captured armed Palestinians as "terrorists" rather than prisoners of war.

Palestine is already a member of international organizations and as a recognized state could join the full panoply of interrational organizations. However, Palestinian attempts to increase trade and obtain the benefits of these organizations remain in the effective control of Israel, making it very difficult for Palestine to actually attain these benefits. Theoretically, if Palestine became a member of the UN, it would be able to draft, propose, table, and vote on its own resolutions at the UN. However, the PLO and Palestinian delegation have enjoyed most of these rights since receiving full observer status at the UN in

1974. Since UN membership is unlikely to be forthcoming, the issue to be considered is whether the risks of going to the Security Council outweigh the benefits of the marginal upgrade membership will provide to Palestine's current status along with the statehood recognition that is certain to pass.

These examples, illustrating the consequences of statehood without independence, show that in the absence of a clear body of soft and hard law to support Palestinian statehood recognition, continued Israeli and US opposition may make recognition an exercise in futility. The Palestinian people will not get what they deem most important: the fulfillment of their individual rights to return, restitution of their properties, collective rights of full recognition as a people connected with their own land, and all the freedoms such recognition ordinarily brings. Over twenty years before actual independence, Namibians and their supporters combined a strong legal strategy with the political and armed struggle. This strategy resolved many of the key issues and allowed the non-rejectionist states to make statehood meaningful by the time actual independence came about. Yet, in the absence of an analogous legal framework for Palestinians, the outcome of their UN bid for statehood is highly uncertain.

3 October 2011

[This is a modified version of a talk delivered by Susan Akram in Beirut, Lebanon in July 2011]

---

[1] International Status of South West Africa, Advisory Opinion (ICJ Report 128,1950); Voting Procedure on Questions Relating to Reports and Petitions Concerning the Territory of South West Africa, Advisory Opinion (ICJ Report 67, 1955); The Admissibility of Hearings of Petitioners by the Committee on South West Africa, Advisory Opinion (ICJ Report 23, 1956); the Legal Consequences for States of the Continued Presence of South Africa in Namibia (South West Africa) Notwithstanding Security Council Resolution 276 (1970), Advisory Opinion (ICJ Report 16, 1971); and South West Africa (Ethiopia vs. south Africa; Liberia vs. South Africa), ICJ Report 6, 1966).

[2] UNSC Res 242, 22 Nov. 1967; UNSC Res 338, 22 Oct. 1973.

[3] Legal Consequences of the Construction of a Wall in the Occupied Palestinian Territory, Advisory Opinion, ICJ Rep. 136 (2004).

[4] Admission of a State to the United Nations, Advisory Opinion, ICJ Rep. 57 (1948).

ICC Rejects Palestine Bid

[The following is a ruling from the Office of the Prosecutor of the International Criminal Court.]

Situation in Palestine

1. On 22 January 2009, pursuant to article 12(3) of the Rome Statute, Ali Khashan acting as minister of justice of the Government of Palestine lodged a declaration accepting the exercise of jurisdiction by the International Criminal Court for "acts committed on the territory of Palestine since 1 July 2002."

2. In accordance with Article 15 of the Rome Statute, the Office of the Prosecutor initiated a preliminary examination in order to determine whether there is a reasonable basis to proceed with an investigation. The Office ensured a fair process by giving all those concerned the opportunity to present their arguments. The Arab League's Independent Fact Finding Committee on Gaza presented its report during a visit to the court. The Office provided Palestine with the opportunity to present its views extensively, in both oral and written form. The Office also considered various reports with opposing views. In July 2011, Palestine confirmed to the Office that it had submitted its principal arguments, subject to the submission of additional supporting documentation.

3. The first stage in any preliminary examination is to determine whether the preconditions to the exercise of jurisdiction under Article 12 of the Rome Statute are met. Only when such criteria are established will the Office proceed to analyze information on alleged crimes as well as other conditions for the exercise of jurisdiction as set out in articles 13 and 53(1).

4. The jurisdiction of the court is not based on the principle of universal jurisdiction: it requires that the United Nations Security Council (article 13(b)) or a "state" (article 12) provide jurisdiction. Article 12 establishes that a "state" can confer jurisdiction to the court by becoming a Party to the Rome Statute (article 12(1)) or by making an ad hoc declaration accepting the court's jurisdiction (article 12(3)).

5. The issue that arises, therefore, is who defines what is a "State" for the purpose of Article 12 of the Statute? In accordance with Article 125, the Rome Statute is open to accession by "all States," and any State seeking to become a

Party to the Statute must deposit an instrument of accession with the Secretary General of the United Nations. In instances where it is controversial or unclear whether an applicant constitutes a "state," it is the practice of the Secretary General to follow or seek the General Assembly's directives on the matter. This is reflected in General Assembly resolutions which provide indications of whether an applicant is a "State."[1] Thus, competence for determining the term "State" within the meaning of Article 12 rests, in the first instance, with the United Nations Secretary General who, in case of doubt, will defer to the guidance of General Assembly. The Assembly of States Parties of the Rome Statute could also in due course decide to address the matter in accordance with Article 112(2)(g) of the Statute.

6. In interpreting and applying Article 12 of the Rome Statute, the Office has assessed that it is for the relevant bodies at the United Nations or the Assembly of States Parties to make the legal determination whether Palestine qualifies as a State for the purpose of acceding to the Rome Statute and thereby enabling the exercise of jurisdiction by the court under Article 12(1). The Rome Statute provides no authority for the Office of the Prosecutor to adopt a method to define the term "State" under article 12(3) which would be at variance with that established for the purpose of Article 12(1).

7. The Office has been informed that Palestine has been recognized as a State in bilateral relations by more than 130 governments and by certain international organizations, including United Nation bodies. However, the current status granted to Palestine by the United Nations General Assembly is that of "observer," not as a "Non-member State." The Office understands that on 23 September 2011, Palestine submitted an application for admission to the United Nations as a Member State in accordance with Article 4(2) of the United Nations Charter, but the Security Council has not yet made a recommendation in this regard. While this process has no direct link with the declaration lodged by Palestine, it informs the current legal status of Palestine for the interpretation and application of Article 12.

8. The Office could in the future consider allegations of crimes committed in Palestine, should competent organs of the United Nations or eventually the Assembly of States Parties resolve the legal issue relevant to an assessment of Article 12 or should the Security Council, in accordance with Article 13(b), make a referral providing jurisdiction.

3 April 2012

---

[1] This position is set out in the understandings adopted by the General Assembly at its 2202nd plenary meeting on 14 December 1973; see *Summary of Practice of the Secretary General as Depositary of Multilateral Treaties*, ST/LEG/7/Rev. 1, paras 81-83.

Imagining Justice Beyond the ICC

Samar Al-Bulushi

The International Criminal Court's acquittal of Congolese militia leader Mathieu Ngudjolo on 18 December did not exactly make headlines in Palestine. Ngudjolo was accused of commanding fighters who raped and hacked to death approximately two hundred people, including children, in a single day in February 2003.

Arguing that witness statements were unreliable, ICC judges determined that the ICC did not have sufficient evidence to prove Ngudjolo's complicity in these crimes. Not surprisingly, the court's verdict dealt a massive blow to the aspirations of thousands of Congolese who had rested their hopes for justice in the ICC.

Though it is not often that Palestinian activists look beyond South Africa to other struggles on the continent, the time is ripe to do just that. Since the UN General Assembly voted overwhelmingly to recognize Palestine as a non-member observer state in November, Palestinian leaders and activists have articulated their determination to pursue a "legal intifada" by joining the ICC in order to seek justice for Israeli crimes.

Although we cannot yet be sure of the various political and legal hurdles that could delay Palestinian membership in this body, an ICC case that seeks to hold Israeli officials accountable for crimes that fall within the court's statute, such as war crimes, genocide, crimes against humanity, and the crime of aggression, would be of immense historic and symbolic significance.

Yet, the Ngudjolo acquittal—and the track record of the court in general—serves as an important reminder not to invest too much hope in the ICC as a source of justice.

Indeed, the court's ongoing cases in Uganda, Sudan, and Kenya reveal a consistent susceptibility to geopolitical interests and local power plays, dynamics that would undoubtedly shape a case against Israel, and which call into question the utility of the ICC as a legal or political weapon.

Every one of the court's indictments since it began its work in 2002 has been against individuals on the African continent. Critics have accused the court of pursuing only the weakest players on the geopolitical spectrum, in part the consequence of the most powerful refusing to join. Relatedly, they point to the power politics at play in ongoing cases that raise doubts about its supposed impartiality and independence.

Less discussed are the challenges and contradictions raised by the court's lack of enforcement powers: namely, who it relies upon to apprehend suspects, and what accountability mechanisms, if any, are in place to prevent further bloodshed in the name of enforcing "justice."

From the protection of victims and witnesses to the apprehension of suspects, the ICC's operational reliance on powerful states ensures that individuals from those states will largely escape scrutiny, and that the court's decisions are often far removed from the very people it was designed to protect.

Perhaps the most dangerous implication of this dependency on "cooperating" states is the potential for manipulation in the service of entirely different objectives. Some analysts draw a parallel between the ICC and the "responsibility to protect" (R2P) doctrine, noting that while both projects claim to challenge impunity in the name of peace and justice, the reliance on powerful states to implement their agendas can turn victims into proxies for military intervention.

The kind of justice that the ICC is in the business of "delivering" is therefore increasingly in question.

The court's cases in Uganda, Sudan, and Kenya have variously encountered these challenges and criticisms. The complexity of each case warrants greater consideration than I provide here, and demands attention not only to the ICC's relationship to structures of power but also to those of the individuals it seeks to hold accountable, many of whom may use their positions of power to escape trial.

The ICC launched its first case in 2004, investigating the rebel Lord's Resistance Army (LRA) in Uganda. Despite widespread documentation of the Ugandan government's domestic crimes—perhaps the most damning being the military's forced displacement of hundreds of thousands of people into camps that rendered them vulnerable to LRA abuses—the prosecutor decided to investigate only the LRA.

While the rebel movement's powers have drastically dwindled over the years, President Museveni has successfully used the ICC indictment against LRA leaders to expand his military capabilities, and to suppress all forms of political dissent.

Thanks to support and guidance from the US Africa Command, the Ugandan military is now a "partner" in the court's efforts to apprehend LRA leader Joseph Kony, who allegedly moves between eastern Congo, the Central African Republic, and South Sudan.

This is not a recipe for the restoration of the rule of law, but for long-term military occupation of a region that has already been subject to Ugandan government-sponsored violence. The US military has been all too happy to point to the ICC's arrest warrant for Kony as the basis for sending special operations forces to the region.

The court's indictment of Sudanese president Omar Al-Bashir four years later was the first against a sitting head of state. Because Sudan is not a member of the ICC, the UN Security Council compelled the court to initiate investigations by issuing a referral in Resolution 1593.

The involvement of the Security Council triggered widespread debate about the selectivity and double standards of permanent council members who refuse to subject themselves to the court's authority. Without disputing Bashir's complicity in grave crimes, some interpreted the referral as a witch-hunt led by Western powers determined to replace Bashir with a leader more amenable to their economic interests.

A 2010 Wikileaks file revealed the former ICC prosecutor's proclivity to use geo-politics to his advantage: In an effort to win China's support for the case against Bashir, Prosecutor Moreno Ocampo suggested that the Americans reassure China that its access to oil would not be jeopardized if Bashir were "removed" from power.[1]

Ultimately, the prosecutor seemed more concerned with serving the interests of external players than with the Sudanese themselves, as many accused him of disregarding the indictment's potential impact on domestic and regional peace-making efforts.

The court has also been susceptible to political maneuvering in Kenya, where it launched investigations in 2010 against individuals responsible for the 2007/2008 post-election violence. British lawyer Courtenay Griffiths has accused his government of meddling in the case against presidential aspirant Uhuru Kenyatta in a deliberate attempt to ensure that British favorite Raila Odinga wins the country's top seat in 2013. Griffiths claims that in this case, the ICC "outsourced evidence-gathering to local intermediaries" who "happened to be well known associates" of "Mr. Kenyatta's long-term political opponent," Odinga.[2]

Kenyatta, however, is not without his own political machinery. He and presidential aspirant William Ruto, also indicted by the ICC, have drawn on their own political networks to push for the postponement of their respective trials in the hopes that victory at the polls might offer them immunity. Both have built considerable momentum for their campaigns on the grounds that the court is meddling in domestic affairs. In the meantime, ICC officials have expressed concerns over the intimidation of witnesses, whose protection seems to depend more on the goodwill of "cooperating" states like the United States and United Kingdom.

Each of the African cases, among them Cote d'Ivoire, Central African Republic, Democratic Republic of Congo, and Libya, is worthy of study as Palestinians weigh their options about possible avenues of justice.

An ICC case could certainly bring further international condemnation of Israeli leaders for their crimes, and for this reason, would be of symbolic value. But the pursuit of justice against top Israeli officials is likely to test the limits of international solidarity, particularly when it comes to advocacy efforts and the protection of victims and witnesses.

Furthermore, it is not entirely inconceivable that Palestinian membership in the ICC would open the door for the prosecution of Palestinians. While this should not be a reason to avoid joining the court, the Ugandan situation is a painful reminder that the apprehension of suspects could serve as a basis for a military operation by external "cooperating" powers, Israeli or otherwise.

Were a case against Israeli officials to proceed as far as trial, an acquittal like that in the case of Congo's Ngudjolo would be a slap in the face to the victims and witnesses who invest their energies, at great personal risk, in the hopes of a guilty verdict. For this reason, it is worth considering what it would mean to rely on the court to confirm or deny the validity of Palestinian suffering. Would "justice" *as defined by the ICC* ultimately be a source of meaningful redress for Palestinians, and would it sufficiently shed light on the broader structures of political and economic oppression that hold Israeli apartheid intact?

The ICC and its more prominent supporters, much like proponents of the "responsibility to protect," generally lead us to believe that the court is the answer to impunity, as though the law were divorced from politics, and as though "peace" and "justice" can simply be delivered at the push of a button.

Yet, the ICC is an institution located within a larger architecture of power that endows some crimes and some victims with legitimacy, and not others. At the same time, its "responsibility to punish" is subject to political manipulation that allows for further exception and impunity, most recently observed in the case of the Security Council referral on Libya.

The extent to which the court is or ever can be a counter-hegemonic project therefore requires careful consideration, demanding questions rather than answers. Perhaps the time has come to engage with our allies on the African continent about the possibilities and limitations of this institution to contribute to our collective struggles, and to grapple critically with how we conceive of justice itself.

10 January 2013

---

[1] "US Embassy Cables: ICC Prosecutor Alleges Bashir Secret Fortune of $9bn," *The Guardian*, 17 December 2010, http://www.guardian.co.uk/world/us-embassy-cables-documents/198641.

[2] Courtenay Griffiths, "The International Criminal Court Is Hurting Africa," *The Telegraph*, 3 July 2012, http://www.telegraph.co.uk/news/worldnews/africaandindianocean/kenya/9373188/The-International-Criminal-Court-is-hurting-Africa.html.

Israel and Palestine: International Law Updates

Sharon Weill

This brief report provides information related to three recent developments in international law related to Israel and Palestine:

1. The International Criminal Court Prosecutor's decision as to whether Palestine qualifies as a state for purposes of accepting the court's jurisdiction;

2. UNESCO's granting of membership to Palestine; and

3. Ongoing investigations concerning Operation Cast Lead.

Israel, Palestine and the International Criminal Court (ICC)

On 20 January 2009, the Palestinian Authority issued a declaration recognizing the ad hoc jurisdiction of the International Criminal Court in accordance with Article 12(3) of the 1998 Rome Statute. The declaration was made in the aftermath of the Israeli military offensive Operation Cast Lead in Gaza, which led to the establishment of a United Nations fact-finding mission (The Goldstone Mission) and its conclusions that Israel had committed war crimes and crimes against humanity.

Article 12(3) allows a state not party to the statute to accept the jurisdiction of the court on an ad hoc basis, in connection to a situation in which war crimes, crimes against humanity, or genocide are alleged to have been committed on the state's territory or by one of its nationals. This provision has previously been invoked by both Uganda and Côte d'Ivoire. Unlike adherence to the Rome Statute, which establishes jurisdiction over crimes committed after the entry into force of the Rome Statute for that state, a declaration under Article 12(3) attributes retroactive jurisdiction since July 2002. In its declaration the Palestinian Authority recognized the competence of the ICC over international crimes committed since 1 July 2002, thereby including Operation Cast Lead.

The legal question posed by the declaration was whether Palestine qualifies as "a State which is not a Party to this Statute" for the purposes of submitting a declaration under Article 12(3) of the Rome Statute.[1] That question spawned a major academic debate, featuring the publication of multiple legal opinions, including by such jurists as Alain Pellet, John Quigley, and Malcolm Shaw. Although the UN fact-finding mission made specific reference to the Palestinian Authority's declaration in its recommendations, noting in its report that "accountability for victims and the interests of peace and justice in the region require that the Prosecutor should make the required legal determination as expeditiously as possible" (paragraph 1970), it took the prosecutor three years to reach a (non)decision on 3 April 2012.

The ICC Chief Prosecutor's (Non)Decision

On 3 April 2012, three years after the Palestinian Authority's declaration was lodged, the ICC prosecutor delivered his opinion on whether it was valid. Instead of deciding on the matter and determining whether Palestine is a state for the purpose of the ICC Statute, the prosecutor deferred the decision to political bodies: the UN Secretary General and the ICC States' Assembly. As none of these bodies are likely to decide soon on the matter, the investigations of the war crimes allegations committed during Operation Cast Lead remain, once again, without any effective mechanism of investigation and prosecution.

Former Israeli Chief Justice Aharon Barak says that any legal question has a legal answer.[2] However, the ICC chief prosecutor chose to avoid deciding on the matter. After three years, the prosecutor concluded, just prior to the expiration of his mandate in June 2012, that he was not competent to make the necessary determination. This decision relies on a rather technical argument, deferring it instead to the authority of the UN Secretary-General and the UN General Assembly (GA) to determine whether an applicant wishing to join the Rome Statute is a state:

> In accordance with article 125, the Rome Statute is open to accession by "all States," and any State seeking to become a Party to the Statute must deposit an instrument of accession with the Secretary-General of the United Nations. In instances where it is controversial or unclear whether an applicant constitutes a "State," it is the practice of the Secretary-General to follow or seek the General Assembly's directives on the matter.[3]

Thus, the prosecutor concluded that the "competence for determining the term 'state' within the meaning of Article 12 rests, in the first instance, with the

UN Secretary-General who, in case of doubt, will defer to the guidance of GA. The Assembly of States Parties of the Rome Statute could also in due course decide to address the matter in accordance with Article 112(2) (g) of the Statute."

According to Professor Schabas, the question of determining what entity is a state for the purpose of joining the ICC is explicitly deferred to the Secretary General by the Rome Statute, and it is of a different nature from determining which is "a State which is not a Party to this Statute" for the purpose of Article 12(3). The latter issue is a question of fact that must be determined by the prosecutor and in second place by the judges. In accordance with that reasoning, Dapo Akande argued that "no one would assert that if the question of statehood came up with regard to immunity of third States under Article 98 [of the Rome Statute], it is the UN Secretary-General that should decide that question."[4]

UNESCO's Recognition of Palestine—Why is this Important?

On 23 September 2011, prior to the ICC prosecutor's determination, Palestinian Authority President Abbas submitted an application for admission to the United Nations as a member state. While becoming a member state of the UN requires the approval of the UN Security Council—which is unlikely in this case given the near certainty of a US veto—the granting of official member state status must be distinguished from being recognized as a state. One hundred and thirty states, a wide majority in the General Assembly, already recognize Palestine as a state. As observed by Michael Kearney:

> Abbas could have ridden the wave and put the recognition of the state of Palestine to the General Assembly and in all likelihood won a large majority vote and ensured Palestine's status as a "non-member state." As things stand it is clear that Abbas was aiming for full UN membership as a political maneuver without any strategic interest in the ICC process. [5]

Importantly, on 31 October 2011, UNESCO (the United Nations Educational, Scientific and Cultural Organization) admitted Palestine as a member. UNESCO is an international organization within the UN, whose membership is limited to states: Article II(2) of UNESCO's constitution provides that a state which is not a member of the UN may be admitted by a two-thirds vote in favor in the General Conference. The legal implication of that recognition is that since Palestine became a member of a UN agency (UNESCO), Palestine can now accede to treaties "open to all States" (including the Rome Statute). As stated above, in cases in which the UN Secretary-General (SG) is the depositary, such as the Rome Statute, and where it is controversial whether the applicant is a state or not, the SG will defer to the determination of the General Assembly. However, according to the practice, these controversial cases would not include "those falling within the 'Vienna formula,' i.e., other than states that are members of the United Nations *or members of the specialized agencies*, or Parties to the Statute of the International Court of Justice." The fact that the Vienna Convention includes members of UN special agencies in the categories of states that are competent to conclude treaties is of major importance. As Professor Schabas noted, "how could the Secretary-General refuse the accession by 'a state' that has already been recognized as 'a state' pursuant to the Constitution of UNESCO?"[6]

Oddly, while the ICC chief prosecutor mentions in his opinion the fact that Palestine was recognized by 130 states, and that the Security Council has not yet made a recommendation concerning its application for UN membership, he did not mention UNESCO's implicit recognition.

The ICC prosecutor's non-decision was not the first time, nor will it be the last, that a legal institution has avoided taking a legal decision because of political controversy, choosing instead to defer to political bodies. However, it is another example of the complex relationship between law and politics at the international level, and how judicial bodies fail to deal with the challenges of credibility and impartiality.

Updates on Israel's Investigations Concerning Operation Cast Lead

If established, ICC jurisdiction could be triggered in cases where local judicial fora are unwilling or unable to prosecute international crimes.

Israel produced five long reports as part of its national follow-up investigations into Operation Cast Lead. In the reports, Israel's state attorneys sought to rigorously refute claims about the state's responsibility for violations of international law, reporting that around four hundred command and fifty-two criminal investigations had been opened (according to the Second UN Report of the Committee of Experts in follow-up to Goldstone, March 2011, page 6). However, three years after Israel launched Operation Cast Lead, prosecution has only been initiated in three cases, all involving low-ranking soldiers and on the basis of violating army orders. Not a single investigation examined the legality of the Israeli government's policies during the operation, or the responsibility of policy-makers. Moreover, all of these investigations have been conducted internally, by military personnel who were involved in issuing and approving orders in "real time" combat.

In its follow-up to the Goldstone report, a Committee of Independent Experts was established by the UN Human Rights Council to assess whether the investigations conducted by the parties complied with international standards.[7] The committee's second report, released on 18 March 2011, stated, *inter alia*, that the investigations conducted by the parties failed to satisfy international law standards as they did not include investigation of high-level officials and did not address all the allegations.[8] According to the Palestinian Centre for Human Rights (PCHR), as of 18 January 2012, despite submitting 490 criminal complaints to the authorities, PCHR had only received responses in twenty-one cases. Israel has not published and will not disclose the status of the ongoing investigations or the evidence that led to the discontinuation of certain inquiries. In a recent example, as published in the Guardian on 2 May 2012, Israel closed its investigation into the destruction of a house which killed twenty-one members of the Samouni family. No action will be taken against any of the soldiers or commanders involved in these killings. Israel's military advocate general stated that the investigation had "comprehensively refuted" allegations that the Israeli army had intentionally targeted civilians or had acted in a reckless manner.[9]

The Turkel Commission

Following the death of nine activists aboard the Gaza Freedom Flotilla, the Israeli government authorized the Turkel Commission[10] to examine, *inter alia*, "whether the investigation and inquiry mechanism that is practiced in Israel in general ... is consistent with the duties of the State of Israel pursuant to the rules of international law."[11] The commission, which was appointed by the government, comprises four Israeli members and two international observers. During the month of April 2011, the Israeli panel heard testimonies from the military and political echelons—including the military advocate general, the attorney general, the head of the General Security Services, and the head of the Military Police—as well as representatives of leading Israeli non-governmental organizations. Of special interest are the testimonies provided by professors Yuval Shany and Eyal Benvenisti, two professors of international law. Both Professor Shany and Professor Benvenisti testified that the reason proper investigations and prosecutions had not been conducted was that there existed structural deficiencies throughout Israel's entire investigative system, which centralized all investigation and prosecution powers in the hands of the Military Advocate General—a body that is neither independent nor impartial.

The commission's report is scheduled to be published in the next few weeks. An article published on 6 May 2012 in Haaretz indicated that:

> The Turkel Committee is expected to recommend significantly augmenting civilian review of IDF probes with regard to Palestinian complaints. The committee discussed the establishment of a department of international law in the Justice Ministry that would answer to the attorney general and supervise both the Military Advocate General and the Military Police. The Turkel Committee is to recommend that the attorney general be granted the power to change decisions by the Military Advocate General with regard to complaints by Palestinians. One chapter of the report, compiled with the assistance of international legal experts, will summarize the way international law deals with investigations of war crimes in order to determine in principle when criminal investigations should be launched in such cases.[12]

Further reading:

- Chantal Meloni and Gianni Tognoni (eds), "Is There A Court for Gaza?—A Test Bench for International Justice" (Asser/Springer, The Hague, 2012).

- FIDH, "Shielded from accountability: Israel's unwillingness to investigate and prosecute international crimes," September 2011.

11 June 2012

[Originally published in Adalah's Newsletter, Volume 93, May 2012]

---

[1] "Rome Statute of the International Criminal Court," 1998, http://untreaty.un.org/cod/icc/statute/99_corr/cstatute.htm.

2 For example, in HCJ 769/02, The Public Committee Against Torture in Israel et al. v. The Government of Israel, et al., [decision delivered 11 December 2005], opinion of Chief Justice Aharon Barak, paragraph 48.

3 "ICC Jurisdiction for 'Acts Committed on the Territory of Palestine Since 1 July 2002' - ICC Prosecutor Declaration," International Criminal Court Office of the Prosecutor, 3 April 2012, http://unispal.un.org/UNISPAL.NSF/0/206D43BAF726DD22852579D50050138B.

4 Dapo Akande, "ICC Prosecutor Decides That He Can't Decide on the Statehood of Palestine. Is He Right?," *EJIL: Talk!*, 5 April 2012, http://www.ejiltalk.org/icc-prosecutor-decides-that-he-cant-decide-on-the-statehood-of-palestine-is-he-right/.

5 Michael Kearney, "The Situation in Palestine," *Opinio Juris*, 5 April 2012, http://opiniojuris.org/2012/04/05/the-situation-in-palestine/.

6 William Schabas, "Palestine Should Accede to the Rome Statute," *PhD Studies in Human Rights*, 1 November 2011, http://humanrightsdoctorate.blogspot.co.uk/2011/11/palestine-should-accede-to-rome-statute.html.

7 See UN Human Rights Council Resolution 13/9, "Follow-up to the Report of the United Nations Independent International Fact-Finding Mission on the Gaza Conflict," UN Doc. A/HRC/RES/13/9, 19 April 2010.

8 Report of the Committee of independent experts in international humanitarian and human rights law established pursuant to Council resolution 13/9, UN doc. A/HRC/16/24, 18 March 2011.

9 Harriet Sherwood, "Israel Closes Inquiry into Palestinian Family Killed During Gaza War," *The Guardian*, 2 May 2012, http://www.guardian.co.uk/world/2012/may/02/israel-closes-inquiry-gaza-family-killing.

10 The Turkel Commission is formally known as the "Public Commission to Examine the Maritime Incident of 31 May 2010."

11 The testimonies on the domestic system of military investigation given by the state authorities, NGOs, and academics are online (in Hebrew) at http://www.turkel-committee.com/connt-153-b.html.

12 Barak Ravid, "Turkel Committee to Call for Stronger Civilian Review of IDF Probes," *Haaretz.com*, 6 May 2012, http://www.haaretz.com/news/diplomacy-defense/turkel-committee-to-call-for-stronger-civilian-review-of-idf-probes-1.428427.

III | US Foreign Policy

Obama's Palestine Problem, and Ours

Anthony Alessandrini

It is shocking, but not surprising, that in the United States the primary way of understanding and analyzing the debate at the United Nations over Palestinian statehood is in terms of its effect upon American politics.

More specifically, the main focus in the US media has been on how the Obama administration would handle the "crisis" at the United Nations, inevitably described as one aspect of the supposed "roiling tensions in the region." Very little thought is being devoted to the question of whether the move by the Palestinian leadership is part of a larger strategy for escaping from the disastrous stasis of the Oslo framework, or what possibilities might arise from potential outcomes at the United Nations. The preferred questions have to do with the effects on the 2012 US Presidential election, including the famous question of the "Jewish vote," variations of which seem to remain eternally fresh and interesting to American journalists and editors. Even the role played by the UN debate in the outcome of the recent special election in the Congressional district of Brooklyn, previously represented by the hapless Anthony Weiner, seems to be of more interest to the US media than the potential effect of that debate upon the lives of Palestinians.

Shocking, but not surprising; the long struggle for Palestinian self-determination and justice has never played much of a role in the dominant narrative of the "conflict" as it gets told in the United States. As Joseph Massad put it recently, "the only game in town has always been Israel's interests," and these interests are simply and unquestioningly linked, in this narrative, to the interests of the US.[1]

The point, at this moment, is not simply to express indignation at this state of affairs. This moment offers some opportunities to take stock of the current status of this dominant narrative of the "conflict," and, ideally, for those of us interested in questions of justice and solidarity, to re-think our strategy accordingly.

One striking aspect of the UN debate coverage is the way that it has been folded into a larger situation in which the state of Israel is described as "besieged" and "isolated." The title of Ethan Bronner's *New York Times* article, which brings the UN debate together with the protests at the Israeli embassy in Cairo and the diplomatic steps pursued by Turkey in the wake of the recent Palmer Report, is explicit about this supposed state of siege: "Beyond Cairo, Israel Sensing a Wider Siege" (it may be worth noting that the article was published on 11 September 2011).[2] John Heileman, in a *New York Magazine* article, uses language almost identical to that used by Bronner: "With the Middle East apparently hurtling headlong into crisis, Israel finds itself increasingly isolated, beleaguered, and besieged: its embassy in Cairo invaded by Egyptian protesters, its relations with Turkey in tatters, its continued occupation of (and expansion of settlements within) the Palestinian territories the subject of wide international scorn."[3]

Does it really need to be pointed out that the state being described metaphorically as under "siege" is in fact a state that has been carrying on an illegal occupation for more than sixty years, and indeed is enforcing a very real state of siege in Gaza? Or that the state being described as "isolated" is in fact protected unconditionally, in the military, economic, and diplomatic sphere, by the world's lone superpower?

Such linguistic inversions and perversions sent me back to the point expressed so beautifully by Mourid Barghouti in his memoir *I Saw Ramallah*:

> It is easy to blur the truth with a simple linguistic trick: start your story from "Secondly."...Start your story with "Secondly," and the world will be turned upside-down. Start your story with "Secondly," and the arrows of the Native Americans are the original criminals and the guns of the white men are entirely the victim. It is enough to start with "Secondly," for the anger of the black man against the white to be barbarous. Start with "Secondly," and Gandhi becomes responsible for the tragedies of the British. You only need to start your story with "Secondly," and the burned Vietnamese will have wounded the humanity of the napalm, and Victor Jara's songs will be the shameful thing and not Pinochet's bullets, which killed so many thousands in the Santiago stadium. It is enough to start with "Secondly," for my

grandmother, Umm 'Ata, to become the criminal and Ariel Sharon her victim.[4]

Barghouti is referring to the speech made by Yitzhak Rabin at the White House on the occasion of the signing of the Oslo Accords, and he sees Rabin's speech as a particularly brilliant example of the reversal of reality affected by starting the story with "Secondly":

> The Israelis occupy our homes as victims and present us to the world as killers. Israel dazzles the world with its generosity toward us….The houses built on top of ours gallantly declare their willingness to understand our odd predilection toward living in camps scattered in the Diaspora of gods and flies…Their generous guns in Deir Yassin forgive us the fact that they piled our bodies high at the sunset hours there one day. Their fighter jets forgive the graves of our martyrs in Beirut. Their soldiers forgive the tendency of our teenagers' bones to break. Israel the victim polishes its hot, red knife with the sheen of forgiveness.[5]

But Barghouti also offers a grudging tribute to the larger international effects achieved through such linguistic violence as that found in Rabin's speech: "This leader knew how to demand that the world should respect Israeli blood, the blood of every Israeli individual without exception."[6]

This is much the same point as that raised by Massad in talking about the context of the current debate at the United Nations:

> It is important to stress at the outset that whether the UN grants the Palestinian Authority the government of a state under occupation and observer status as a state or refuses to do so, either outcome will be in the interest of Israel. For the only game in town has always been Israel's interests, and it is clear that whatever strategy garners international support, with or without US and Israeli approval, must guarantee Israeli interests a priori.[7]

The principle that underwrites all discussions of "the conflict" in US discourse is the notion of Israel's security. This emphasis on security has two unspoken aspects: that such security is constantly under threat, constantly "besieged" (despite Israel's incontestable military superiority in the region), and that such security is the paramount concern of the United States. It is never directly stated that Israeli lives, in this narrative, are given more value than Palestinian lives. It is just that in discussions of Israeli security, Palestinian security never seems to come up as an issue.

The second key aspect of this narrative is the taken-for-granted place of the United States at its center. After all, when Rabin and Arafat had their famous handshake, it was at the White House, with Bill Clinton grinning in their midst. Likewise, the equally famous Sadat-Begin handshake overseen by Jimmy Carter, and even the (admittedly less frequent and less friendly) Netanyahu-Abbas handshakes, marshaled by a clearly strained Barack Obama.

One possibility raised by the current debate at the UN, whatever its outcome, is the challenging of this taken-for-granted role of the United States at the center of all things. The absurdity of this perceived centrality has been brought out quite nicely by Mouin Rabbani, who notes that in the dominant US media discourse, the Palestinian leadership's decision to go to the UN, which is "the very definition of multilateralism," has been portrayed again and again as "a unilateral move, and therefore illegitimate."[8] Through the same twisted reasoning, as Obama's speech to the UN made clear, the only viable alternative to this supposed "unilateralism" on the part of the Palestinian leadership was the form of "bilateralism" represented by direct negotiations. It never even needs to be said out loud that such negotiations (part of the "peace process" that is constantly invoked, although no such process currently exists) would be conducted under the aegis of the US government.

My purpose is not to take a position on the UN debate itself. I agree with those who suggest that UN recognition might present certain strategic gains, particularly in the realm of international law (although, as Massad notes, the problem in the past has not been with a lack of international legal instruments with which to challenge Israeli actions, but rather with the failure of international institutions to enforce any sort of legal sanctions against Israel, largely because of the intervention of the US to ensure Israeli impunity). But I also agree very strongly with Noura Erakat's suggestion that the UN strategy is being put forward by a Palestinian leadership that, while purporting to represent the Palestinian people as a whole, has refused to be part of any sort of truly democratic process that would allow for popular participation in these sorts of strategic decisions. So the real question, whatever the outcome at the UN, will be, as it always has been, the nature of the ongoing popular struggle of the Palestinian people for justice and self-determination.

It is in this context that I would like to see a reinvigorated discussion of the forms of solidarity that will be required in the days to come. In particular, what sort of solidarity can begin to work against the twin bulwarks of the dominant narrative of the "conflict" in the United States: the emphasis on Israel's victim status and thus of the primacy of its security needs, and the taken-for-granted role of the United States as central to the situation of Israel-Palestine?

Another way to ask the question would be: What sort of solidarity can help to advance the goals that Rabbani sees as the most positive potential outcomes that may follow from the debates at the UN? As he puts it:

> Two decades of negotiations have achieved nothing except the further consolidation of Israeli control over the occupied territories, in large part because of consistent American support for Israeli impunity. It is therefore high time for an alternative and more effective approach to resolve this conflict and achieve a credible two-state settlement. Given the systematic failure of bilateral Israeli-Palestinian diplomacy under unilateral American sponsorship, returning the Question of Palestine—in all of its dimensions—to the multilateral forum of the United Nations is an essential first step. Serious questions can and should be raised about the manner in which this is being approached by the Palestinian leadership. But the era in which the US and other Western powers profess support for the principle of Palestinian statehood while thoroughly undermining it in practice must come to an end.[9]

Speaking from within the US context, I would put this as the question of how we can work to most effectively remove US influence from the equation, or, at the very least, lessen US involvement, especially when this involvement entails the ensuring of Israeli impunity and the funding of Israeli atrocities.

This means revisiting our intellectual and activist agendas and rethinking the modes of solidarity that will be most effective in the new struggles that will arise. For example, the Boycott, Divestment, and Sanctions (BDS) movement has arguably been the most exciting and effective mode of international solidarity over the past few years. One of the key accomplishments of BDS (among many) has been to raise the question of Israeli impunity, and to force individuals (particularly in their role as consumers) to address their own implication in the atrocities committed by the Israeli government and funded and enabled by the United States and other governments.

In this, the BDS movement has been an unqualified success. But, at least in the United States, these efforts have not (yet) effected any major changes in the workings of the dominant narratives about Israel-Palestine. I would also argue that they have to a great extent supplanted other sorts of actions aimed more directly at the US government's role in underwriting Israel's actions. I think Adam Shapiro's description of the evolution of strategies of solidarity in the United States over the past decade is largely accurate:

> In the United States…lobbying elected officials seems both impossible and meaningless, given the vast support for Israel from the US government (and US taxpayer money). Whereas groups like Stop US Taxpayer Aid to Israel Now (SUSTAIN) emerged in 2000 and 2001 and ran out of steam by the middle of the decade, by 2009 there were vibrant and active boycott, divestment, and sanctions groups emerging in communities, cities, and on college campuses around the United States.[10]

Without in any way wishing to suggest that the work of the BDS movement be curtailed, it may be time to revisit, at least in the United States, some of those earlier strategies, particularly those aimed at US funding to Israel. Certainly the need to maintain international BDS actions (not to mention forms of international solidarity work in Palestine) is crucial. But it may be that the most effective acts of solidarity now, in the wake of the movements of the Arab Spring and whatever forms of popular struggle will follow from the strategies of the Palestinian leadership at the UN, would take the form of directly addressing the US government's role in the region, with the goal of neutralizing it as effectively as possible.

To be clear, this is not a matter of requesting that the US government take a more "positive" role in Israel-Palestine, or in the region more generally. It is a matter of working to remove US influence from the region, insofar as that influence has generally consisted of maintaining US interests at the expense of the interests and aspirations of the majority of the people living there. This process has, of course, already begun, thanks to the uprisings of the Arab Spring; thus, the repetition of crisis narratives in the US media, the handwringing about the "tumultuous" changes ongoing in the region, and the open expressions of fear regarding the effects these popular uprisings will have on US interests and influence. Solidarity, in this case, would consist of doing whatever is possible to speed this process along—to "expedite the day of liberation," to cite the title of Shapiro's essay.

While writing this I learned of the execution of Troy Davis by the state of Georgia, after his stay of execution was denied by the US Supreme Court and after President Obama refused to intervene in the case. According to a White House spokesperson, the president had determined that "it is 'not appropriate' to become involved in specific state cases." It is telling that this horrific miscarriage of justice was carried out by the US legal system only a few hours after the president of the United States stood before the UN to lecture the world on the proper methods by which Palestinians should and should not pursue justice. To become involved in the "specific state case" of Palestine is, apparently, quite appropriate, in President Obama's view.

What will happen at the UN in the days to come remains to be seen. Meanwhile, the struggle for justice in Israel-Palestine, and throughout the region, continues. Here in the belly of the beast, as always, there is work to be done.

22 September 2011

---

[1] Joseph Massad, "State of Recognition," *Institute for Palestine Studies*, 15 September 2011, http://palestine-studies.org/columndetails.aspx?t=1&id=115.

[2] Ethan Bronner, "Beyond Cairo, Israel Sensing A Wider Siege," *The New York Times*, 11 September 2011, http://query.nytimes.com/gst/fullpage.html.

[3] John Heilemann, "The Tsuris," *New York Magazine*, 18 September 2011, http://nymag.com/news/politics/israel-2011-9/.

[4] Mourid Barghouti, *I Saw Ramallah* (Random House Digital, Inc., 2008).

[5] Ibid.

[6] Ibid.

[7] Massad, "State of Recognition."

[8] "Interview with Jadaliyya Co-Editor Mouin Rabbani on Palestinian Statehood," *Jadaliyya*, 20 September 2011, http://www.jadaliyya.com/pages/index/2675/interview-with-jadaliyya-co-editor-mouin-rabbani-o.

[9] Ibid.

10 Adam Shapiro, "Expediting the Day of Liberation," in *Midnight on the Mavi Marmara: The Attack on the Gaza Freedom Flotilla and How It Changed the Course of the Israel/Palestine Conflict* (OR Books, 2010), 286.

United States Should Step Aside as Mideast Broker

Mouin Rabbani

When it comes to Arab-Israeli diplomacy the American monopoly on mediation needs to be terminated. The reason is simple. Washington's systematic failure over several decades has disqualified it from acting without adult supervision.

Rather than the marriage counselor who must be balanced because both spouses are angry, the United States is the arbitrator who sleeps with and solicits bribes from the more powerful disputant, and fixes outcomes accordingly. Given the US mantra that it cannot want peace more than the parties themselves and that negotiations without preconditions are the only acceptable formula—meaning that Israel has a veto over every decision large and small—it is high time the Obama administration makes room for the many who value peace more than occupation.

In November 1947, the United Nations General Assembly recommended the establishment of separate Arab and Jewish states in Palestine. Israel was established the following year, and currently occupies all of the territory allotted by the world body to both states. It is a reality that could not exist without consistent and increasingly uncritical American support of Israel.

Since the 1970s, the international community has routinely prescribed a two-state settlement to resolve this prolonged conflict. It took the United States until the 21st century to join the community of nations in endorsing a Palestinian state, though this never went beyond the declarative level. Indeed, the main achievement of the diplomatic process initiated by Washington in 1991, and monopolized by it ever since, has been the exponential acceleration of Israel's illegal settlement enterprise. The reality is that a process carefully designed to fragment and disenfranchise Palestinians to the largest extent possible, and consolidate Israeli control over Palestinian lives, would not have proceeded differently.

Last month, the Palestine Liberation Organization (PLO) submitted an application for UN membership for the missing state to the Security Council. In response, Washington all but declared a global state of alert. The ferocity of its campaign to deny Palestinian statehood, including the credible threat of yet another veto on Israel's behalf, the incessant bullying of friend and foe alike, and punitive Congressional sanctions, conclusively demonstrate that the United States is incapable of mediating anything other than a one-state outcome, comprising perpetual Israeli domination from the river to the sea rather than equality between them.

American claims of support for Palestinian statehood ring more hollow than ever. Consider President Obama's September 2010 proclamation from the UN rostrum that he hoped to see Palestine as a member of the world body. Yet, he has stopped at nothing to prevent it. Similarly, Washington consistently enables further settlement expansion and systematically shields Israel from censure and consequences, while verbally opposing Israeli colonization of Palestinian land.

This begs the question: Why does Washington remain so committed to extending its perfect record of abysmal failure? The answer increasingly provided by Palestinians and Arabs alike is that the United States is devoted to its monopoly precisely because it views its involvement as a success—for itself and Israel, at the Palestinians' and the international community's expense. If there are indeed other factors that explain why Washington opposes even a symbolic Palestinian diplomatic initiative, and goes rabid at the very suggestion of multilateralism, these have yet to be persuasively presented.

For those Arabs who still listen to President Obama's speeches, the contrast between his proclaimed support for Arab self-determination and determined opposition to its Palestinian variant was at least as clear as daylight on a cloudless afternoon.

Obama fools only himself if he thinks Palestine will not be the litmus test of American intentions towards the region's peoples. By yet again sabotaging a Palestinian attempt to break free of perpetual Israeli domination, he has made a mockery of American claims to support not only Palestinian but also Arab aspirations. In Tunisia, Obama at least had the sense to hail the uprising once Ben Ali's plane reached 30,000 feet. In Palestine, he poured copious amounts of fuel on a raging regional fire despite repeated warnings from the four corners of the world.

While Obama's total embrace of Israel was as objectionable to Arabs as it was delightful to Avigdor Lieberman, it was the US president's insistence on business-as-usual yet again that grated most. Denouncing diplomacy at the United

Nations as "unilateralism" in order to preserve America's monopoly over the "peace process" only added insult to injury.

Not all successful mediators are neutral, yet America's seemingly limitless devotion to the colonizer against the colonized cries out for a counterweight. To the extent Washington succeeds in excluding other actors from the equation, it will increasingly be called to account by the region's citizens. As Ben Ali, Mubarak, and other trusted friends of America are forced to make room for more representative leaderships, Washington's startling incongruence with the spirit of the times is creating a massive problem for itself.

It is anyone's guess when, how, and by whom American interests in the region will pay the price of US Middle East policy. In order to minimize that cost, and retain what prospects remain for a constructive relationship with the Arab world, Washington's politicians would do well to at least stop digging. To paraphrase Obama's message to Syria's Asad: If he cannot lead, he should follow, and if he refuses he must get out of the way before being forced aside.

23 October 2011

[A shorter version of this article was published on Northjersey.com's The Record]

An Apocalyptic Air of Approaching Peril: Zionism at the United Nations

Sherene Seikaly

Bibi sauntered. He swaggered. He spoke freely, seemingly unguided by any text. He irreverently made circles with his fingers. He called the group of diplomats and interns assembled in front of him actors in "a theater of the absurd." He proudly modeled his thick coat of indifference, just as he called the United Nations a "house of lies." Indeed, so capable was the UN in presenting the false as true, Bibi gestured assuredly, they could go so far to declare that the sun set in the West.

Realizing that the sun did in fact set in the West, Bibi calmly stepped back from the rhetorical precipice and began what he came for: to speak the truth, the truth about Israel, the truth about a Palestinian state, and the truth about civilization.

For good measure, he informed the audience that he had just laid a wreath on the September 11 memorial; he was deeply moved. He went on to provide the General Assembly with his philosophical understanding of the challenges the enlightened world faces from its benighted other. Those who worried that eight months of popular revolt in the Middle East signaled the final nail in the coffin of the shallow, essentialist readings of the late Samuel Huntington were comforted. Bibi assured the world that the West and East were still on their way to an inevitable civilizational clash. Echoing Huntington, Bibi reminded his audience that the Cold War was over and done with (thanks for the update) as was the very idea of politics, now replaced, he explained, by religious strife. The ugly head of the real, mortal enemy, the "malignancy" threatening civilization as we know it, was none other than the "insatiable crocodile" of militant Islam.

Had the years dulled Bibi's capacity to creatively conjure the monstrous embodiment of the other? A crocodile? Really?

Bibi persisted. He dug. He blew air into the figurative corpses of the September 11 decade. Leaping from the clash of civilizations to the ever-delayed "final status" location of Israel's never declared borders, Bibi then unearthed the old "constructive ambiguity" argument about Resolution 242. He explained (for those of us who have not been following this inane debate since 1967) that the UN resolution specified Israeli withdrawal from *territories* not *the territories*. Thus, armed with the powerful weapon of a definite article, Bibi, like many before him, justified the now century-long denial of Palestinians' inalienable right to self-determination.

Bibi went on to channel his predecessors, echoing Abba Ebban that day in 1967 when the foreign minister stated:

> In short, there was peril for Israel wherever it looked. Its manpower had been hastily mobilized. Its economy and commerce were beating with feeble pulses. Its streets dark and empty. There was an apocalyptic air of approaching peril. And Israel faced the danger alone.[1]

Bibi revived the idea of an island of fear; a "tiny country, surrounded by people sworn to its destruction and armed to the teeth by Iran."

He then effortlessly named the West Bank "Judea and Samaria," without which, he pleaded, "Israel is all of nine miles wide....That's about two-thirds the length of Manhattan. It's the distance between Battery Park and Columbia University." Having extended his hand to the Egyptians, Jordanians, Iranians, Lebanese, Syrians, and *even* the Palestinians, Bibi went on to disparage them: "And don't forget that the people who live in Brooklyn and New Jersey are considerably nicer than some of Israel's neighbors."

Bibi did not utter the word "Zionism" at any point in his forty-minute speech. As he sliced through the UN's "unjust condemnation" of Israel he indirectly defined Zionism as the "age-old yearning of my people to restore our national life in our ancient biblical homeland."

It was this national life, this "age-old yearning" that Bibi explained was under threat. "We just don't want the Palestinians to try to change the Jewish character of the state." Thus, the Palestinians' yearning (of the last sixty-three years) to restore their national life on their homeland and realize their right to return was in Bibi's speech a "fantasy" that "we want the Palestinians to give up."

What was most surprising about Bibi's performance was neither the arrogance nor the condescension. It was not his confident and relentless commitment to expansionist policies that have and will continue to uproot, occupy, oppress, imprison, and *attempt* to erase the Palestinians. It was not even the gestural and rhetorical assurances that the only two states in the world that truly matter are the United States and Israel. There is nothing new in any of this.

What was surprising was the flaccid emptiness of Bibi's ideology. When he said: "in Israel peace never wanes," what he meant to say was that Zionism, or so he hoped, never wanes. But his performance in front of the world personified that very waning. It is true that the members of the US Congress obsequiously stood and clapped when Netanyahu mourned the "painful compromises" of making "peace" with the Palestinians since: "In Judea and Samaria, the Jewish people are not foreign occupiers." But the General Assembly was not so servile.

Indeed, Mahmoud Abbas far outranked Bibi in argument and reception. This outranking had nothing to do with charisma, a quality that Abbas could never be accused of possessing. It had to do with words. Abbas delivered the language of the Palestinian opposition. In voicing the terms *apartheid, ethnic cleansing, the racist separation wall,* he, if only momentarily, called the Oslo process what it is: an intensification of Israeli occupation that has pulverized Palestinian land and society. He used the very words that critics and organizers have deployed against the Palestinian Authority, in its role as the subcontractor of the Israeli occupation.

But Bibi used old words. And they fell flat. His confidence, his righteousness, and his indifference were so ripe that he did not resort to ideology or argument. In his derision for international opinion, he was outmoded and out of step. He declared the death of politics at the very moment when people all over the world (including his very own constituency) are taking to the streets demanding social and economic justice. But it is perhaps this constituency that is most to blame for the flaccidity of Bibi's rhetoric, for they have no words to oppose the occupation.

Bibi's attempts to continue the long Israeli tradition of presenting an earnest David against the big bad Arab-Muslim-Palestinian Goliath won him no love at the UN. The audience was left instead with the image of that malignant crocodile and his insatiable appetite. Indeed, it is difficult to imagine any of Bibi's predecessors offering a two thousand year old ring with their name on it as evidence to support the last one hundred years of colonialism.

21 October 2011

---

[1] "Statement to the Security Council by Foreign Minister Eban- 6 June 1967," *Israel Ministry of Foreign Affairs*, http://www.mfa.gov.il/mfa/foreignpolicy/mfadocuments/yearbook1/pages/19%20statement%20to%20the%20security%20council%20by%20foreign%20mi.aspx

IV | Representation

Roundtable on Palestinian Diaspora and Representation

Naseer Aruri, Sherene Seikaly, Seif Da'na, and Karma Nabulsi

Part I: Palestinians Organizing in Diaspora

Q: Palestinians are not unique for organizing themselves in diaspora. The Tamils of Sri Lanka have recently elected their transnational government. Other ethnic polities, like indigenous communities in Latin America, including the Mayans of Zapata, have organized themselves within their homelands, as opposed to without. How can the Palestinian national body be contextualized in a legacy of diasporic politics and calls for self-determination more generally? Can a "people" be adequately represented in diaspora? What lessons can be drawn from other case studies for organizing Palestinians in diaspora and inversely, what lessons can be drawn from the Palestinian experience?

Naseer Aruri

Given the relationship between the Palestinian body politic and its adversary, we need to raise a few questions relating to the settler colonialist nature of Zionism and the state of Israel. First, when did settler colonialism emerge as a framework of analysis? How has the Palestine Liberation Organization's (PLO) shift in strategy from liberation through resistance to independence through negotiations and statism been reflected in the shift in analytical and strategic paradigms on Palestine, Palestinian liberation, and modes of resistance and representation? How did the movement strategize its analytical framework following the loss of land as a result of Zionist settler colonialism, and how was this framework intellectually neglected, politically abandoned, and lost with the passing of time? For us, Palestinians, who are going through a second Nakba, today is yesterday.

ABORTED STATE?

Seif Da'na

True, every diaspora experience is unique. The Palestinian experience of living in and experiencing the diaspora has been shaped by a variety of factors that need to be highlighted in order to comprehend the experience and draw necessary lessons for the future course.

1- Colonial Zionism

The expulsion of the Palestinian Arabs that led to the formation of many Palestinian communities in exile has been critical for the formation and transformation of the specific Zionist colonial genre. The pure settlement-colony, which is distinguished from other colonies of settlement (mixed settlement, plantation, and ethnic plantation) in its conquering of both land and labor (a condition that ineluctably shapes identity and brings about the erasure and negation of the other) dictated from the start the expulsion of Palestinians.

The shift from the ethnic plantation colony, the form that Zionist colonization took at the beginning, to the pure-settlement colony, which has characterized Israeli state and nation building since 1904 with the second wave of Jewish European "immigration," had serious implications and led to the Nakba.[1]

The ethnic plantation colony is based on land control, similar to the mixed settlement and plantation colony, yet "unlike the plantation colony, it employed local rather than imported labor, [and] in distinction to the miscegenation prevalent in the mixed colony, it possessed a full-blown European national identity and opposed ethnic mixture."[2]

The pure settlement colony represents the underlying structural arrangements that have shaped every aspect of the colonial experience since the second wave of Jewish-European settlement in Palestine in 1904. Fredrickson explains that "the pure form, in which European settlers exterminated or pushed aside the indigenous peoples, developed an economy based on white labor, and were thus able in the long run to regain the sense of cultural or ethnic homogeneity identified with a European conception of nationality."[3] Thus, the difference between the ethnic plantation colony and the pure settlement colony resides in labor; in Palestine, this meant a shift from Arab to Jewish labor.

As such, pure settlement colonies involve the conquering not only of land, but of labor as well, excluding the natives from the economy. These colonies,

141

therefore, are "inherently genocidal,"[4] and rest on the principle of "replacing a nation with another nation and a culture with another culture by means of extermination,"[5] and have the "purest form of racist impulse."[6]

Colonial Zionism prepared the foundations for the expulsion of the Palestinian Arabs, shaped the Israeli culture that imagined the diaspora Jew, not the Palestinian, as the other (negation of exile), and, therefore, excised the Palestinians from the Jewish European awareness and Zionist discourse ("a land without a people for a people without a land").

The PLO strategy and the hegemony of the state discourse or the two-state solution (at least since 1974 and the adoption of the ten-point plan, or since the late 1950s for Fateh) ignores this fundamental fact (see discussion below).

2- Al-Nakba and its consequences

The outcome of uprooting almost a whole nation was not limited to the creation of the refugee problem, and refugees as a new social and political category that composed the majority of the Palestinians. New political, social, economic, and spatial realities were created in which the old regime of power relations and the traditional political elite, consisting mainly of competing groups of landowners and urban elite, collapsed. The disintegration of the traditional elite and the new realities offered a political space for new elite groups to form.

While most Palestinians living in the area controlled by Israel were expelled or dislocated, the West Bank came under direct Jordanian control and was isolated, until 1967, from Gaza, which came under Egypt's control. In both areas the composition of local political elite groups varied since 1948. The aftermath of the 1948 War, or Nakba, led to the creation of four separate realities (and many sub-realities) for the Palestinians where various elite groups would be formed in exile, the West Bank, Gaza, and inside "Israel."

The relationship between and within the political elite in the four areas would determine the politics of the Palestinian national movement and the PLO's discomfited fate. Although the most obvious tension within the Palestinian movement seemed to have taken place between political organizations and within the institutions of the PLO in exile, some experts stress the "tensions inherent in the dynamics governing the relationship between those sections of Palestinian society that remained on the land (in Israel, the West Bank, and Gaza) and those dispersed in other countries, primarily Jordan, Syria and Lebanon."[7]

Prior to 1948, Palestinians did not compose an undifferentiated mass. Sociologically, Palestinians were and remain sharply bifurcated. The Nakba and diaspora were and are, therefore, felt and experienced differently across Palestinian communities. While many prosperous members of the fortunate few managed to deposit and transfer large sums of their wealth, accumulated before but certainly during the early 1940's economic recovery, in foreign and Arab banks, the majority retained no more of their property than they inadvertently carried into the cruel exile in the chinks of their battered attire. Although immovable assets and urban buildings constituted two-thirds of the national wealth and were robbed by ruthless conquerors, bank records and estimates of movable assets show that millions of pounds sterling were either transferred or have already been deposited in English and Arab banks.[8]

Not only was exile experienced differently, a few even made fortunes out of the national tragedy. Therefore, many Palestinian communities existed in exile, not one. The separation was geographic, economic, social, and political. Those who acquired employment, especially as civil servants, and investment opportunities in the underdeveloped but oil rich Arab Gulf states, such as Kuwait, grew to form the richest and most influential Palestinian community in exile. Together with their wealth and political sway, the Palestinian community in Kuwait, the real birthplace of Fateh, would play a decisive role in the history of the Palestinian national movement and the PLO.

In the West Bank, the Jordanian administration's discriminatory policies and favoritism would deform the local economy and produce a dependency of novel form. More advanced in every standard, and "far outstancing neighboring Arab countries on almost every economic indicator,"[9] the West Bank, mutilated under the new regime, was reduced to no more than a satellite of the impecunious East Bank. After annexing the West Bank, a few of the local political elite retained commitment and remained dedicated to the "Government of all Palestine" established in Gaza by the former elite attempting to consolidate and extend their power into the new age. "Other prominent Palestinians either retired into obscurity or were absorbed into the political life of the kingdom of Jordan."[10] The latter's influence extended throughout the Jordanian governance of the West Bank, delimiting the political spectrum. Despite political oppression, dissent existed, but at a level narrower than that of Gaza.

A cataclysm of refugees inundating the Gaza Strip altered the local demography in a manner unprecedented. Gaza's population increased three folds, almost seventy percent of whom were newly arriving refugees, becoming one of the most densely populated areas in the world. While fifty percent of Gaza's population lived in refugee camps, "the agricultural lands in the strip were concentrated in the hands of nineteen percent of the original population, who were the only ones able to sustain a living from it."[11] Due to deteriorating economic conditions and the elites' monopoly over land ownership, tension between refugees and the local elite reached severe levels at certain times. Politically, however, and due to the Egyptian political rhetoric, the political spectrum was spectacular: communists, Arab nationalists, Ba'athists, and Islamic groups. Unlike Jordan, Egypt did not annex Gaza, but also neither allowed the "consolidation of a local political force independent of the will of Cairo... [nor] endorse[d] the traditional leadership."[12]

Inside the area controlled by Israel, Arab Palestinians were the odd man out. Not only had they "found themselves on the lowest rung of the social and economic ladder... they became citizens of a state that celebrated its independence around the event that they considered their biggest catastrophe."[13] Facing an overwhelming power and now an oppressed minority in their homeland, Palestinians would render Israel's de-Palestinianization and de-Arabization policy a total failure. Attesting to a robust non-chauvinist-nationalist tradition that, contrary to Israeli propaganda, preceded Israel's establishment, they marvelously proceeded to take up every possible hue in the political spectrum in order to defend an identity under attack.

In addition to Arab and Arab identity-oriented movements, Palestinian Arabs would make up the core of the few non-racist Israeli movements such as the Israeli Communist Party. Astounding opposition to Israel's policies led by Al-Ard, Abna'a Al-Ard, and Abna'a Al-Balad movements would legendarily enter Palestinian history and the history of the Palestinian national movement. Ghassan Kanafani's examination of the "Literature of Resistance" of Palestinians under Israel's military rule illuminates artistically innovative and nationally and historically conscious writers since 1948. Mahmoud Darwish's grand poem "Al-Ard" commemorated the confrontation of "Land Day" of 30 March 30 1976, in which Israel murdered six Palestinians defending their land.

The forcible de-peasantization of the would-be refugees and dispersion of Palestinians induced, among many things, the collapse and demise of the Palestinian political elite that led the Palestinian struggle against Britain and the Zionist movement before 1948. Prior social arrangements such as clan structure, land ownership, and religious clerkship and offices that constituted the power bases of traditional leadership were eliminated by the 1948 War. The

Government of All Palestine, established by Haj Amin Husseini and former political leaders, was the last attempt to consolidate the traditional elite into the new arrangements but died soon after the war. It was discredited by Palestinians for mishandling resistance, and sanctioned by some Arab regimes, such as Jordan's King Abdullah, that perceived it as a competing force .

Karma Nabulsi

There is a long and very rich mobilizing tradition of peoples who have organized collectively against their repression in exile over the centuries. Struggles for liberation against tyranny and unrepresentative rule historically, and quite typically, have had a large exile component. It becomes even more pronounced in the cases like that of the Palestinian people who were subjected to ethnic cleansing on such a massive scale. Yet, when you cross the borders of your country and become a refugee, you do not lose your humanity. What I mean here is that you do not become reduced merely to a legal status as a refugee (as much as you need to hold fast to that status, since it expresses the absence of particular rights you are claiming as a refugee).

However, at that moment and from that day forward, your political agency, your role in struggling to overcome that predicament becomes even more essential, more integral as a person, and especially as part of a people. Actually, it is this that is at the heart of the Palestinian cause: the Palestinian revolution was created by Palestinian refugees who were insisting on a return to their homes. They were not claiming this right as refugees, but as a people dispossessed altogether; the claim is a collective one. It is important to highlight this point because the liberal model of the state comprised of individuals—refugees—with individual rights neither captures the collective predicament nor solves it. It is as a people with political and civic rights—collective rights—that we struggle to overturn the injustices together. This leads us to the question of political representation of course and—as in any struggle to liberate ourselves—the question of freely representing ourselves as the first step becomes the key challenge we must address together.

It is also why I never much liked the term diaspora, although it is the term that most readily comes to mind. By implication, it denies the political predicament we are in, and of our unity as a people who are seeking to overturn the ethnic cleansing of the Nakba. Accordingly, I find the term *al-shatat* more sympathetic and more inclusive of our current state of affairs. Once Palestinians

145

who are part of the core body politic can return to their homes, and choose to do so, then what remains of those who do not choose to return home (and there will be some) will then make up what will become the Palestinian diaspora. But until that moment, those Palestinians in forced exile outside of Palestine are the people—and indeed happen to be the majority of the people. So, it is vital not to implicitly accept the outcomes of this ethnic cleansing, or the language that has emerged from this violent coercion; one which frames our predicament as being one of "people" inside Palestine, and a "diaspora" with refugees outside of it.

This central quest—to free ourselves and to represent ourselves freely—has been the dual challenge facing Palestinians since the Zionist colonial project began at the start of the twentieth century. The violent combination of colonial and apartheid forces, together with the comprehensive, constant, and brutal repression by the Arab regimes, has meant that the urgent task of Palestinians is to overcome the geographic and physical fragmentation imposed by ethnic cleansing. This means that those Palestinians under occupation, who under the Oslo framework might have more privileges in terms of political voice (especially in the West Bank), do not claim that voice, or seize the role of representation that belongs to all Palestinians, equally. This is a complex task given the current pressures. But here one takes great heart from the fact that the young generation of Palestinian activists in the West Bank and Gaza are increasingly aware of their responsibilities in this regard. They understand their role in ensuring that the voices of the millions who are excluded are indeed heard, and have equal value and weight to their own.

Given this analysis, most of my own work, especially since the mid-1990s, has out of necessity focused exclusively on exploring and establishing the precise mobilizing and representative mechanisms that can overcome this violent fragmentation, in the study of the philosophy and practices of democratic revolutions of the past and present. My own sense is that we can only overcome our current predicament through the force that the democratic will and mass mobilization of all our people—all—bring to this battle: with their energy, their commitment, and life. It is also because I believe that the struggle, the land, and the claims to it actually belong to the people, myself being a committed adherent to the principle of popular sovereignty. This means that our cause cannot be run by an elite or a vanguard or a group who are as unrepresentative as the current few unelected officials currently holding the reins of official power in Ramallah.

Sherene Seikaly

The Oxford American Dictionary defines "diaspora" as first and foremost "the dispersion of the Jews beyond Israel" and second as "the dispersion of any people from their original homeland."

The notion of "diaspora" was central to Zionist understandings of the Jewish people as "abnormal." Three foundational myths (the negation of exile, the return to the land of Israel, and the return to history) constituted Zionism's colonial-settler project.[14] In understanding de-territorialization as a condition of abnormality, Zionism constructed the territorial nation as the necessary historical subject on the path to self-fulfillment.

I appreciate Karma Nabulsi's move away from diaspora when she says: "it denies the political predicament we are in." I am interested in how we can begin to imagine a politics that demands Palestinian self-determination *in*, liberation *on*, and return *to* the land of Palestine, while dismantling the territorial nation-state as the natural and irreducible form of human collectivity. Seif Da'na's point that "many Palestinian communities existed in exile, not one" is central here. How do we critique the inherited essentialism and elitism of Palestinian nationalism, while still recognizing and demanding the nation-state as an object of struggle?

Zionist scholars explain that the mantra "a land without a people for a people without a land" did not in fact imply that Zionists were unaware that there were *people* on the land of Palestine. They were more precise. Palestinians were not *a people*. These "inhabitants" were disparate, an amalgam, a motley crew. It was the very denial of the Palestinians' status as a people, a unified collective with legitimate political demands that was the basic infrastructure for British colonial rule. In November 1917, the British government instated its commitment to a Jewish National Home in Palestine through the Balfour Declaration, which pledged to facilitate Jewish immigration and land settlement while promising to safeguard the "civil and religious rights of existing non-Jewish communities in Palestine." Thus, from its inception, the facilitation of the Zionist enterprise was premised on the invisibility of the native people, who are neither named, nor possess even the potential for political rights. Through the dual policies of land settlement and Hebrew labor, and under the political and economic facilitation of British colonial rule, the Zionist movement began partitioning Palestine in the first half of the twentieth century as farmers and sharecroppers were increasingly dispossessed from their lands and livelihoods.

Despite the denial of their collectivity, Palestinians forged a multiplicity of registers to resist this project of enforced invisibility. These included various efforts of political and economic elites, women, laborers, farmers, villagers, youth, and local leaders to mobilize their aspirations and demands for self-determination. These at times disparate efforts found their culmination in the Arab Revolt of 1936-1939 that included national boycotts and armed struggle against both British colonialism and Zionist settlement. British colonials' tactics to suppress the revolt such as collective punishment, mass arrests, house demolitions, and torture were painful harbingers of what was to come.

Some Zionist conventional scholarship continues, until today, to portray the Nakba as a result of Palestinian "political deficiency" and the absence of an adequate "national spirit." For over five decades now, scholars from all walks (Palestinian, American, European, and Israeli) have responded to this blame-the-victim approach by providing incisive accounts of Palestinian nationalism, urban life, literary and cultural production, populist politics and mobilization, the women's movement, the struggle for labor rights, constructions and experiences of religiosity, and much more. Such scholarship has seared a critical light through the accusation that Palestinians lacked the characteristics of a collectivity; that they stood outside of history.

Yet, in a sense, historiographic debate continues to revolve around the relentless specter of the nation's success or failure. Has the time now come to begin to imagine stepping out of the nation-state as the ultimate framing device? This labor could potentially allow us to dismantle and transcend the paradigm of Palestinian failure versus Israeli success as a civilizational and developmental fact on the ground. Indeed, the nagging and intrinsic problem that Zionism faced in the 1880s continues apace today: How can the vision of a democratic Jewish state be realized as long as Palestinians live in, around, underneath, or between the borders of the state of Israel? As Joseph Massad has put it: "Israel's inability to complete its mission of thoroughly colonizing Palestine, of expelling all Palestinians, of 'gathering' all Jews in the world in its colony, keeps it uneasy and keeps its project always in the present continuous." Moreover, the question of the authenticity of Palestinian nationalism and collectivity seems to miss a basic point. People struggled against the process of their dispossession from lands that they and their families had continuously resided on for hundreds of years, regardless of their adherence, or lack thereof, to a nineteenth century European understanding of identity as bound to constructed myths and carefully drawn borders.

Part II: A Positive Model or Doomed for Failure?

Q: Is it fair to say that, prior to Oslo, Palestinians had effectively organized themselves in a transnational governing body in the form of the PLO and the PNC? What are some elements of this historical experience that may be taken for granted in the current discourse on representational politics? What is the value of representational government today, in the form of reviving the PNC for example, and are there different, more forward-looking models, worth considering?

Karma Nabulsi

Rather than look at comparative cases (and there are many that can and will continue to be useful here), the richest experience we need to draw upon first and foremost is our own. We have a quite extraordinary and truly epic tradition of collective organizing in our own revolutionary history, and one that provides us with principled guidelines to both liberation and representation.

In exploring representative and revolutionary mechanisms, one that was directly related to overcoming the Oslo framework's physical, geographic, and political fragmentation took place in the early years of the last decade. Dozens of civic and political organizations in refugee camps and in exile engaged in a mobilization from 2002 to 2006 involving tens of thousands of Palestinians in the more than twenty-four countries where our people now live and struggle. It also now provides us with an extremely useful template, as its conclusions go directly to the questions we now ask ourselves that we must answer. The results were plain: Palestinians everywhere seek direct representation in our national struggle, and see the only institutional framework within which it can have that representation is through reclaiming the national parliament of all Palestinians, the Palestine National Council of the PLO. This demand has already been synthesized into a collective one, and it has already been articulated by a broad base of our people.

At this moment we also now possess a forceful appreciation that only through reclaiming our national political institutions can we, as Palestinians, fashion our own destiny. And here the Arab Spring has played a great role in clearing the minds of a generation of young Palestinians to understand that rather than engaging as solidarity activists with an existential Palestine, the task before us is to organize democratically and reclaim our national liberation institutions ourselves for ourselves. This reorientation in consciousness has been pivotal. We have not liberated Palestine, so we are not requiring of ourselves to create either a government or a state. The aim is simpler and more profound: to determine for ourselves together, collectively, our strategy for liberation and return. And since it is the only principle that puts popular sovereignty at its core, it is therefore the only truly revolutionary one.

During the previous era when the resistance organizations captured the PLO institutions from the notables and elites in the late 1960s, it functioned according to the ethos of the time, based upon the model employed by national liberation movements worldwide in the anti-colonial struggle for liberation. This means that those traditional organizing features of the period—underground resistance movements, unions, and mass institutional representation, were broadly popular and representative, and certainly legitimate. This is far from the case today. The PLO is empty of both the spirit and the will of the masses of struggling Palestinians. For example, most of our young people do not belong to any party, unlike the previous generation who filled the parties with their energy, commitment, and service, and gave the revolution its mandate. Most people belonged to one or more of the unions. In this way the PNC reflected a popular mandate. Today's demands of direct enfranchisement of every Palestinian through constituency-based democratic voting are reflective of this same principle of popular sovereignty, but expressed through the forms that are legitimate and collective today. And, actually, the issue here is both intrinsic and instrumental, for it is the only model that can work. A PNC based on factional quotas is not representative of the people, and only a directly elected national parliament can make the platforms and strategies of liberation that can represent the general will. So the demand is direct, and simple, and manageable. We have done it before, and we can easily do it again.

Seif Da'na

I disagree that Palestinians had effectively organized themselves in a transnational governing body in the form of the PLO and the PNC. The PLO and the PNC were dominated since 1968 by wealthy members of the Palestinian community in Kuwait and the oil producing Arab states and formed the backbone of Fateh. For example, Arafat's employment at the public work ministry in Kuwait put him in touch with the members of the wealthiest

Palestinian community in exile, some of whom played important roles in Palestinian politics and PLO institutions since 1968.

In the aftermath of the collapse of the PLO's first regime after the 1967 war, an interim chair of the executive committee, Yehya Hammoudeh, began an effort to reorganize the Palestine National Council with active participation of guerrilla organizations that have just declared a strategy of armed struggle. Hammoudeh's efforts together with strong influence from Fateh would result in an agreement that favored Fateh. The new Palestine National Council would consist of one hundred members distributed as follows: thirty-eight members for Fateh, ten for the Popular Front, twenty members for the Palestine Liberation Army, three for the popular and civil organizations (students, workers, and women), and twenty-nine independents.

During the PLO's 5th Palestine National Council meeting on 1-4 February 1969, Fateh and the PFLP failed to reach an agreement regarding power sharing and control of the PLO, and the PFLP decided to boycott the meeting, insisting instead that "the existing PLO be completely dismantled to give all resistance movements equal voice in the leadership of the armed struggle."[15] Fateh took control of the PLO's key positions and Yasser Arafat was selected as the head of the PLO executive committee. In effect, the privilege and power baton traditional elite relinquished was passed to Fateh's leadership and their supporters.

Fateh's encroachment and control of the PLO was a significant political transformation in the history of the Palestinian National Movement, in which the orientation of the PLO's agenda and even charter will have significant political and social impacts on the Palestinian national movement as a whole. Fateh's control of the PLO's key positions "gave the movement (Fateh) an advantage in the contest for supremacy within the Palestinian national movement. This step by the more conservative and pragmatic members of the national elite led to the marginalization of the other segment, which was more secular and more radical in its social views."[16] So, the PLO (and PNC) was a powerful apparatus used to justify, or attenuate, the agenda of the right wing of the Palestinian movement.

The quest of the group that dominated the PLO and Fateh from the beginning was the establishment of a state. Fateh accepted and supported the idea of entity (*kayan*) in the late 1950s, two decades before the ten-point plan of 1974: "The establishment of a Palestinian revolutionary authority in the parts of Palestine that were put under Arab control after 1948 as an initial national step toward the liberation of all Palestine."[17]

Social, political, and economic transformations within the Palestinian communities, especially in exile, transformed the notion of a mini state (*kayan*) from a treasonable notion into a "national necessity." The failure of the Palestinian elite to integrate into the Arab countries, and assimilate their growing economic power with the rising Arab elite in the oil producing countries, despite being accepted at the beginning, was the root cause underlying the quest for a political entity. This period of the history of the Palestinian national movement and PLO demonstrates not only the effective control and power the Palestinian elite in exile had on the PLO, but also the nature of the PLO as a revolutionary organization. The refugees, however, could not and did not integrate from the beginning.

Naseer Aruri

Is the situation reversible? Can the PLO return from its status as a virtual regime to a national liberation movement? Perhaps not with the same leadership, the PA should remain with powers as a large municipality. Nothing more. The PLO, which has lost its structure, must be rebuilt.

One of the tragic mistakes is that we did not focus on the demand for the right to self-determination that encompasses everything. Instead, they concentrated on the idea of a state. A state? Netanyahu, Obama, and Ariel Sharon also talked about a state, without land, water, and borders. Everything is enclaves. Dr. Mamdouh Akr, head of a major human rights organization in the occupied territories, put it this way:

> As far as I'm concerned, they can call that an empire. I can feel the seeds of change. There are demonstrations in the villages, the BDS [Boycott, Divestment and Sanctions against Israel], the boycott on settlement products, defying the PA on the Goldstone report. What has happened in Tunisia and Egypt will expedite the process of change, revitalize the Palestinian cause and bring it back to where it belongs —not to a government or a "state," but as a movement of national liberation.[18]

I would add: "...as a representative movement of national liberation."

Today, US imperialism and hegemony are on the rise. Israel is governed by Iron Wall adherents, and thus unrestrained. The Arab states, which were inept in 1948, have been downright complicit. Egypt and Jordan not only enforced the Israeli siege on Gazan civilians, but they also provided training camps to the new quislings, in order to enable them to do the job of the Israeli army, and camouflage the occupation.

But this collaboration will be gone, no doubt, particularly after the great Arab Revolt of the spring 2011. This Arab awakening, which is still ongoing, is bound to reverse the earlier trends and create a milieu of emancipation and liberation. Egypt is no longer a symbol of subservience and collaboration; its revolution has already placed it on the path of Arab nationalism.

At this juncture, one hopes that a regional milieu would create a more suitable environment for turning complicity back to resistance (perhaps the ongoing resistance in the form of BDS, and other means of non-violent struggle, together with serious efforts at unification of Fateh and Hamas). The backbone, however, would have to be the non-violent mobilization. It would have to serve as the framework for the new resistance, the rebuilding of new institutions, and the injection of democratic representation—not that which governed the previous recruitment by appointment and the balancing of factions (*fasail*) in which Abu Ammar played the principal role.

Sherene Seikaly

I would agree with Seif Da'na that Palestinian elites played a dominant role in the PLO and PNC. I would also emphasize that the character of those elites necessarily shifted, and that is an important question to further explore. Additionally, it is also important to trace when and how Palestinian refugees constituted and challenged Palestinian politics. From today's standpoint, the PLO's turn to accepting a two-state solution and its recognition of 242 (the language of which reduces the Palestinian struggle to that of nameless refugees) are critical turning points, when the PLO's ostensible base, Palestinian refugees, became marginal to the very terms of the struggle.

Additional Comments:

Karma Nabulsi

I would like to add some historical comments about the PLO. I raise these now because I believe that a clear understanding of our past can help us better confront our many present challenges; a fair appraisal of the revolutionary elements in our history can certainly help us to organize revolutionary action and thought in the future. Too many black legends are propagated about the history of the Palestinian revolution. The remarkable world of that revolution has been presented to our young people as being nothing more than a series of betrayals, corrupt acts, and nasty leaderships. Besides its inaccuracy, this alienates Palestinian youth from their own history, and creates a demobilizing atmosphere, guided as it is by the principle that everything was always wrong and nothing was ever right. Such narratives negate all the sacrifices, everyday heroism, and positive elements that flourished in the Palestinian revolution (pre-Oslo Fateh included), and especially of the contribution and actions of the tens of thousands of cadres it was comprised of.

First, it is not accurate to argue that the "state discourse or the two state solution" had been hegemonic within Fateh since the late 1950s. This claim relies on a single quote from an article in the magazine *Filastinuna*, taken out of context, and presented in a secondary source that itself has a very problematic teleological reading of Palestinian resistance. Any serious reader of *Filastinuna* will notice that it advanced an absolute and unquestionable commitment to the idea of total liberation of Palestine from the river to the sea. Fateh at that time believed that the liberation struggle was to be led by the Palestinian people from Gaza and the West Bank, the Palestinian areas that were under Egyptian and Jordanian administration. Those that spoke of a Palestinian *kayan* were interested in a fighting entity that could mobilize the entirety of the people in the battle for liberation. That is partly why they used the word *kayan* (entity) and not *dawla* (state). Those interested in understanding Fateh's ideas in the fifties should go back to the original sources, the two most important being *Bayan Harakatuna* (Our Movement's Manifesto) and *Haikal al-Binaa al-Thawri* (The Structure of Revolutionary Building). The first goal of Fateh was outlined in its founding *bayan* without any ambiguity: "the liberation of Palestine in a total manner, and liquidating the Zionist occupying state politically, militarily, socially, and intellectually." Every other Fateh principle, argument, article, pamphlet, or book from this period was built on this principle.

Actually, the same goes for Fateh of the sixties. Fateh was the first to call for armed struggle during this period. To call it "right wing" is not entirely accurate, as it included numerous leftist (as well as rightist) elements that were committed to that principle. In fact, Fateh was the closest thing to a broad "national front" at the time, inspired in particular by the Maoist experience in China and by Ho Chi Minh's example in Vietnam (for intellectual articulations of this fact see the following 1960's Fateh publications: *Al-Tajruba al-Vietnamia* and *Al-Tajruba al-Seenia*, as well as *Tahreer al-Aqtar al-Muhtala*; for its concrete application check the lists of major cadres that were active during this period, reflecting communist, nationalist, and Ba'athist, as well as Muslim Brotherhood backgrounds). This is not to defend the Fateh of today by any means, but it is to salvage the revolutionary legacy of the movement. Rejecting Oslo and its defeatist logic should not amount to rejecting the history of the Palestinian revolution. Indeed, reclaiming the history of the revolution should be a matter of concern for anyone serious about emphasizing the importance of revolutionary struggle in the present and future.

Those who have experienced the revolutionary spirit of the past find claims that "the PLO and the PNC were dominated since 1968 by wealthy members of the Palestinian community in Kuwait and the oil producing Arab states and formed the backbone of Fateh" to be quite alien. Sure, the Palestinian community, including the bourgeoisie and the businessmen in Kuwait, played an important role in financing Fateh (as well as the PFLP by the way). But to claim that this amounts to "wealthy" or "Kuwaiti" dominance over the PLO and PNC is not only inaccurate, but incorrect. Most of the Fateh leadership and cadres came from families that were out of the orbit of the traditional politics of the notables. In fact, the 1960s witnessed quite a shift in the Fateh leadership from the Gulf-based group to those located in Syria, Jordan, Palestine, and Lebanon.

As for the reasons behind the PFLP's initial attitude to the PLO, these are complicated. There was a traditional mistrust of the PLO on the part of the groups that were committed to armed struggle (indeed, Fateh's entry to the PLO was itself made with hesitance and after much internal debate). There were also differences over the percentage of seats that each party would get (the PFLP demanded a larger quota than Fateh was prepared to give, that did not represent its diminished weight in the post-Karameh period). Those interested in the debates of the period should go back to PFLP publications from those days rather than Western secondary literature on the topic. A good sense can be gained from the PFLP's 1969 pamphlet *Al-Jabha al-Sha'biya Li Tahreer Filasteen Tuwadeh Mawqifaha Min al-Ishtirak fi al-Majlis al-Watani wa Al-Lajna al-*

Tanfithya wa Qiyadat al-Kifah al-Musalah (The PFLP Clarifies its Position Regarding Participation in the PNC and the Executive Committee and the Leadership in the Armed Struggle). The evolution of these positions can also be seen in the post-Black September period in such writings as *Al-Bayan al-Siyassi al-Muqadam ila al-Dawra al-Tasi'a Lil Majlis al-Watani al-Filasteeni* (The Political Communiqué Submitted to the 9th Session of the PNC), which explains why the PFLP participated in the PNC for the first time. The PFLP's history with the PNC has ebbed and flowed, but it has always accepted the principles of the PNC, and for many years it has regretted its early positions on it. Certainly, those positions were not shared by the entirety of the Palestinian left (including the left-faction within Fateh and the DFLP).

What is important to emphasize, however, is that whereas the PNC at the time operated on the basis of "revolutionary legitimacy" (accepted as a concept and guiding principle by PFLP, Fateh, DFLP, and everyone else at the time and common to anti-colonial liberation movements of the period), what is relevant today is to shift the basis of representation to "electoral legitimacy," by enfranchising all Palestinians including those living in the places of refuge and exile. Our strength does not lie in either negating or disposing of our entire political heritage, but rather in reclaiming its proper resources and strengthening it through common principles and purposes. Structures like the PNC and the PLO were established after a long and arduous process of struggle with the Israelis, the Arab regimes, and the Western states, and, most importantly, in spite of them. These structures afford Palestinians struggling for liberation and return the necessary mechanism for representation—once re-energized with our people's popular will—in spite of their current emptiness and unrepresentative character.

Seif Da'na

I argued that the PLO did not only fail, but enfolded the seeds of failure from the beginning in its political thoughts, structure, and social orientation and background of its leadership. My concern in this very short exercise (to call for reconstructing the history of the Palestinian national movement, PNM, and the PLO) is to explain the political present of the PNM and its leading force, the PLO. Failure alone not only does not suffice in neither explaining the tragic conclusion of the PLO venture nor the political present. It does not provide any insights for any promising alternative future. In other words, my concern with an alternative past is not to explain the causes of the failure per se but also to seek

156

principles of a view for an alternative future (this, of course, requires more space and effort than this very short synopsis).

I inserted the term "tragic" above to characterize the PLO's failure in order to highlight the amazing heroism and great sacrifices of the Palestinian people and the cadres and members of the PLO's factions despite the disastrous outcome. In this sense, there is a need to distinguish between history (which explains the present, or should be reconstructed to do so should we continue to seek the envisioned promising future of the first generation of Palestinian rebels) and historical literature. Slipping into idealism and holding onto the romantic optics to perceive the PLO and the history of the PLO's venture might have been necessary in the early period of the Palestinian revolution—like any revolution at the beginning (David Scott's "Conscripts of Modernity: the Tragedy of Colonial Enlightenment" reading of C.L.R James account of the Haitian Revolution in the "The Black Jacobins" might be useful to consider). Retroactively, however, it is possible now to see that underneath the shrill of the revolutionary lexis of defiance, there was always a tacit, and sometimes explicit, willingness to compromise and accept a political settlement to the contrary. Both Arafat's 13 November 1974 UN speech and 15 November 1988 Declaration of Independence of the State of Palestine are good examples. (I dealt with both in more details elsewhere in Arabic in the "State Discourse" and "Tragedy of the PLO.") We live in a new era, however, that requires highly critical lenses to perceive the PLO experience in order for the liberation, not state, scheme to remain alive.

In short, given what seems to many as an undisputed outcome, or failure, (unless we can pinpoint concrete success or if we consider the establishment of the Palestinian Authority as a historical achievement) any recounted history might show that, at its kernel, the PLO germinated conditions and enfolded forces that spearheaded its demise. The PLO failed because of factors similar to those that rendered earlier independence and development attempts in the Arab homeland (and elsewhere) ephemeral, calamitously departing the nationalism and independence age. Similarly, the PLO's failure was immaculate. Post-Nakba rising social forces that took over the PLO led a fundamental reconstruction of the whole political and cultural landscape underlying the PLO's national and democratic liberation cause.

Changing global, regional, and local structural conditions coincided with the highly pragmatic, but hegemonic nonetheless, Palestinian elite to produce the co-optation of once the most spectacular manifestation of revolutionary vigor in the modern history of the Middle East. An evener, an alternative to dwarf the effects of the inescapable social nature of the leading forces the post 1948 war realities sprouted, was not missing and the elites' ascendance to and grip on power was not without a fight internally and beyond the PLO's institutions (e.g., Fateh vs. PFLP; PLO vs. the 1970s National Front and National Guidance Committee in the West Bank and Gaza). Failure, however, was a matter of history, not in spite of it. With the exception of a few cases, literature on the Palestine question has ignored this highly important dimension of the conflict within the PLO.

However, this is not and cannot be the end of the story of the Palestinian struggle. Given that the specter of Palestine appears to be occupying a central status in the ongoing Arab revolts that definitely signify the beginning of a new era, one should remain highly optimistic. The beginning should be a shift in the political discourse towards restoring the original and true view of the conflict (anti-colonial struggle rather than border conflict), a discourse of liberation rather than state. This is a great step.

Part III: Whither Palestinian Resistance?

Q: For many Palestinians who had hitherto been involved in the Palestinian Liberation Organization and its associated bodies, like the Palestinian National Council, the advent of the peace process, and particularly the terms of the Oslo Accords, signaled a collapse in a resistance platform and instead a turn to complicit accommodation of Israeli colonialism and apartheid. Do you agree with this sentiment? If so, what factors do you believe contributed to the collapse of the resistance platform and do you believe it can be rehabilitated? If not, what do you believe constitutes a resistance platform today? In either case, how can the Palestinian national body continue its struggle for self-determination in light of the peace process's most recent collapse?

Naseer Aruri

The Palestinian struggle for "independence" or self-determination since the 1967 occupation passed through three stages: paramilitary, known as "armed struggle;" diplomatic/political; and statist. Initially, the armed struggle was declared as the means to establish a single democratic secular state in all of Palestine in which equality among Christians, Muslims, and Jews would prevail.

That was a short-lived endeavor, which effectively came to an end in the early 1970s. The PLO and the Arab states then reached an unwritten agreement: The PLO agreed to tone down its revolutionary rhetoric, give up the "armed struggle," and launch a form of diplomatic struggle jointly with the Arab states in pursuit of a mini-state in the West Bank and Gaza.

The diplomatic struggle proceeded since 1973 (following the Algiers and Rabat summits, which recognized the PLO as the sole legitimate representative of the Palestinian people). But while pseudo diplomacy was the major focus of the PLO's work during the 70s, 80s, and 90s, there was an important political struggle going on inside the occupied territories. It was the endeavor of a civil/political society applying a non-violent struggle under the banner of the Palestinian National Front (PNF) during the 1970s. Their techniques varied from non-payment of taxes to boycotts, demonstrations, and other peaceful means designed to not only declare the occupation illegal, but to demand an independent state. For the next two decades, this unwritten agreement, and the search for a "two-state solution," was to consume the combined energies of Palestinians and Arabs.

The third phase is the statist. The search for statehood began with the PLO's quest for international recognition as the sole legitimate representative of the Palestinian people. The PLO claimed the largest portion of Arab and Palestinian resources, and went on to embark on a quest that came at the expense of fundamental national and human rights, including refugee rights and interests. The PLO was easily enticed to embark on the Oslo process, just as it had been persuaded to enter into the joint diplomatic struggle for a futile two-state solution two decades earlier. Israel's aim was to side-line the political/civil society struggle going on inside the occupied territories. From there the road to Oslo was paved for an unprepared PLO, and the result is the present disaster.

For the millions of Palestinians scattered outside pre-1948 Palestine, Oslo meant that there would never be restitution or a right of return, there would never be adequate representation. For the Palestinians inside Israel, Oslo meant that they would have to accept, for all times, their status as second-class citizens —the cutters of wood and hewers of water.

Oslo succeeded in dismantling the fabric of civil society and destroying its grassroots political struggle. In its place, we now have a state apparatus without a state. Thus, Oslo's biggest damage was the one inflicted on civil society.

Peace may never be at hand as long as the 1948 Nakba is not recognized for what it is—a form of ethnic cleansing, a colonial settler enterprise, which covets the land without the people.

The ultimate goal of the colonial settler regime is to destroy the political and national existence of a whole community of people, and thus deny it the possibility of self-determination. It is a process of politicide, one that has as its ultimate goal the dissolution of the Palestinian people's existence as a legitimate national, social, and economic entity, which may also include partial or total ethnic cleansing.

This is what Israel has been doing to the Palestinian people, persistently between 1948 and the present—destroying the very fabric of the Palestinian nation and obliterating the Palestinian *wujoud* (presence).

Of course, the so-called peace process could never succeed in these conditions. First, a colonial-settler regime is inconsistent with peace and so is the pursuit of politicide. A two-state solution is not in the offing, given the lack of intent to withdraw from occupied land, and to permit any sovereignty other than Israeli sovereignty on any piece of land lying between the Jordan River and the Mediterranean Sea.

Consequently, a real state in the West Bank and Gaza is simply not in the cards. That also goes for Salam Fayyad's 2011 project.

Seif Da'na

Yes, I agree. Actually, a tacit willingness to accommodate the Zionist colonization of Palestine existed since the early 1970s. The quest for a mini-state by the Palestinian elite began much earlier and became possible after this group took over the PLO. The Palestinian elite control of the PLO since 1974 was truly nothing less than a coup d'état. It replaced the liberation discourse that enfolded early Palestinian revolutionary thoughts with the state discourse, which entails not only a tacit recognition of the Zionist colonial scheme, but clearly showed that Palestinian (and Arab) elite shared structural interest with the Israeli elite. This, at least partially, explains not only much about the Oslo era (an agreement intended originally to prepare the foundations for a neo-liberal Middle East rather than achieve alleged peace), but also the futility of all attempts to reform and rehabilitate the PLO. The story of the Palestinian elite in exile since the

Nakba is important and is worth narrating to understand the sequence of events from 1970 on.

In the aftermath of the Nakba, wealthy and influential Palestinians embarked on economic schemes and extended their economic base to the rest of the Arab world and beyond. The economic success story of the Palestinian bourgeoisie after the Nakba is more than just impressive. In less than five years after the Nakba, Palestinian-owned firms dominated the Arab economy and were the central player in enormous economic ventures that were regional in scale. The story of the Contracting and Trading Industry (CAT), one of several ventures that operated at the regional level and had international connections, testifies to a significant impact these ventures had on the development of Palestinian and PLO politics later.

It all began with the early 1940s economic recovery. A Palestinian venture called CAT that was established by Emile Bustani, a Lebanese businessman who was residing in Palestine, received major construction contracts from the British Army during World War II. After the war, CAT extended its operation to the rest of the Middle East, operating in the construction of, among other things, oil pipelines and oil installations. In the early 1950s, CAT formed a partnership with the British Motherwell Bridge and Engineering Company. The new breed, MotherCat, specializing in the construction of refineries, pipelines, and oil tank farms, was the only one in the world that was capable of providing the kind and size of pipe needed for the Middle East oilfields.[19]

Successfully performing major construction work for British Petroleum and Shell (such as the construction of the Iraqi Petroleum Company—IPC—in the early 1950s), CAT's operation extended to all British controlled Arab Gulf states. CAT and MotherCat won

> major contracts for the construction of oil pipelines, oil terminals and storage depots, roads, power plants, water-supply installations, port and harbor works, pumping stations and commercial buildings in Kuwait, Qatar, the Emirates and later, in Saudi Arabia and Oman as well. In Qatar, CAT obtained a virtual monopoly on foreign trade and construction for the oil industry in the early 1950s.[20]

Scores of Palestinian firms and Palestinian businessmen embarked on other ventures that would also extend their operations to the rest of the Middle East.

Investors from the pre-war Arab Bank branch in Haifa would establish the Arabia Insurance Company, with branches in most Arab countries, and even in Britain, the Cortas Canning and Refrigeration Company, Al Mashriq Financial Investment Company of Beirut, and the Beirut-based Intra Bank that became the largest financial institution in Lebanon with assets amounting to just under one billion Lebanese pounds (325 million US dollars) in 1965. In addition to their actual specialization, these corporations would own airlines (Middle East Airline operating from Lebanon), casinos, publishing houses, and radio and TV interests.

The power of this group was not only in being the best and most suitable instrument for a possible integration of the Arab economy, but also in their access to political power in Egypt, Kuwait, Saudi Arabia, Jordan, Qatar, Lebanon, Libya, Bahrain, and their political involvement in Palestinian politics and the PLO since the beginning. Fuad Saba of the Arab Bank, and the founder of the Al Mashriq Financial Institution that handled businesses for CAT, Arabia Insurance, and other Palestinian-owned firms, was responsible for setting up the Palestine National Fund and was appointed Secretary of the Arab Higher Committee.[21] Emile Bustani's death in a crash while campaigning for the presidency in Lebanon, in addition to other seemingly unexplainable accidental deaths of several Palestinian businessmen, initiated many conspiracy theories regarding their fate. The Palestinian elite not only created a structure for a possible economic integration of the Arab world, but assumed that they had successfully integrated into the Arab surroundings.

The success of the Palestinian bourgeoisie in exile, engrossing the envy of rising local bourgeoisie in the recently independent Arab countries, led to a series of new measures adopted by the Arab countries favoring compatriots for holding supervisory positions in the economy, and local companies, rather than Palestinian-owned firms, for major contractual work. Such a strategy would stabilize these regimes and eliminate such structures that might make Arab unity in the future conceivable. Many Arab countries amended their agreements with oil corporations giving priorities to their nationals to hold key positions in oil ventures, while others, like Kuwait, gave this favoritism the power of the law, as in the 1965 Industrial Law. In the exceptional cases, in which Palestinian firms could still acquire contracts and were allowed to operate, they were required, as foreigners, to pay hefty fees. The new measures, coupled with the nationalization of firms, resources, and assets in many countries such as Iraq after the Qasem revolution, Syria, and Libya, and even the arrest of Palestinian businessmen as in the case of Libya, bankrupted many of these firms, while others lost holdings to rising Arab businesses, especially in the Arab Gulf states.

The last of these pernicious measures took place in Jordan. Forced by the decision made during the Arab Summit Conference held in Rabat, Morocco in 1974 to recognize the PLO as the sole and legitimate representative of the Palestinian people, and following the failure of the United Arab Kingdom initiative to unite the West and East Bank, King Hussein temporarily abandoned his quest for controlling the West Bank and embarked on the program of Jordanizing the East Bank. As a result, influential Palestinians lost their powerful political posts in the government and civil administration. Thus, "Palestinian merchants, financiers, and industrialists who depended on the government for contracts and funds found themselves at a disadvantage vis-à-vis their Jordanian rivals."[22] Losing ground in exile, many prosperous businessmen and ex-Jordanian loyalists switched allegiance to the PLO. The Palestinian bourgeoisie began their long quest for a state of their own, and the PLO was the effective instrument.

It is fair to conclude that the PLO did not really fail miserably, one might say, but enfolded the seeds of failure from the beginning. The destiny of diaspora activism was ill-fated from the beginning as well. It failed to either contribute to the national liberation scheme or build community in the diaspora. Entwined structurally and politically with that of the PLO's scheme, the fate of diaspora activism was sealed.

Karma Nabulsi

Not to be too dialectical, but this same strategy to free ourselves and to represent ourselves freely is also the same self-mobilizational mechanism to unite ourselves. This is why a reconciliation of the factions (although always welcome) neither addresses nor solves the Palestinian predicament. Without the force of popular will coming together in the equivalent of our own national public square, we cannot liberate ourselves. As this core aim is what binds us, the calls for direct elections to the PNC has taken new life. And I am confident, within the fold of the Arab revolutions that are currently underway, that it will succeed.

Many other strategies and frameworks that have either distracted us from our national responsibilities, or have not been able to have the strong effect they must, can function properly when emerging directly from a body comprised of the people themselves. It is here, too, that the early revolutionary generations' work can provide useful models. Our people, as we know, possess an extraordinary amount of talent, determination, and courage. Within a loose framework of the institutional unity that the PNC provides, all of these independent initiatives and gestures, all the civic activities in the realm of intellectual initiatives, of student activism, of workers' mobilizations, of culture production, of collective and individual enterprises and campaigning, of resistance through popular and legal strategies, can take both strength and direction. For we absolutely need this kind of intellectual, ideological, and sectoral pluralism, this vitality, this debate and contestation within the national architecture of our liberation struggle.

Here, the differences and divergences become a real strength, rather than simply adding to our current fragmentation and frustration. In our own revolutionary history at its best, and in every revolution's history, it is within the collective framework that the unique contributions of each find their home inside the collective. For me, this is the essence of political freedom.

Sherene Seikaly

Naseer Aruri makes a powerful point in reminding us of the PLO's shift from armed struggle, to pseudo-diplomacy, to pseudo-state strategies. I would add here that the Arab Spring offers some lessons and reminders for the course of Palestinian politics. Grassroots mass mobilization was the force that inspired, executed, and undertook the uprisings and revolutions of Tunisia and Egypt. We are now witnessing various leadership figures scrambling to catch up to the will and strength of popular demand. Similarly, in 1936 the elite Palestinian leadership was at pains to harness the popular resistance to British colonialism and Zionist settlement. In the 1970s and later with the beginning of the intifada, grassroots organizing led and the political leadership followed in the struggle against the occupation. This is the case today, as broad efforts in the West Bank and Gaza and beyond call for boycott, divestment, and sanctions. As we witness the unlikely sight of courageous Palestinians, Syrians, and Lebanese lining that invented and impermeable border that has interrupted lives and families, the possibility of another moment of popular politics is upon us.

26 May 2011

---

[1] For details see: Gershon Shafir, *Land, Labor and the Origins of the Israeli-Palestinian Conflict 1882-1914* (Cambridge: Cambridge University Press, 1989).

[2] Ibid., 9.

[3] G.M. Fredrickson, "Colonialism and Racism," in *The Arrogance of Race: Historical Perspectives on Slavery, Racism, and Social Inequality*. (Hanover: Wesleyan University Press, 1988), 220-21.

[4] Ward Churchill, *A Little Matter of Genocide: Holocaust and Denial in the Americas, 1492 to the Present* (San Francisco: City Lights Books, 1997).

[5] Munir Al Akash, *The Right to Sacrifice the Other: America and Genocide (Haq Al Tadhiya Bil Akhar: America Wa Al Ibadat Al Jamaiyya)* Beirut: Riyad Al Rayyes.

[6] Fredrickson, 221.

[7] Salim Tamari, "No Obvious Destination," *Al Ahram Weekly*, no. 656 (2003).

[8] Pamela Ann Smith, *Palestine and the Palestinians, 1876-1983* (London: Croom Helm, 1984), 117-22.

[9] Barukh Kimmerling and Joel Migdal, *The Palestinian People: A History* (Cambridge: Harvard University Press, 2003), 138.

[10] David Waines, *The Unholy War: Israel and Palestine, 1897-1971* (Wilmette: Medina University Press International, 1971), 170.

[11] Amal Jamal, *The Palestinian National Movement: Politics of Contention 1967-2005* (Bloomington and Indianapolis: Indiana University Press, 2005), 20.

[12] Ibid., 21.

[13] Kimmerling and Migdal, 169.

[14] Gabriel Piterberg, "Erasures," *New Left Review* 10 (July-August 2001).

[15] Smith, 195.

[16] Jamal, 19.

[17] Ibid.

[18] Amira Hass, "Why Isn't the PA Supporting the Egyptian Uprising?" *Haaretz* (3 February 2011).

[19] Smith, 137.

[20] Ibid., 135.

21 Ibid., 132-3.

22 Ibid., 142.

Guy S. Goodwin-Gill Legal Opinion on Palestinian Statehood Bid

[The following legal opinion on the Palestine statehood bid was issued by Guy S. Goodwin-Gill on 10 August 2011.]

Opinion

Re: The Palestine Liberation Organization, the future State of Palestine, and the question of popular representation

By Guy S. Goodwin-Gill, Senior Research Fellow, All Souls College, Oxford--Barrister

Introduction

1. I have been asked for my opinion on certain issues relating to popular representation (that is, the representation of the views of the Palestinian people) which may arise incidentally to the current proposal to seek recognition of the State of Palestine and observer status for the state in the United Nations.

2. This opinion seeks only to identify problems potentially affecting the right of the Palestinian people to self-determination and the manner by which that right can or may be exercised, due account being taken of the will of the people. The purpose is simply to flag the matters requiring attention, if a substantial proportion of the people (having a particular interest in, among others, the right of return) are not be to be accidentally disenfranchised.

3. I am advised that one possibility being debated involves the replacement of the Palestinian Liberation Organization (PLO) and its substitution, within the United Nations, by the State of Palestine as the "legitimate" representative of the Palestinian people. In my view, this raises, first, what I will call constitutional problems (in that they engage the Palestinian National Charter and the organization and entities which make up the PLO); secondly, the question of the capacity of the State of Palestine effectively to

take on the role and responsibilities of the PLO in the UN; and thirdly, the question of popular representation.

The constitutional issue

4. The PLO was established in 1965, bringing together various groups united initially for the purpose of liberating Palestine. Its governing instrument is the Palestine National Charter. The PLO's nominal legislative body is the Palestinian National Council, which currently comprises some 669 members, of whom some 483 represent the diaspora; since 1996, forty percent of the membership has been directly elected. In practice, "political power" resides with the Executive Committee, the eighteen members of which are elected by the Palestinian National Council.

5. When the Palestinian National Council is not in session, policy is determined by the Palestinian Central Council, whose 124 members are drawn from the Executive Committee, the Palestinian National Council, and other Palestinian organizations.

6. Following the Oslo Accords of 1993, the PLO, with the subsequent endorsement of the Palestinian National Council, established the Palestinian Authority as a short-term, administrative entity charged with the limited governance of those areas of the West Bank and Gaza which were placed under Palestinian responsibility. Its mandate, originally five years, was extended in 1998. The Palestinian Authority thus has limited legislative and executive competence, limited territorial jurisdiction,[1] and limited personal jurisdiction over Palestinians not present in the areas for which it has been accorded responsibility.

7. Within the constitutional structure of the PLO and the governance of the Occupied Palestinian Territory, therefore, the Palestinian Authority is a subsidiary body, competent only to exercise those powers conferred on it by the Palestinian National Council. By definition, it does not have the capacity to assume greater powers, to "dissolve" its parent body, or otherwise to establish itself independently of the Palestinian National Council and the PLO. Moreover, it is the PLO and the Palestinian National Council which derive their legitimacy from the fact that they represent all sectors of the displaced Palestinian people, no matter where they presently live or have refuge.

8. In addition, the possibility of reconfiguring the self-determination unit by substitution, and without the consent of the competent institutions, raises the "external" question of its consistency with the long-standing acceptance of the PLO, by the UN and the international community at large, as the sole, legitimate representative of the Palestinian people; see below, paragraphs 11-17.

The "statehood" issue

9. Until such a time as a final settlement is agreed, the putative State of Palestine will have no territory over which it exercises effective sovereignty, its borders will be indeterminate or disputed, its population, actual and potential, undetermined and many of them continuing to live under occupation or in states of refuge. While it may be an observer state in the United Nations, it will fall short of meeting the internationally agreed criteria of statehood, with serious implications for Palestinians at large, particularly as concerns the popular representation of those not currently present in the Occupied Palestinian Territory.

10. The significant link between the Palestinian National Council and the diaspora has been noted above in paragraph 4. They constitute more than half of the people of Palestine, and if they are "disenfranchised" and lose their representation in the UN, it will not only prejudice their entitlement to equal representation, contrary to the will of the General Assembly, but also their ability to vocalize their views, to participate in matters of national governance, including the formation and political identity of the state, and to exercise the right of return.

The "representation" issue

11. A number of elements of international and UN practice must be recalled. First, the United Nations (the General Assembly, the Security Council, the International Court of Justice) and member states of the UN, including Israel, accept that the Palestinian people are entitled to self-determination.

12. The General Assembly has also repeatedly stressed that "the Palestinian people is the principal party to the question of Palestine...,"[2] and that the Palestine Liberation Organization is, "the representative of the Palestinian people."[3]

13. Moreover, it is the Palestinian people who possess the inalienable rights to self-determination, national independence and sovereignty, and the right to return to their homes and property from which they have been displaced and uprooted.[4]

14. In the practice of the UN, neither the Palestinian people nor the right to self-determination is territorially limited to the space currently referred to as the Occupied Palestinian Territory. Even though it may be challenging to identify "the people" in this context, at least pending a viable and effective system of registration for the purposes of voting or referendum, the intent of successive General Assembly resolutions has been clearly to include both Palestinians in the Occupied Palestinian Territory, and those who remain displaced in other countries.

15. Secondly, the PLO is accepted by the United Nations and by the international community of states[5] as the sole representative of the Palestinian people, and in this capacity it has been accepted as an observer by the UN and its specialized agencies.

16. As the sole representative of the Palestinian people, both inside and outside the United Nations, the PLO's mandate thus encompasses the totality of issues arising from the continuing displacement of Palestinians and the struggle for self-determination—this includes, among others, the questions of return and compensation highlighted in UNGA resolution 194 (III), and the question of national boundaries, which is implicit in Security Council resolution 242. These, necessarily, are matters for the Palestinian people as a whole, irrespective of their present place of residence.

17. The exercise of the right to self-determination is closely linked to "representation" and the right of the people to make known their views. Article 21(3) of the 1948 Universal Declaration of Human Rights provides in straightforward language that "The will of the people shall be the basis of the authority of government." An inherent aspect of the principle of self-determination today is representative and democratic government, and it is increasingly recognized that there is an essential link between the state (e.g., as a member of the United Nations), and the people it claims to represent.[6] The best evidence of that link—representative government—is through elections which are based on the enfranchisement of the people at large.

Conclusion

18. The right of the Palestinian people to self-determination has been clearly recognized as a matter of international law.[7] The peaceful and effective exercise of this right in accordance with the UN Charter has further been recognized as requiring the representation of the Palestinian people in the work of the United Nations.

19. In my opinion, current moves to secure recognition of statehood do not appear to reflect fully the role of the Palestinian people as a principal party in the resolution of the situation in the Middle East.

20. The interests of the Palestinian people are at risk of prejudice and fragmentation, unless steps are taken to ensure and maintain their representation through the PLO, until such time as there is in place a state competent and fully able to assume these responsibilities towards the people at large.

GUY S. GOODWIN-GILL
BLACKSTONE CHAMBERS
BLACKSTONE HOUSE
TEMPLE, LONDON EC4Y 9BW
10 August 2011

---

1 At present, the Palestinian Authority does not in fact exercise effective government even in some of the areas assigned to it.

2 UNGA res. 3210 (XXIX), 14 October 1974; UNGA res. 3236 (XXIX), 22 November 1974, §4; UNGA res. 3375 (XXX), 10 November 1975.

3 UNGA res. 3236 (XXIX), 22 November 1974.

4 UNGA res. 3237 (XXIX), 22 November 1974.

5 See, for example, League of Arab States, Seventh Arab League Summit, Rabat, Morocco, "Resolution on Palestine," 28 October 1974, §2, affirming the PLO as, "the sole legitimate representative of the Palestinian people."

6 Note also the reference to a government representing "the whole people" in UNGA res. 2625 (XXV), 24 October 1970, "Declaration on Principles of International Law concerning Friendly Relations and Co-operation among States in Accordance with the Charter of the United Nations."

7 International Court of Justice, *Legal Consequences of the Construction of a Wall in the Occupied Palestinian Territory*, Advisory Opinion, 9 July 2004, para. 118.

John Quigley Critique of Goodwin-Gill Legal Opinion on Palestine Statehood Bid

[The following critique by John Quigley was issued on 28 August 2011, in response to a legal opinion by Guy S. Goodwin-Gill on the Palestine statehood bid at the United Nations.]

To: Interested parties
From: John Quigley
Re: Legal Opinion of Guy S. Goodwin-Gill on the representation issue
Date: 28 August 2011

The Goodwin-Gill legal opinion provides no sound basis for not pursuing any of the initiatives contemplated for autumn 2011 at the United Nations.

Paragraph 1: Goodwin-Gill says that he has been asked for an opinion not about UN membership but about the possibility of gaining recognition and observer-state status via appropriate resolutions that could be adopted by the UN General Assembly. That scope means that the opinion does not relate to the question of seeking UN membership, or to consequences that might flow from gaining UN membership. The opinion thus does not purport to have any relevance to the issue of UN membership. In particular, Goodwin-Gill is not giving an opinion on the issue of whether UN membership might hold advantages, and how the situation of UN membership would compare with the current situation in regards to the ability to promote the rights and interests of the Palestinian people.

The paragraphs on the "constitutional issue" (paragraphs 4 to 8) dealing with the status of the PA are not relevant to the issue of the representation of Palestine at the international level. Goodwin-Gill is correct as to how the PA was constituted, but he does not explain any significance for representation of Palestine at the UN. By using the term "constitutional issue," Goodwin-Gill inadvertently undermines his own argument. It is precisely a "constitutional," namely an internal, issue for Palestine as to how and in what way the rights and interests of the diaspora will be ensured. It is not an issue at the international level. Institutional mechanisms to ensure a voice for the refugees need to be maintained, whether that is by their being nationals of Palestine or some other mechanism. But that is an internal matter of governance.

Paragraph 8: Goodwin-Gill is suggesting that what is being done now is against the PLO. But it was the PLO that decided (1988 declaration of statehood) to constitute itself as the government of the State of Palestine, making clear that all Palestinians would be represented by it and that status as a state of the international community was being declared. The implication was that Palestine would function fully as a state, including as a member of the UN. The determination made at the time by the PLO was that for there to be any real protection for Palestinians there needed to be a state, even if its borders were less than those of mandate Palestine. The PLO could not forever remain a national liberation organization. The statehood initiative thus is not an idea devised by the PA, rather the PLO project of 1988 is being pursued.

Paragraph 9: Here Goodwin-Gill says, incorrectly in my view, that Palestine is not a state. He argues that state under occupation is not a state. His argument ignores the widespread recognition of Palestine by other states and the practice of UN main bodies that treat Palestine as a state. Goodwin-Gill asserts that even if Palestine becomes a state observer (here again reflecting the fact that Goodwin-Gill's opinion does not purport to deal with UN membership), it will not really be a state. Here, Goodwin-Gill argues that becoming a state observer gains little but risks the representation of the refugees. An upgrade to state observer status—if that alternative is pursued—would solidify the present international understanding that Palestine is a state. (It would make it very difficult for the ICC prosecutor to say that the international community is uncertain on the statehood of Palestine.)

Paragraph 10: Goodwin-Gill says the diaspora would lose its representation at the UN. It matters little to other states at the UN whether it is the PLO or the State of Palestine that pushes for respect of the rights of the Palestinian diaspora. Goodwin-Gill says this would be contrary to the will of the General Assembly. To pose the issue in this way is pointless. The General Assembly accepted the PLO as the representative of the Palestinian people because that was what the organized Palestinian community was asking it to do. If it is now the State of Palestine that fulfills that role, the GA will accept that just as easily. It is not as if some violation of the will of the GA is occurring.

Paragraphs 11 to 17: Similarly, the GA is not going to try to impose on the Palestinian people who should represent them. The GA accepted the PLO in the 1980s. In 1988, the PLO constituted itself as the government of the State of Palestine. Thus, the GA will not be concerned over this.

Goodwin-Gill writes as if the government of Palestine will not be recognized at the international level as having legal capacity to promote the rights and interests of the Palestinian diaspora. This omission is the fundamental flaw in his document. He ignores the role that the State of Palestine can play as promoter of the interests and rights of the Palestinian people, whether diaspora Palestinians are or are not nationals of the state. Palestine (like any other state in the world) has a "legal interest" (see Articles on "Responsibility of States for Internationally Wrongful Acts," art. 48) in protecting individuals from violation of their rights. Palestine can pursue international remedies, or raise the issue at the diplomatic level in its capacity as a state of the world.

The concern of many is whether it will in fact do so, or whether it will promote the interests of those in the territory (West Bank/Gaza) to the detriment of the interests of those outside. That is a matter of internal governance for Palestine, but not one that is relevant to representation of Palestine at the international level. To date, while there may be cause for concern, there is also indication that the interests of the diaspora will be promoted (Chairman Arafat did not cave on the issue of repatriation at Camp David 2000, despite pressure to do so). The diaspora is not shy about making its voice heard. But again, this is an internal matter that does not relate to what status Palestine has at the international level. A state of Palestine, particularly one that is a member of the UN, is better positioned to promote the rights and interests of the diaspora than is true of the PLO or PA. A state of Palestine will be interacting with other states on a myriad of issues. It will do favors for other states. It can demand favors in return from other states. A Palestine state can pursue the prosecution at the ICC of Israeli officials for war crimes such as settlements in occupied territory, thereby putting pressure on Israel on an issue that has been the principal obstacle to a peace settlement. Palestine will have leverage that it presently lacks.

The Goodwin-Gill opinion is limited to the issue of enhancement to state observer status, but even in this limited scope it makes no valid arguments. Nothing in it should be considered an impediment to pursuit of the contemplated initiatives at the UN.

31 August 2011

A Note on the Palestinian Diplomatic Initiative at the United Nations

[The following statement was issued by a group of Palestinians on 29 August 29 2011.]

Your excellences,

The chairman and members of the executive committee of the Palestine Liberation Organization (PLO)
Leaders of Palestinian political parties and factions
Leaders of Palestinian trade unions and NGOs:

Emphasizing the importance of the Palestinian diplomatic initiative at the UN, and in order for it to succeed in shaping a strategic turn and a new political and resistance path in light of the impasse bilateral negotiations have reached, and based on achieving national reconciliation and the rehabilitation of national representation within the framework of the PLO, this initiative must be linked to the transfer of the Palestinian issue in all its dimensions and aspects to the UN, in a way that ensures preserving national rights, including those contained in UN resolutions since the beginning of the conflict until now, at the forefront of which are UN resolutions 181 and 194, with the need for the UN to assume its responsibilities under its charter. This initiative must renew the emphasis on the following:

Reaffirm that Palestinians are a people with fundamental national and human rights, foremost among them the right of return of the refugees to their homes and properties from which they were forcibly displaced and uprooted, the right to self-determination, including the right to national independence and sovereignty. These rights are recognized by the United Nations as inalienable rights held by the Palestinian people, based on UNGA resolution 194, 11

December 1948; and UNGA resolution 3237 (XXIX), 22 November 1974. The right to self-determination is a collective right of all Palestinians, irrespective of their geographic location.

The PLO is the sole legitimate representative of the Palestinian people, and its legitimacy derives from the people in exile and the homeland. The PLO is recognized as the representative of the Palestinian people by the League of Arab States and the United Nations, based on UNGA Resolution 3236 (XXIX), 22 November 1974.

In its role as the legitimate representative, the PLO is responsible to protect and advance the human rights of the Palestinian people, foremost the inalienable rights to return as an individual and collective right, and self-determination as a collective right for Palestinians wherever they are.

All diplomatic initiatives, including the initiative at the United Nations this September, must preserve the status of the PLO as the sole representative in the United Nations and protect and advance the inalienable rights of the Palestinian people.

Based on the above, the Palestinian leadership, on the level of the PLO and the parties bear the historic responsibility of taking all needed steps and policies to ensure that the PLO remains the sole and legitimate representative of the Palestinian people wherever they are, and to preserve it in the UN in September and after, and to commit to transparency and the right of the Palestinian public to view all the political steps and decisions that are related to its future, including the content of any draft resolutions related to Palestinian diplomatic initiatives at the UN.

Endorsed by:

Mohammed Abu Dakka - Hani al-Masri - Jamil Hilal - Talal Al-Sharif - Shawan Jabarin - Karma Nabulsi - Mohammed Abu Mahadi - Khalil Abu Shamala - Hind Awwad -Oraib Rantawi - Mamdouh Aker - Walid Allouh - Munib Masri -Mohsen Abu Ramadan - Mohammed Maqadma - Mouin Rabbani - Muhammad Hijazi - Yusri Darwish - Khalil Shaheen - Gaza - Khalil Shaheen - Ramallah - Ibrahim Abrash - Omar Shweiki - Abdul Razzaq Al-Takriti - Bassam Darwish - Talal Okal - Nadia Hijab - Tayseer Muheisen - Hani Habib - Noura Erakat - Nasser Abu Atta- Akram Al-Ajaleh- Ziyaad Abu Shawish - Camille Mansour - Mohammed

Arouqi - Sami Abu Sultan - Sami Abu Salem - Rajab Abu Sireyeh - Mamoun Sweidan - Muhammad Dahman - Zakaria Muhammad - Akram Atallah - Bashir Bashir - Lama Abu Odeh - Maged Kayali -Samira Al-Natour - Ali Abu Shahla - Saad Abdul-Hadi - Faiha Abdul- Hadi – Hasan Jabareen - Hafez Omar - Ismat Quzmar -Antoine Shalhat - Awad Abdel Fattah - Ibrahim Shikaki - Ahmed Yacoub - Issam Younis - Akram Salhab - Anas Abu Oun – Salah Abdul-Ati – Taisir Nasrallah – Ziyad Khaddash – Zeinab Al-Ghonaimi – Issam Al-Yamani, Ismail Al-Zabri, Haitham Al-Azabri – Nadim Ruhana – Hazim Abu-Hilal – Samia Bamia – Mazin Al-Masri – Rima Tarazi – Mustafa Ibrahim – Rami Saigh – Saed Abu-Hijla – Bisan Ramadan – Nadia Abu-Nahla – Abdullah Al-Najjar – Mohammad Masoud.

31 August 2011

Statement by Palestinian Youth Movement on the September 2011 Declaration of Statehood

[The following statement was issued in both English and Arabic by the Palestinian Youth Movement on 22 September 2011.]

We, in the Palestinian Youth Movement (PYM), stand steadfastly against the proposal for Palestinian statehood recognition based on 1967 borders that is to be presented to the United Nations this September by the Palestinian official leadership. We believe and affirm that the statehood declaration only seeks the completion of the normalization process, which began with faulty peace agreements. The initiative does not recognize nor address that our people continue to live within a settler colonial regime premised on the ethnic cleansing of our land and subordination and exploitation of our people.

This declaration serves as a mechanism for rescuing the faulty peace framework and depoliticizing the struggle for Palestine by removing the struggle from its historical colonial context. The attempts to impose a false peace with the normalizing of the colonial regime has only led us to surrender increasing amounts of our land, the rights of our people, and our aspirations by delegitimizing and marginalizing our people's struggle and deepening the fragmentation and division of our people. This declaration jeopardizes the rights and aspirations of over two-thirds of the Palestinian people who live as refugees in countries of refuge and in exile, to return to their original homes from which they were displaced in the 1948 Nakba (catastrophe) and subsequently since then. It also jeopardizes the position of the Palestinians residing in the 1948 occupied territories who continue to resist daily against the ethnic cleansing and racial practices from inside the colonial regime. Furthermore, it corroborates and empowers its Palestinian and Arab partners to act as the gatekeepers to the occupation and the colonization of the region within a neocolonial framework.

The foundation of this process serves as nothing more than to ensure the continuity of negotiations, economic and social normalization, and security cooperation. The state declaration will solidify falsified borders on only a sliver of historic Palestine and still does not address the most fundamental issues: Jerusalem, settlements, refugees, political prisoners, occupation, borders, and resource control. We believe such a state declaration will not ensure nor promote justice and freedom for Palestinians, which inherently means there will be no sustainable peace in the region.

Additionally, this state declaration initiative is being presented to the United Nations by a Palestinian leadership that is illegitimate and has not been elected to be in a position of representation of the Palestinian people in its totality through any democratic means by its people. This proposal is a political production designed by them to hide behind their failure to represent the needs and desires of their people. By claiming to fulfill the Palestinian will for self-determination, this leadership is misusing and exploiting the resistance and sacrifices of the Palestinian people, particularly our brothers and sisters in Gaza, and even hijacking the grassroots international solidarity work, such as boycott, divestment, and sanctions efforts and the flotilla initiatives. This proposal only serves to squander all efforts made to isolate the colonial regime and hold it accountable.

Whether the proposal for statehood recognition is accepted or not, we call on Palestinians inside our occupied homeland and in countries of refuge and exile to remain committed and convicted to the worthiness of our struggle and inspired by their rights and responsibilities to defend it. We call on the free people of the world and the Palestinian people's allies to truly practice solidarity with the Palestinian anti-colonial struggle by not taking a position on the state declaration but rather continuing to hold Israel accountable, by means of boycott —in all forms economically, academically, and culturally—divestment, and sanctions.

Until Return and Liberation,
International Central Council
Palestinian Youth Movement

22 September 2011

[Originally published on pal-youth.org]

US Palestinian Community Network's Response to the Palestinian Authority September Statehood Bid

[The following statement was issued in both English and Arabic by the US Palestinian Community Network on 27 August 2011.]

Liberation and Return are the Demands of the Palestinian People:
A note of caution to our people and our allies

In recent months, the Palestinian Authority has intensified diplomatic efforts to declare statehood at the United Nations. Wasting no avenue, the PA has been seeking to mobilize popular forces in Palestine and in the *shatat* (diaspora) behind this initiative. Students, community associations, solidarity campaigns, and organizers across the United States have all been called upon to "make Palestine the 194th state."

While the call sounds attractive, many community members wonder what to make of it. Will this initiative bring Palestine closer to liberation? Will it help Palestinians achieve their right to return? Some have remarked that, if nothing else, it will not hurt.

The US Palestinian Community Network, a grassroots community-led network of democratically elected chapters across the US, asserts that such initiatives, in fact, do hurt. They are not benign exercises, but can cause great damage to achievements made through the hard, brutal, struggle of generations of Palestinians.

As has been recently revealed, this initiative in no way protects nor advances our inalienable, and internationally recognized, rights—namely, our right to return to the homes and properties from which we were forcibly expelled, our right to self-determination, and our right to resist the settler colonial regime that has occupied our land for more than sixty-three years. The Palestinian people, wherever they are, hold these rights. They are non-negotiable. No one can barter them away for false promises of "peace" and "stability." The cynical irony of turning a UN resolution enshrining our right to return under international law (UNGA Resolution 194) into a rhetorical ploy should give anyone pause. That it is being advanced at a time when the PA does not even have the political mandate of Palestinians in the West Bank and Gaza through Palestinian Legislative Council elections must also give us pause.

Our inalienable rights give us the foundational principles with which we seek liberation and return. When these two things are achieved, it is then that we will achieve independence. Not before, and not without the mandate of the entirety of the Palestinian people. Indeed, it is in struggle and the emboldening of our emancipatory spirit that we free ourselves. Resistance is our first independence.

But, the question remains. Who protects our inalienable rights? Who speaks in the name of the Palestinian people?

In our long Palestinian revolutionary struggle, no matter where we lived, we fought for our right to determine our own destiny; pave a path to freedom that would be of our own design, our own democratic will. In 1968, we rescued the Palestinian Liberation Organization from Arab regimes, and through a generation of struggle and sacrifice, transformed it into the sole legitimate representative of the Palestinian people, recognized by the Arab League and by the United Nations.

Through the PLO, and its countless popular committees, associations, unions, and camp formations, many (though not all) Palestinians had a voice within their movement. Indeed, it is that popular democratic mobilization that gave the PLO its legitimacy. And, in its continued role as legitimate representative, the PLO, and only the PLO, has the legal mandate to advance the political will of the Palestinian people.

Any diplomatic initiatives, including the initiative at the United Nations this September, must therefore preserve the status of the PLO as the sole representative of the Palestinian people at the United Nations *and* protect and advance our inalienable rights. The current Statehood initiative does neither, and is therefore an unacceptable threat to the Palestinian national movement.

We say this knowing full well that, in the last few decades, the PLO has been decimated by corruption, ineptitude, collaboration, and betrayal. It must be reclaimed, cleaned, revived, and rebuilt. It is we, the Palestinian people, across the *shatat* and in the homeland, who will do it. It is ours. We will not allow it to be stolen from us. The PLO must expand to truly represent all Palestinians, inside Israel, in the West Bank and Gaza, in the camps, and across the *shatat*. It is we who give it legitimacy; it is we who give political mandate to our leadership; it is we who will breathe new life into our long too dormant national institutions through popular democratic mobilization.

In the meantime, we hold the current occupants of PLO positions ultimately responsible for protecting the PLO's role as the representative of the Palestinian people. A failure to do so must have consequences.

We call on all Palestinian and Arab community associations, societies and committees, student organizations, and solidarity campaigns, to reject fully and unequivocally the Statehood initiative as a distraction that unjustifiably and irresponsibly endangers Palestinian rights and institutions.

We need not be concerned that to do so would be to stand with the interests of the US or Israel. Lack of US and Israeli support for the statehood initiative is a red herring, meant to distract us from the continued support that both have provided for an authority and "peace process" that daily cost the Palestinian people their liberty, self-determination, and lives.

However, such an initiative nonetheless has potential to positively impact our struggle. It clarifies for us that we must return to a framework we once had, but one that has been thwarted by decades of endless and cynical negotiations, diplomatic stunts, and "peace deals." We must return to a framework of genuine struggle and a cohesive and coherent strategy built upon our inalienable rights.

The first step in such a strategy must be an escalated focus on Palestinian mobilization for direct elections to the Palestinian National Council (PNC), the legislative body of the PLO. It is the PNC that holds the mechanism by which Palestinians can collectively determine the strategy the PLO must execute in our name. Its democratization is key to cohering us, bringing back to us our collective force. Indeed, democratization of our movement must reach into all aspects of our political work, in each of our community associations, and all our student, labor, and popular formations.

We therefore call on all Palestinians across the United States to participate in strengthening the campaign for direct elections to the Palestinian National Council by participating in Palestinian Movement Assemblies and Community Meetings for Democratic National Representation. Held throughout the summer, these meetings will continue through the fall and throughout the country. They

183

will grow as the campaign grows, building a critical mass for our demand for democratic representation.

Organize an assembly, community meeting, or town hall in your area. USPCN will be with you every step of the way, with support, guidance, and coordination. We can only demand of our struggle what we put into it. We are indivisible from the Palestinian people. We must activate and elevate our role in the *shatat* for our common liberation and return.

To students, solidarity campaigns and allies, we caution you against this distraction of resources, time, and energy. The path for solidarity and mutual struggle is clear. We must continue the work of building our common struggles for all forms of emancipation and liberation. We must continue to isolate Zionism, and strengthen the Boycott, Divestment, and Sanctions movement in the United States by getting involved in the growing campaigns across the country. We must return to international institutions with our inalienable rights intact, and utilize all legal instruments, vigorously, to challenge Israel's impunity for its continued and unceasing crimes in Gaza. We must support the legal campaigns against Israeli war criminals, shame them, hound them, and try them at the International Criminal Court for their continued crimes against our humanity.

And we must also take to the streets. Let us all rally at the United Nations on September 15. The march will take place on Thursday, September 15 in New York City, with a 4:30 gathering in Times Square followed by a 5:30 march to Grand Central and the United Nations. We demand the United Nations hear our voice. We are the people of Palestine, we are the allies of Palestine, and we will be heard by the General Assembly.

To our beautiful brave Arab people, from Tripoli to Cairo to Homs to Sana'a to Amman to Manama, we salute you and stand with you. In devoting ourselves to our liberation, we honor your sacrifices and struggle for our Palestine and for our Arab future. Stand with us, open the gates and crossings that besiege us, and rest assured: we will not stop until the banner of freedom flutters above the skies of our Jerusalem.

Until liberation and return.
US Palestinian Community Network

27 August 2011
[Originally published on USPCN.org]

BNC Reiterates Its Position on September

[The following statement was issued by the BDS National Committee on 8 August 2011.]

In the midst of the debate on Palestinian diplomatic initiatives aimed at securing membership of "Palestine" in the United Nations, many legitimate questions on strategies and tactics have arisen among people of conscience around the world who support freedom, justice, and equality for the Palestinian people. As in the struggle against apartheid in South Africa, Palestine solidarity groups and activists are convinced, as we are, that only concerted, effective, and sustained forms of solidarity, especially in the form of Boycott, Divestment, and Sanctions (BDS), can hold Israel accountable to its obligations under international law and lead to the realization of comprehensive Palestinian rights.

The Palestinian BDS National Committee (BNC), the largest Palestinian civil society coalition, reiterates and further explicates below the main principles which have informed its position on this matter, as expressed in our statement issued on 1 June 2011.

(1) Self-Determination

The most fundamental, inalienable right of the people of Palestine is the right to self-determination. Ending the occupation is one pillar in exercising that right. The right to self-determination, which in the case of Palestinians is represented by the Palestine Liberation Organization (PLO), is commonly defined as the right of "all peoples ... freely to determine, without external interference, their political status and to pursue their economic, social and cultural development."[1] It is a right held by all Palestinians, irrespective of their current location, by virtue of international law and the principles of popular sovereignty and democracy. All Palestinians, including refugees in the *shatat* (diaspora) and Palestinian citizens of Israel, have a right to participate in and be represented by—in the UN and elsewhere—a democratic PLO that determines the political status and pursues the economic, social, and cultural development of the entire Palestinian people.

At a minimum, exercising the right to self-determination by all Palestinians entails

1. ending Israel's occupation and colonization of all Arab lands occupied in 1967;

2. honoring the right of Palestinian citizens of Israel to full equality by ending the Israeli *system* of legalized and institutionalized racial discrimination (which conforms to the UN definition of apartheid); and

3. respecting and enabling the implementation of the UN-sanctioned right of Palestinian refugees to return to their homes and lands from which they were expelled.

(2) PLO

Until the Palestinian people exercises its right to self determination, the PLO remains the sole legitimate representative that represents all Palestinians in the UN and in other international, regional, and multinational forums. No alternative will be accepted by the great majority of the Palestinian people.

(3) Complicity and Accountability

States that have recognized the Palestinian right to statehood are even more obliged to end their complicity in maintaining, covering up, or even strengthening Israel's regime of occupation, colonialism, and apartheid against the Palestinian people. States that offer recognition of Palestinian statehood and continue business as usual with Israel are beyond hypocritical; they betray their own basic legal and political obligations to end Israel's grave and persistent violations of international law and Palestinian rights.

[Excerpts from a June 2011 statement issued by the BDS National Committee (BNC), the largest coalition in Palestinian civil society]

Before and After September: The Struggle for Palestinian Rights Must Intensify

This September will mark the twentieth anniversary of the start of the Israeli-Palestinian "peace process" that is widely recognized as a total failure, by any objective standard. This sham process has served as a cover for Israel's intensive colonization of Palestinian lands, continued denial of Palestinian basic rights, and gradual ethnic cleansing of Palestinians, while simultaneously giving a false impression of peacemaking. In this context, the BNC welcomes the recognition of a great majority of states around the world that the Palestinian right to statehood and freedom from Israeli occupation are long overdue and should no longer be held hostage to fanatically biased US "diplomacy" in defense of Israeli expansionism. However, recognition of Palestinian statehood is clearly insufficient on its own in bringing about a real end to Israel's occupation and colonial rule. Neither will it end Israel's decades-old system of legalized racial discrimination, which fits the UN definition of apartheid, or allow the millions of Palestinian refugees to return to their homes of origin from which they were violently uprooted and exiled.

Diplomatic recognition must result in protection of the inalienable right to self-determination of the entire Palestinian people represented by a democratized and inclusive PLO that represents not just Palestinians under occupation, but also the exiled refugees, the majority of the Palestinian people, as well as the discriminated citizens of Israel. For it to go beyond symbolism, this recognition must be a prelude to effective and sustained sanctions against Israel aimed at bringing about its full compliance with its obligations under international law. As shown in the struggle to end apartheid in South Africa, as well as in the current struggles for freedom and justice in the Arab region, world governments do not turn against a patently illegal and immoral regime of oppression simply on ethical grounds; economic interests and hegemonic power dynamics are far weightier in their considerations. In fact, Israeli Prime Minister Benjamin Netanyahu's militant and war-mongering speech before the US Congress, coupled with US President Barack Obama's latest humiliating submission to Israel's will, shows beyond doubt that anyone still holding onto the hope that Washington is able or willing to contribute to building a just peace in our region is delusional.

The key lesson learned from South Africa is that, in order for world governments to end their complicity with Israel's grave and persistent violations of human rights and international law, they must be *compelled* to do so through well organized mass grassroots pressure by social movements and other components of civil society. In this context, BDS has proven to be the most potent and promising strategy of international solidarity with the Palestinian people in our struggle for self-determination, freedom, justice, and equality.

In light of the above, and inspired by the will and the power of the people which have given rise to the Arab Spring, the BNC calls upon people of conscience and international solidarity groups to proceed with building a mass BDS movement in the US and elsewhere in the world's most powerful countries before and after September. Only such a mass movement can ensure that whatever diplomatic recognition that transpires at the UN in September on Palestinian statehood will advance the rights of the Palestinian people and raise the price of Israel's occupation, colonialism, and apartheid by further isolating it and those complicit in its crimes. A mass solidarity movement that can hold elected officials, especially in the United States, accountable to the people, rather than to a Zionist lobby serving Israel's colonial and belligerent agenda that directly conflicts with the interests of the peoples in these countries, is the only hope for a comprehensive and sustainable peace based on justice.

8 August 2011

[Originally published on BDSmovement.net]

---

[1] Declaration of Principles of International Law Concerning Friendly Relations and Co-operation Among States in Accordance with the Charter of the United Nations: UN General Assembly Resolution 2625 (XXV) of 24 October 1970.

Beyond Sterile Negotiations: Looking for a Leadership with a Strategy

Noura Erakat

In Search of a Collapsed Palestinian Leadership

Palestinian leadership briefly returned to the weathered tables of diplomatic niceties to negotiate a path to negotiations. The return signaled an alarming regression from the confrontational stance the leadership made in September 2011, when it took its case to the United Nations (UN). Then, notably buoyed by President Mahmoud Abbas's liberation message to the global community, Palestinians thought it possible that the leadership would remove its self-determination struggle from the sterile confines of bilateral negotiations and place it on an international stage. In the event, the Palestine Liberation Organization (PLO) decision to resume negotiations for a while dashed any hope that the Palestinian leadership has a strategic vision for national liberation. During the eighteen years of the "peace process" the settler population has more than doubled, the Jordan Valley has been all but declared a closed military zone, the annexation wall has expropriated twelve percent of the West Bank, with sixty-two percent of the West Bank beyond Palestinian control, the Gaza Strip has been reduced to destitution under the heavy-handedness of war and an ongoing blockade, and the ethnic cleansing of Jerusalem has dramatically accelerated. In these circumstances, any return to negotiations, however brief, can neither be justified nor forgiven. Absent a Palestinian national liberation strategy, negotiations are counterproductive to Palestinian national interests.

The Palestinian Authority's (PA) electoral mandate of the West Bank's two and a half million Palestinians has long expired and, even were it in force, the PA "represents" only a quarter of the global Palestinian population. Thus, it may be fair to ask whether some other body can responsibly develop a national liberation strategy that will be more representative than what either the PA or PLO has been able to offer for more than two decades, and if so, what its goals should be.

The lack of a political program representing Palestinian national aspirations follows the steady erosion of the PLO in the aftermath of the Oslo Accords. In his unpublished paper, "The Rise and Fall of the PLO: A History of the Palestine Liberation Organization," Seif Da'na writes the following:

> The Oslo agreement prepared the grounds for the demise of the PLO, both as a structure and program, initiating a conflict inside the PLO between the bureaucrats interlinked with the new ruling class, and figures professing PLO ideals and liberation and independence. This inevitable rivalry intensified as the Palestinian Authority has gradually replaced the PLO as a political structure and the nature of the Palestinian question was significantly redefined.

The tensions between the aims and structure of the PA with those of the PLO has sharpened with Hamas's electoral victory in January 2006, and again, when the PA, under the auspices of the PLO, approached the UN in its bid for to become a member state.

In immediate response to Hamas's legislative victory, the United States, Israel, and the European Union imposed sanctions on the PA, having already declared Hamas a "terrorist organization." This exacerbated tensions between Fateh, the once-dominant secular political party led by the late PLO Chairman Yasser Arafat, and the PA. Tensions reached their apex—when Hamas routed Fateh from Gaza in June 2007—in what can be described as a preemptive coup, which resulted in a politically and geographically bifurcated Palestinian government. Thereafter, the United States and Israel resumed their financial and diplomatic support of the Fateh-dominated PA thereby affording Fateh considerable influence over the official Palestinian political agenda.

Mired in an internecine conflict, Palestinian leaders dedicated more effort to asserting their control over the occupied territory, than they did to combatting settler-colonial occupation or apartheid. Neither Hamas nor Fateh, nor their short-lived government of national unity, has ever represented the entirety of the Palestinian nation. The conflict has led friends and foes alike to ask, "Who speaks for Palestinians?"

Palestinians asked this question again in the lead-up to September 2011, when the PA/PLO applied for membership in the UN. Since 1974, the PLO, which likes to remind the world that it is the "sole and legitimate representative of the Palestinian people," has had UN observer status, when the UN General Assembly passed resolution 3236. The statehood bid raised concerns that if the UN granted Palestine membership, the PA, which only represents the Occupied Palestinian Territories (OPT), would supplant the PLO as the Palestinian representative body to the global community. Palestinians living in the diaspora feared that they would be excluded from Palestinian national representation altogether. The threat of such exclusion prompted many Palestinians in the diaspora to reject the statehood bid in unequivocal terms.

The Rise of the BNC and Diaspora Networks

In the wake of the 2005 Palestinian Civil Society Call for Boycott, Divestment, and Sanctions (BDS), endorsed by over 170 civil society organizations, the BDS National Committee (BNC) emerged as the leader of a global movement coalescing around the need to respond with specific non-violent economic measures to Israel's violations of international law. In addition to representatives of civil society organizations, the BNC now includes representation from Palestinian political forces in the form of the Coalition of National and Islamic Forces. By providing a central Palestinian reference point and authoritative guidance to global solidarity, the BNC has partially filled a void left by the disappearance of a once commanding PLO—even though it makes no claims to do so.

In addition, the 2005 BDS call grounded Palestinian self-determination within the universal frame of international law and human rights norms. It was based on three demands: 1) ending the occupation and colonization of all Arab lands, 2) full equality for Israel's Arab-Palestinian citizens, and 3) the right of return of Palestinian refugees. It did not, however, offer a political vision or program. Omar Barghouti, a founding member of the BDS movement and the BNC, explains, "The BNC does not take sides in the one-state versus two-state solution debate among Palestinians." Indeed, the three rights-based demands enshrined in the BDS call are necessary, but not sufficient, for the achievement of national self-determination. In addition, they do not correspond to a particular political program among Palestinians.

By contrast, the US Palestinian Community Network (USPCN), a non-sectarian network of Palestinians living in North America, emerged in 2006 in an effort to provide representative and accountable leadership for Palestinians and Arabs in the United States, in response to their exclusion from the PA/PLO. Andrew Dalack, a leading member, explains that the "USPCN [responds] to a need from the Palestinian national body by providing a vehicle through which

Palestinians in the Diaspora can exert influence over their own self-determination and Palestine's future." In response to the statehood bid, the USPCN called on allies to "reject fully and unequivocally the Statehood initiative as a distraction that unjustifiably and irresponsibly endangers Palestinian rights and institutions."

Similarly, the Palestinian Youth Movement (PYM), a grassroots movement of young Palestinians in Palestine, as well as eleven other countries in the Arab world, Europe, and North America adopted a political program from the very start. PYM's International General Coordinator Loubna Qatami recalls: "From the early days of PYM's formation… we knew we were trying to fill a void: a political vacuum that no present body or solution was seemingly addressing." PYM opposed the statehood bid, too, and chastised the PA/PLO for "misusing and exploiting the resistance and sacrifices of the Palestinian people, particularly [those] in Gaza, and even hijacking the grassroots international solidarity work." According to PYM, "[The bid] only serves to squander all efforts made to isolate the colonial regime and hold it accountable."

Like the USPCN and the PYM, the BNC has also tried to fill a political void. Unlike these other organizations, however, the BNC does not seek to represent the collective will of the Palestinian national body but instead to establish a trustworthy reference for international solidarity. Though it distinguishes itself from diaspora and transnational networks, the BNC also strongly criticized the statehood bid declaring it "insufficient" and urged "people of conscience and international solidarity groups to proceed with building a mass BDS movement in the United States, United Kingdom, and elsewhere in the world's most powerful countries before and after September."

Of all these organizations in the diaspora, the BNC presently comes closest to representing comprehensive national interests. However, it has steadfastly refused to fulfill such a political mandate. Barghouti insists, "The BNC is not, and does not, aspire to become an alternative political body. The political leadership of the Palestinian people must remain within the structures of the PLO." However, because the BNC only seeks to be an authoritative reference with regard to BDS, the tactic—along with the lexicon that surrounds it—has often been mistaken for a national liberation strategy.

The BNC position, thus, raises two primary challenges for the Palestinian body politic. First, because the BNC does not claim a representational mandate equivalent to that of the PLO, this creates confusion among solidarity groups who can consequently and simultaneously adopt a call for human rights without being held accountable to developing a political program. Second, in the absence of a national liberation strategy, BDS's major successes can only expand the call for Palestinian rights. They cannot achieve Palestinian self-determination.

Qutami highlights the danger of conflating BDS as a strategic tactic with the purpose of the movement itself. She attributes this risk to the lack of a broader national strategy, offering that "There is no base, no project, no trajectory, no collective conviction, and no strategy to ensure the continued sense of accountability to the movement."

Human Rights without a Political Program?

In short, the pressing questions regarding representation and a strategy for national liberation remain to be answered by Palestinians the world over. A few of those questions could include:

1. Should Palestinians go so far as to support annexation of the Occupied Palestinian Territories in order to usher in an era of struggle for equality within a singular territory and legal regime?

2. Should settlements be racially integrated or completely demolished?

3. Will the amendment of Israeli laws to ensure equality ever suffice to change its character from Jewish to secular?

4. Should Palestinian citizens of Israel focus on an equality struggle or should they articulate a comprehensive frame to combat ethnic cleansing within Israel proper as well as the OPT?

5. What is the role of the PA, as an outcome of Oslo, if any? Should it be boycotted, dismantled, or leveraged as recently suggested by PLO executive committee member Hanan Ashrawi?

6. What type of economy should Palestinians advocate for?

7. With which states and international movements should Palestinians ally for economic, political, and security support?

8. What is the role of armed resistance? If it is still salient, how does it relate to nonviolent direct action?

It is interesting to note that, in 2011, PYM removed the language of a rights-based approach from its charter because—according to a consensus among its members—it made them lose sight of the need for a direct grassroots mobilization among Palestinian communities. A similar approach inspired the

Freedom Riders action, when a group of independent Palestinian activists defiantly boarded settler buses bound for East Jerusalem to demonstrate against the insidious nature of Israel's institutionalized segregation of public and private spatial territories. The action drew international attention and praise for highlighting Israel's apartheid system. It also drew controversy among Palestinians who mistakenly read it as a demand to end segregation amongst settlements and their exclusionary transportation systems rather than to liberate the lands upon which they sprawl. The controversy sparked a healthy discussion amongst Palestinians about the limitations of human rights language. Both approaches speak to the tension between a rights-based approach and a political program clearly aimed at achieving self-determination and national liberation.

Despite these internal Palestinian tensions, a rights-based approach remains the salient reference for international solidarity activists. Hannah Mermelstein, a leading member of Adalah New York and a longtime human rights activist, notes, "Not every Palestinian person on the street is necessarily active in BDS but it is a platform that very few Palestinians would disagree with. It is a bottom line: a set of rights and a framework. And to me, that is just as important as the tactic itself." Though the BNC's rights-based approach may arguably represent a common denominator amongst Palestinians, the lack of a political program that it can advance structurally limits its ability to achieve self-determination.

Lessons Learned from South Africa

Does the experience of struggle against apartheid rule in South Africa offer a way beyond the tensions between a human rights-based approach and a political program for national liberation? There are of course differences between the Palestinian and apartheid South African cases. For example, the call to boycott apartheid South Africa was made by African states in 1961 and adopted by the UN General Assembly in 1962 (Resolution 1761). By contrast, the 2005 BDS call was made by a large coalition of Palestinian civil society associations and networks. The call was only partially endorsed by the Palestinian Authority and has not been embraced by any Arab regimes, let alone by the UN General Assembly.

And yet, despite its apparent cohesion, the South African boycott movement also suffered from internal divisiveness. Bill Fletcher Jr., scholar and past president of the TransAfrica Forum, notes that although the African National Congress (ANC) was the most widely known South African political party in the United States, other parties included the Pan-African Congress (PAC) and Azania People's Movement (Azapo). Each party represented distinct movements influenced by international and domestic politics. As in the case of Palestine, international solidarity had many choices for an authoritative reference. Unlike the case of Palestine, however, Fletcher explains, "Solidarity was very broad, and there was never a need to pick sides or to choose which organization to ally with." Instead, solidarity activists committed themselves to end apartheid. Although, Fletcher notes, "no one was quite sure what the end of apartheid would mean." Despite lacking a shared political vision, solidarity activists agreed that victory would include black majority rule, an end to segregation, land redistribution, and the release of all political prisoners.

The challenge to the South African call for boycott did not emerge from internecine tension but instead from African-American-led solidarity efforts. In particular, forces that opposed the radical call for boycott coalesced around the Sullivan Principles, drafted by Reverend Leon Sullivan. Despite their celebrated legacy, Sullivan's "blueprint for ending apartheid" was a "distraction." As Fletcher puts it, "Sullivan was aiming to delegitimize the ANC and PAC....The people that advocated the Sullivan Principles were opposed to the BDS forces in the United States and the revolutionary forces in South Africa."

Barghouti points to similar struggles within the BDS movement against Israel. He notes, "Some soft Zionist groups have tried at various stages, sometimes desperately, to dilute the demands of the BDS call, limiting them to ending the 1967 occupation and to obscure the Palestinian reference of the global BDS movement. But their efforts were decisively aborted." Although these "soft Zionist" attempts clearly have their own political agenda, they also highlight the problem of the absence of a political program and BDS dependence only on a rights-based approach. In this context, activists can and are often encouraged to express their support for human rights, irrespective of the political will of the people they claim to support.

Non-Revolutionary Political Solutions

The possibility that rights could be attained without achieving a revolutionary solution also loomed as a threat for the South African anti-apartheid movement. Fletcher notes that although activists recognized that the African-American struggle for equality was addressed legislatively and without a revolutionary solution, "It was common for people to assume that because the ANC and PAC had armies...there would be a sweeping away [of repressive systems]."

Of course, today, people's movements with armies are marginalized as "terrorist organizations." In any case, the potential for revolutionary transformation will arguably have to emerge from a political, economic, social, and civic platform. The most pressing challenge at this juncture is to decide who will engender this platform, and how they will do it, and to define the scope of its geographic reach, and the salience of its political representation.

To this end, the movement to revitalize the Palestinian National Council (PNC) may prove significant. Following Al Jazeera's release of the infamous *Palestine Papers*, Palestinians from Lebanon, Britain, the United States, and the Occupied Palestinian Territories, as well as those residing within Israel demanded more accountable political leadership. The resuscitation of the PNC stood out among this decentralized movement's demands. That demand has since crystallized into a global, coordinated movement to register Palestinians by October 2012, and then to hold elections for the PNC. Even after registration is complete, and assuming that PNC elections are accepted as legitimate by an identifiable Palestinian national body, the "what next" question will continue to loom large.

Nour Joudah, a DC-based graduate student and Palestinian activist, notes that these questions are more likely to be answered in practice than in meeting rooms. She comments, "We are going to work from all sides and angles—BDS campaigns, protests, international solidarity, press connections, and public relations. We will thus continue to have the conversation of 'what next?' even if in a 'state of limbo' with a political leadership seemingly uncommitted to resistance."

Joudah's response appears closest to the South African model for revolutionary transformation: to work on all fronts while addressing the core question of a national liberation strategy and the leadership necessary for its achievement. The Palestinian political arena currently encompasses a non-representative political body (PA/PLO) that claims leadership in international circles, a powerful civil society movement that seeks Palestinian rights without claiming representation or a political program (the BNC), a smaller but growing network of diaspora groupings that do seek political representation (the USPCN and PYM), and a budding effort to seek national representation through universal elections to the PNC. In this context, the most effective strategy does seem to be the struggle for human rights, while still working on a political program and engendering a representative leadership, especially at a time when an increasingly sympathetic world is gradually expanding its support for the Palestinians' national aspirations.

6 February 2012

[This article first appeared as a policy brief on Al-Shabaka]

V | Back at the UN Again 2012

Statehood Bid One Year Later: No State, No Bid, No Freedom

Noura Erakat

In early August 2012, Palestinian Authority President Mahmoud Abbas vowed to renew the United Nations statehood bid in September:

> Even if this step conflicts with other parties' interests . . . [W]e will not step back. . . . Israel neither halted settlement activities, nor recognized the Palestinian territory occupied in 1967 as occupied territory. Thus, the only choice we have is to go to the UN equipped with a united Arab mandate.

Yet, only a few weeks later, the Palestinian Foreign Ministry announced that it would not submit an application to the UN General Assembly session set to begin in mid-September. Alternatively, it will make an informal call for recognition in a speech. Analysts say that the Palestinian leadership will wait until after the US presidential elections to resume a more forceful campaign at the United Nations. Be that as it may, the timing has become virtually irrelevant because the statehood bid as advanced by the current Palestinian leadership has proven to be fruitless.

September 2012 marks one year since the Palestinian leadership introduced its bid for membership and recognition at the United Nations. Then, an international community—comprised of UN member states, NGOs, and Palestinians—watched the Palestinian leadership with apprehension and hope, eager that it would use the UN platform to embark on a new chapter of the Palestinian struggle for self-determination. One year onwards, it is clear that this leadership is more committed to preserving its rule in a truncated statelet than achieving national liberation.

Withdrawing from Oslo's Terms: A Prerequisite

Since establishing the terms of the Oslo peace process in the early and mid-1990s, the Palestinian Authority and Israel, together with the United States, have been managing a colonial reality rather than working towards its

199

dissolution. The Oslo Accords suffer from three fundamental and enduring flaws: they deliberately omit the rights enshrined in international law from the terms of reference aimed at resolving the Israel-Palestinian conflict; they confine negotiations to bilateral talks brokered by the United States, an unwilling and unable agent of change; and they transform transitional Palestinian self-governance into a permanent arrangement. The terms of Oslo structurally prioritized Israeli security interests—as defined by Israel—above Palestinian rights—as codified by the international community—by making any progress towards Palestinian freedom dependent upon an Israeli certificate of good conduct that the Palestinians were never going to obtain.

Palestinians protested these terms well before January 2011, when the *Palestine Papers* revealed the deleterious course steered by the Palestinian leadership. In 2006, fifty-eight percent of the Palestinian electorate voted for Hamas in Palestinian Authority parliamentary polls, in what can be described as a triple referendum: on Fateh's management of the Palestinian Authority and the national movement more broadly; on conditions of daily life in the Occupied Palestinian Territory; and on the Oslo peace process.

Consider that by 2006, almost a decade after the Oslo process was slated for completion, serious Israel-Palestinian negotiations had all but collapsed and had yet to genuinely address the core issues separating the two sides. As it became increasingly clear that Israel had no intention to enable a genuine process of decolonization, the second intifada raged between 2000 and 2005, resulting in the killing of thousands of Palestinians, many of them civilian non-combatants, as well as the destruction of no less than five thousand Palestinian homes. Furthermore, Israel in 2002 began construction of the West Bank wall. In 2005, Israel had also unilaterally disengaged from the Gaza Strip, relocating its twelve thousand settlers to either side of the Green Line. Finally, the number of Israeli settlements in the West Bank practically doubled during the decade after Oslo. The "peace process" enabled and facilitated, rather than deterred, these developments.

A Palestinian approach to the United Nations would therefore have been meaningful only if it simultaneously consisted of a clear withdrawal from Oslo and its terms. To be successful, the statehood bid would have needed to clearly challenge continued Israeli colonialism and apartheid along with the international economic and political relationships that sustained them. Such a strategy would have included the termination of security cooperation with Israel, removing the conflict and its resolution from the purview of bilateral negotiations, and engaging in tactics designed to isolate Israel and expose its settler-colonialist structure and policies. Yet, as various international analysts and Palestinian organizations observed, the statehood bid was designed in a manner to improve the Palestinian leadership's position *within* the terms of Oslo, rather than one aimed at shifting decisively away from it.

Failure to Change Course in the Intervening Twelve Months

If this latter criticism was not entirely obvious in 2011, the Palestinian leadership has confirmed its validity many times over in the intervening twelve months. Consider first that the bid for full membership status died a quiet death in the Security Council. Full UN membership requires a positive Security Council recommendation to the General Assembly, which the United States adamantly opposed. To save face, the US and Palestinian leaderships agreed to spare the statehood application from a vote and the US veto it would have entailed. The standoff would have embarrassed the United States, which proclaims support for a two-state settlement, as well as the Palestinian leadership, because it has not disavowed the US-brokered peace process. What has survived this process, and what remains at stake, is recognition within the General Assembly, which would upgrade Palestine from its "observer mission" status at the United Nations to an "observer state" one. In order to break away from Oslo's framework, the Palestinian leadership could and should have used this opportunity to confront the United States' intransigent support of Israel. Instead, it chose not to and continued to pursue a political program under American tutelage in the hope that a global superpower would deliver independence.

Since leaving UN Headquarters, the Palestinian leadership has done little to indicate a move away from Oslo's debilitating terms. Even its most significant achievement of earning acceptance as a member state within the United Nations Educational, Scientific and Cultural Organization (UNESCO) became another opportunity to reify Oslo's structure. Palestinian diplomats used its state status within UNESCO to add the Church of the Nativity in Bethlehem to the list of endangered world heritage sites. While recognition of the church as a Palestinian site is indeed positive, doing so also marks a missed opportunity for Palestinians to use their UNESCO membership to add other sites that are under graver threat within the West Bank. For example, as Ryvka Barnard highlights, it would have been optimal for Palestinians had their leadership used the opportunity to add Battir, a village in the Bethlehem district that sits in Area C, to the list of World Heritage Sites. Most of Battir is now under threat because it is about to be consumed by the route of the annexation wall. The Jewish National Fund (JNF) has also designated lands alienated from the village by the Israeli state as a green park for exclusive use by Israeli citizens—in effect, Jewish settlers and their fellow travelers. By contrast, the Nativity Church is located within Area A, which is under full Palestinian civilian and security jurisdiction and not in imminent danger.

The Palestinian leadership also lobbied the International Criminal Court (ICC) to approve its application, submitted in January 2009, requesting to be recognized as a state within its jurisdiction. This would have enabled Palestinians to bring lawsuits for war crimes against Israel for its winter 2008/9 onslaught on the Gaza Strip. Not surprisingly, the ICC rejected the application and did not admit Palestine as a state even for jurisdictional purposes. This marked the end of the Palestinian leadership's pursuit for accountability. Its paralysis was unnecessary as it had other available options to pursue accountability for Israeli war crimes committed in Gaza. These included advocacy to make actionable the recommendations of the 2009 Goldstone Report. Despite Judge Richard Goldstone's subsequent attempt at disavowal of elements of his own work, the report is and remains an official Human Rights Council document. Therefore, it can be legitimately supported. However, even this small measure within the United Nations has not been pursued, indicating a myopic quest for self-rule by the Palestinian leadership.

Strengthening Security, Entrenching the Occupation

In addition to the missed and neglected opportunities at recognition as a state, the Palestinian leadership has strengthened its Oslo-engendered security apparatus. In early July 2012, the Palestinian Authority invited then-Israeli vice prime minister Shaul Mofaz—who as chief of staff in 2002 was responsible for the pummeling of Jenin refugee camp—to visit Ramallah. Palestinian youth, organized under the banner of "Palestinians for Dignity," launched protests against this invitation. In response, PA security forces beat youth activists, and the journalists covering them, with repressive force.

More recently, the Palestinian Authority has extended its detention of Zakaria Zubeidi, the Freedom Theater co-founder, for nineteen more days. The Palestinian security forces detained Zubeidi on 13 May 2012, but have yet to charge him with any crime. Zubeidi, who is on hunger strike and has vowed to continue until the end, proclaimed: "This decision is unjust and means you want to kill me, but I want to choose how I will die. In four days, there will be a funeral from Jericho to Jenin." In non-ironic protest, onlookers screamed "shame" and accused the Palestinian leadership of being "no better than the Israelis."

Indeed, Zubeidi's protest emulates the campaign waged by thousands of Palestinian detainees in Israeli custody earlier this year. Political prisoners, beginning with Khader Adnan, launched hunger strikes to protest their "administrative detention." A euphemism for indefinite incarceration, this draconian measure allows Israel to arrest a Palestinian without charge or trial for up to six months, renewable indefinitely. Adnan was on hunger strike for sixty-six days before Israel agreed to release him. Several other Palestinian prisoners followed his example and in April 2012, 2,500 Palestinian prisoners engaged in a mass, collective hunger strike. On its own, it threatened to severely disrupt and (if strikers had died) sever the state of normalcy prevailing in the Occupied Palestinian Territory. Only months later, and days before the purported resumption of the UN statehood bid, the Palestinian Authority is faced with its own hunger striker.

Restoring Agency

By initiating the statehood bid, the Palestinian leadership was able to extend its shelf life by another year. It does not have another life preserve available to it today. In light of its adamant pursuit of a self-defeating and harmful "peace process," the Palestinian leadership has proven itself irresponsible and inadequate. If it does not find the means to mitigate the economic brunt of its austerity measures, it will surely lose all remaining favor among even a majority-patron West Bank population. In which case, it will assert its control by authoritarian rule and continue to vie for swaths of land that it can dutifully govern.

Moving beyond this impasse is the responsibility first and foremost of the Palestinians themselves, who have the agency both to deny the Palestinian leadership's legitimacy as well as to insist upon alternative paths forward. The most promising of these are rights-based approaches aimed at achieving the human and national rights enshrined by norms and law, and which cannot be truncated by the imbalance of power, dutifully preserved by unconditional US support for Israeli colonialism. Beyond the shade of US-afforded impunity, and under the scrutinizing eye of a universalist discourse, Israel cannot withstand the demand for equality of its non-Jewish citizens, of civilians under military occupation, and of an exiled indigenous population. Even if it could maintain its institutionalized discriminatory practices, it will be forced to do so without legitimacy of being the "only democracy in the Middle East," and with the stigma of an apartheid regime instead. Admittedly, this is not a plan or a liberation strategy. It is, however, a vision, which is much more than the current Palestinian leadership has to offer.

21 September 2012

Quick Thoughts on the Significance of the November 2012 Palestine UN Bid

Noura Erakat

The Palestinian UN bid for non-member observer status will certainly pass today as the majority of UN member states have expressed their support for the initiative. The positive vote will do little to alter the course of Israel's ongoing settler-colonial expansion in the West Bank, or its racially motivated policies aimed at the forced population transfer of non-Jewish Palestinians throughout Israel and the Occupied Palestinian Territory. Still, the significance of Palestine's bolstered status is three-fold.

First, it diplomatically affirms the Palestinian cause for self-determination as a just one among the community of nations, thereby rebuffing Israel's insistence that the conflict is a national security issue. Unfortunately, those states will not place the necessary pressure upon Israel to thwart its structurally violent practices.

Second, it saves the Fateh-dominated Palestinian Authority from the specter of complete irrelevance at a moment when Hamas has emerged as a viable political player in the region together with the admission that the peace process has failed. This will not only benefit the PA, but also Israel, whose occupation costs have been significantly reduced thanks to the PA's security apparatus as well as the United States, which has been its primary financier.

Finally, the new status will allow Palestine to appeal for International Criminal Court jurisdiction, thereby enabling it to hold Israel to account for its alleged war crimes committed in, now two, Gaza operations, as well as its settlement colonial project in the West Bank.

The bid will not, however, work to salvage the two-state solution, which has long been declared dead. Israel has civilian and military control over sixty-two percent of the West Bank; the apartheid wall has further confiscated another thirteen percent of the West Bank; and the Jewish-Israeli settler population now numbers six hundred thousand. East Jerusalem, which is part of the West Bank, has been the site of rapid ethnic cleansing where Israel is explicitly pursuing a Judaization campaign. Meanwhile, Gaza is territorially separated, isolated, and besieged. The World Health Organization says it will be unlivable by 2020.

The next steps forward include dealing with the one-state reality. There exists one political entity between the Jordan River and the Mediterranean sea. This area is home to an inextricably linked population made up of Jewish Israelis as well as Muslim and Christian Palestinians, which the Israeli state distinguishes between based on religion, irrespective of their specific territorial location within Israel or the Occupied Palestinian Territories.

29 November 2012

More Quick Thoughts on Palestine at the United Nations

Mouin Rabbani

The outcome of a United Nations General Assembly vote on enhanced membership status for Palestine has never been in question. The Palestinians will win, probably handily, because the international community overwhelmingly supports the Palestinian right to self-determination and opposes Israel's occupation of Palestinian territory. Those openly opposing this vote can easily be counted on the fingers of an amputated hand: Israel; the United States, which is more pro-Israel than Israel itself; Canada, which is more pro-Israel than even the United States; and perhaps one or two Pacific islands casting one of their final UN votes since they will be rewarded for their obeisance by further North American carbon emissions and an attendant rise in the sea level.

Rather, this event should be considered on the basis of a number of related issues:

1. *Will Abbas do it?* For much of the past year there has been justified skepticism about Abbas's intentions. He repeatedly delayed. First, Abbas parked the application at the UN Security Council, where it was guaranteed to languish under US custodianship. Then, he postponed it until after the US presidential elections. Finally, he appeared to want to procrastinate further until after the January 2013 Israeli elections. Since Abbas remains confident Obama will commence the liberation of Palestine in 2013 or 2014, he most likely would have continued delaying matters.

What then happened was that events (and Abbas's own conduct) essentially forced his hand. First, he informed Israeli television of his personal disinterest in the right of return in order to assuage Israeli fears about Palestinian rights. This created an instantaneous firestorm among Palestinian public opinion, and put Abbas in the position of needing a quick fix to arrest the rapidly accelerating collapse of his remaining legitimacy. Then came the recent Israeli assault on the Gaza Strip, and the resulting perception that Hamas is successfully confronting

207

Israel while Abbas is hapless, helpless, and (more dangerous yet) irrelevant in equal measure. This left him no choice but to go to New York. Presumably, he came under significant pressure from what is left of Fateh to act and act speedily as well.

2. *This is about quality not quantity.* With the outcome of the UN vote never in doubt, the real question is whether the Palestinian UN bid will gain significantly more support, and garner significantly less opposition, than the 1988 proclamation of independence. There are already very encouraging signs in this respect. France is leading a very respectable group of EU member states to vote in favor. Germany, which is no longer the determined obstructionist within the EU it has been in years past, is abstaining. It seems no more than one or two insignificant EU members, if any, will vote against the status upgrade. Further beyond, even Australia is abstaining.

Within Europe, the British position is of particular interest. London has made its vote conditional on a Palestinian commitment to unconditionally resume participation in a peace process that does not (and that within the framework advocated, simply cannot) exist, as well as a Palestinian pledge to ensure Israeli impunity at the International Criminal Court (ICC) with respect to its war crimes. It appears to have obtained neither condition, but is nevertheless abstaining rather than voting against. For this, Abbas has Ahmad Ja'bari rather than David Cameron to thank.

The above notwithstanding, it has been painful to watch the unbridled glee and haste with which the Harper government is flushing Canada's international reputation for neutrality and support for international law—built up over decades—down the toilet and into the sewer.

More amusing have been US efforts to restrain the Israeli response to the UN vote. Since Palestinian success will trigger automatic US sanctions, the Obama administration wants to prevent the Netanyahu government from doing the same lest the Palestinian Authority collapses. The prospect of Washington pleading with Israel to limit sanctions against the PA to lessen the impact of US sanctions is, to say the least, utterly bizarre. But given the EU's total abandonment of Israel on this specific issue, Israel's freedom of action in the coming weeks will in any case be constrained. To be sure, a formal Israeli annulment of Oslo would have been icing on the cake. However, it is far from clear that Israel's security establishment would have let Netanyahu and Lieberman run amok on election eve.

3. *The real issue is what comes next.* Anyone familiar with the position of Western governments knows that, for them, what this issue is really about is not the United Nations or Palestine's status in the General Assembly but rather the International Criminal Court (ICC). They desperately do not want to have to make a choice between their commitment to Israeli impunity and their support for the ICC. That has worked so long as the ICC only goes after Africans. They are simply mortified that this may now change. Not only should they make that choice, they should be forced to make that choice in full public view. If this means the demise of the ICC and its inability to continue with the exclusive prosecution of Africans, so be it. We need a real court, and a willingness to prosecute Israeli war crimes is for many, and quite rightly, the litmus test of the court's efficacy and utility. Parenthetically, it is interesting that the same governments getting all bent out of shape about a UN vote and particularly the prospect of Israel having to account for its crimes have a policy of total indifference on Israeli settlement expansion and total support for "Israel's right to self-defense" every time it launches a murderous assault on the Palestinians. Indeed, when is the last time Victoria Nuland even alluded to the latest Israeli settlement announcement? Obama's record in this respect has been significantly worse than even that of George W. Bush.

For the Palestinians, the key question is whether Abbas is using this as cover to resume utterly meaningless negotiations with Israel that serve only to consolidate occupation, or whether it is a step towards the internationalization of the question of Palestine and therefore an irrevocable move away from the Oslo framework. There is in this respect an urgent requirement for a Palestinian national strategic consensus, so that this tactical move becomes part of a comprehensive national strategy rather than an initiative that is taken for personal or factional considerations.

The not unrelated point is that to the extent the PA is punished (particularly financially) for this move, it reduces foreign leverage over the Palestinians to undertake absolutely essential maintenance work on the national movement, particularly insofar as ending the schism between Fateh and Hamas is concerned. To the extent it is not punished, it should serve as an object lesson in how to call a bluff and stand up to foreign pressure.

The key issue here is internationalization.

29 November 2012

Citizenship and the New "State of Palestine"

Lauren Banko

In his second attempt to obtain United Nations recognition of Palestine as a state, on 29 November 2012 Palestinian Authority (PA) president Mahmoud Abbas requested the General Assembly to accept the bid for non-member observer state status. An overwhelming majority of countries—138 of them—voted yes. The vote's implications are largely symbolic for the time being, but it does mean that "Palestine" signifies the Palestinian territories occupied by Israel in 1967.

Now, rather than "Palestine" signifying a nation, it can be considered an official state within the parameters of international law. The aftermath of the vote will demonstrate that even decades after most states attained independence and recognition, the differences and tensions between *nation* and *state* remain crucial.

Symbolic Implications of the UN Vote

The symbolism of the UN vote is clear. The status of the PA was upgraded to that of a non-member state. However, in as far as the Palestinians' ultimate goal is independence and sovereignty, the new status means very little. The State of Palestine is nothing close to historic Palestine, which Abbas tossed aside recently when he disavowed the Palestinians' right of return. Statehood in this case may just be little more than a slight change in wording to the non-member observer status that the Palestinian Liberation Organization (PLO) held since November 1975. A majority of UN members previously recognized Palestine as a state, and many did so after Yasser Arafat's unilateral declaration of Palestinian statehood in 1988.

The symbolism is also embedded in the status of President Abbas and the PA itself: PA authority is only accepted in the West Bank since the split between Fateh and Hamas in 2007. Moreover, Abbas's term of office expired in 2009, but because of the split (among other factors), there have been no Palestinian elections since 2006. The PA's provisional mandate as the "self-governing authority" in the territories expired in 2000. In fact, Abbas had no popular mandate even to ask the UN to recognize a state.

Another symbolic implication of the vote is that it precludes the PA from considering a one-state solution. Even further, since Israel does not have internationally-recognized borders, it is hard to envision how to draw the borders of a Palestinian state.

Practical Implications of Statehood

A major implication of statehood is that the Palestinian Arabs themselves must be transformed from members of a non-sovereign nation into the actual citizenry of a state. While an implication such as this is indeed real, historic, and practical, it needs to be fleshed out in the coming months and years. A good place to start on this transformation, along with other practical implications of statehood, can be found within a number of discussions that have taken place since the prior UN bid in September 2011 before the Security Council— promptly vetoed by the United States—for full membership. For instance, in April, a conference took place at Hebron University in the West Bank that brought together a number of academics and policy-makers from the West Bank, Gaza (via video link), Jerusalem and Israel, the United States, and Europe to discuss the political and legal implications of Palestinian statehood.

Several recent discussions make clear the need to understand Palestinian citizenship now that a state has been recognized. Citizenship deserves analysis in terms of its legal and internationally-recognized status as well as the relation of citizenship to nationality and documentary identity. The issue at hand, then, is the meaning of the Palestinian *national* vis-à-vis the Palestinian *citizen* and how each fits into the state of Palestine.

Demands and proposals for an independent Palestinian state that incorporated the Arab nationality of the majority of its inhabitants have been presented by Palestinian Arab leaders to various governments and international organizations since 1918, the year Great Britain started to administer the territory it defined as Palestine. Not since the end of the British Palestine Mandate in 1948 has "Palestine" had a status close to that of a state with recognized borders and citizenship legislation, and thus not since the mandate have the inhabitants themselves been Palestinian citizens (albeit colonial citizens).

The Semantics of Palestinian Nationality and Citizenship, Post-1948

After 1948, the Palestinian citizen ceased to exist and the Palestinian national, both in the diaspora and within the occupied territories, took its place as the internationally-recognized identity status of all Palestinians. The existence of only Palestinian nationality, and not citizenship, has implications for the creation of Palestinian citizenship for a second time in history, after the UN recognition of the Palestinian Authority as a state. Indeed, recognition of the PA as a state is not the same as recognition of the nation of Palestine as a state. The state, not simply the PA's reach within the West Bank, must become the sole grantor of rights and duties to all citizens. It remains the responsibility of the state to enact legislation of citizenship and to regulate nationality through *jus sanguinis* (by descent), *jus soli* (by birth in a territory), or naturalization provisions. Currently of course, Israel regulates the documentary identity of Palestinians in the occupied territories.

In 1947, UN Resolution 181 proposed that Palestinian Arabs and Jews would become citizens of the state of their residence upon a future partition of Palestine. Obviously, the events of 1948 did not happen in accordance with the UN partition resolution. From 1948 until the promulgation of the 1952 Nationality Law of Israel, Palestinian Arabs in Israeli territory were deprived of nationality and citizenship in contravention of the international laws of state succession.

Following Israel's occupation of the remainder of historic Palestine, in 1968, Article 4 of the Palestinian National Charter affirmed that Palestinian identity passed by blood, *jus sanguinis*, and refugee status did not negate this. Article 5 defined the Palestinians as "those Arab nationals who, until 1947, normally resided in Palestine regardless of whether they were evicted from it or have stayed there. Anyone born after that date, of a Palestinian father—whether inside Palestine or outside it—is also a Palestinian."[1]

Currently, Israel issues identity cards to Palestinians living under occupation —in the territory meant to be under administration of the State of Palestine. The PA issues passports after Israeli approval, but passports are not equated with citizenship status. Neither documents identify their holders as citizens or nationals; rather they are identified as residents of a certain territory.

Practical Questions of Citizenship in the State of Palestine

Fast-forwarding to 1995, the PA drafted a citizenship law but had no authority to regulate citizenship since it operated under Israeli occupation. Following that, the third Draft Palestine Constitution gave citizenship to any Palestinian resident of Palestine before 1948, by both paternal and maternal descent. The most recent official mention of Palestinian citizenship and nationality is in the PA's 2003 Basic Law: Article 7 states that "Palestinian citizenship shall be regulated by law" and nationals who are not citizens will be given representation within "Palestine."[2]

Statehood, however, presents problems. Guy Goodwin-Gill's legal opinion on Palestinian statehood highlights questions of citizenship for Palestinian nationals in the diaspora. He notes that refugees and emigrants will lose representation with the coming of statehood as the Palestinian National Council, their official representative, could be dissolved. This means Palestinian nationals will not have the right to participate in matters of government as citizens.

The UN vote brings to light elementary issues such as whether statehood for Palestine can bring a Palestinian citizen into being. In the case of an independent Palestinian state, the criteria for citizenship must be delineated in order to give Palestinian nationals clear terms of membership. But what of the territorial fragmentation of Palestine and the fragmentation and dispersal of those who are nationals? Victor Kattan has argued that all Palestinians were denationalized following the end of 1948, and remain without nationality due to the need for a Palestinian state to provide such nationality.

If nationality is the criteria for Palestinian citizenship, it is essential to also recognize that the Palestinian national and the Palestinian citizen are two different statuses. The right of return is the means for extending citizenship to nationals living abroad; under international law, all Palestinian nationals have the right to return, and those who return to the State of Palestine would be deemed citizens.

Finally, the question remains whether citizenship and the electorate in the Palestinian state must be officially and internationally made clear first, or whether prospective citizens (i.e., nationals abroad) would be provided a means of participating in the formulation of a new basic law. The more likely alternative, given Abbas's abandonment of the right of return, is that citizenship qualifications will be imposed by the executive or determined by the PA electorate.

The expiration of the PA's mandate will play a significant role in decisions on citizenship if the symbolically-recognized State of Palestine is to be transformed into a practical, meaningful state.

2 December 2012

---

1 "The Palestinian Charter," *Palestine Ministry of Information*, June 1999, http://www.pac-usa.org/the_palestinian_charter.htm.

2 "2003 Amended Basic Law," *Palestinian Basic Law*, 18 March 2003, http://www.palestinianbasiclaw.org/basic-law/2003-amended-basic-law.

The Palestinian Authority, UNESCO, and the Illusion of Triumph

Ryvka Barnard

Over one weekend, two seemingly incongruous sets of images dominated the news from Palestine: one set displayed local tourism operators and Palestinian Authority (PA) officials in Bethlehem celebrating the designation of the Nativity Church as a UNESCO World Heritage site. The other set of images, coming from Ramallah, showed PA police and thugs beating protestors, who had taken to the streets in anger over a scheduled (but later cancelled) Ramallah meeting between Israel's vice premier Shaul Mofaz and PA president Mahmoud Abbas. The two sets of images together depict the sad and poignant reality of the occupation and the PA statehood bid. That reality is of an unelected and unrepresentative leadership, which is more committed to staging spectacles for the Israelis and Americans than resisting the occupation.

A few weeks ago, the Palestinian representative to United Nations Educational, Scientific, and Cultural Organization (UNESCO) submitted a file for the Church of the Nativity in Bethlehem to be added to the list of "World Heritage Sites in Danger," and to the consternation of Israel and the United States, it was accepted. In October 2011, Palestine's admission to UNESCO as a full member took place in the context of the controversial statehood bid, prompting the United States to withdraw funding from the organization. The Church of the Nativity's addition to the list is the first result of the Palestinian admission to UNESCO. It was hailed by the PA and many supporters of Palestinian rights as a great victory, and even, according to Prime Minister Salam Fayyad, "a triumph of justice." Israeli and American officials frowned and expressed disapproval, adding fuel to the notion that this move was somehow deeply controversial and even an act of resistance. If only that had been the case.

Last Fall, critics of the statehood bid warned that it was a PA move to retain power, to further disenfranchise Palestinians not under PA jurisdiction, and to create an international spectacle of the PA as a resistance force. Some astutely observed that the statehood bid could be redeemable if it resulted in using increased status in international forums to challenge Israel's violations of international law. Unfortunately, the choice of the Church of the Nativity as the first site to recognize is nothing but a restatement of the status quo of occupation, and will likely be meaningless, if not destructive, to Palestinian communities in the West Bank.

The Church of the Nativity sits squarely in Area A, one of the small parts of the West Bank that is under full PA control (that is, control under occupation). It is visited by millions of foreign tourists every year, the great majority of whom are bussed in from their hotels in Jerusalem, past the apartheid wall, past the refugee camps, past the recently destroyed homes and businesses. The tourists are shuttled to an alternate reality in Manger Square, where they can see the ancient birthplace of Jesus without having to acknowledge that it is situated in a city, a city with people in it, people who are struggling under an ever-tightening occupation. Most tour operators carefully avoid any talk of politics or anything contemporary, not wanting to scare away these apparently delicate tourists.

Palestinian tourism operators all agree that at the end of the day, under the current conditions, the Church of the Nativity is a loss for Palestinian tourism. The tourism industry has a major leakage problem. This is not in reference to the leaky roof of the church (a problem UNESCO will perhaps solve), but rather the fact that the tourism industry does not generate real income, and certainly not from visitors to the church. The money lost is money gained by the Israeli tourism industry. It is Israeli tour operators that meet groups in the airport while Palestinian tour operators wait for them behind the apartheid wall, hoping, usually to no avail, that they might spend more than an hour in the West Bank, and at least a few shekels, before leaving Bethlehem in a cloud of dust from their charter buses.

Of course, Palestinian tour operators that get any business related to the Church of the Nativity are the luckiest of the lot, particularly in comparison with tourism operations in the more rural parts of the West Bank, outside of the PA controlled enclaves. Area C, which is more than sixty percent of the West Bank, is under full Israeli control, meaning that Palestinians have extremely limited access and no decision making over zoning in those areas. They cannot build or even renovate without an almost impossible to obtain permit from the Israelis, whether it is for a person to dig a well on her own personal property, or to renovate a historic site which could be used for tourism development. Because of the PA's limited control in Area C, some sites, such as the historic ruins in

Sebastiya, have sought international sponsorship in renovations, to at least make their projects a bit more visible lest they be quietly swallowed by Israeli expansion.

One fantastic tourism venture underway in the Bethlehem municipal area is in the village of Battir, which straddles the Green Line in the Jerusalem hills. Battir and its neighboring village of al-Walaja are home to a vast spread of two-thousand-year-old Roman agricultural terraces, which include an intricate system of stone-lined channels that bring water from the village springs to cultivated plateaus. The beautiful landscape, which is not only the heritage but also the livelihood of these villages, is scheduled to be cut off from the villagers by the impending construction of the apartheid wall. The landscape would then be included into a "Green Park" fashioned by the Jewish National Fund, which has already begun to boast of how the landscape tells the story of agriculture and settlement in "the Land of Israel." Both villages have been mobilizing tirelessly to halt the construction of the wall. In fact, Battir has already prepared a file on these landscapes in accordance with UNESCO standards, and won a UNESCO award for their conservation activities and promotion of preserving the ancient agricultural practices.

Battir, most of which is Area C, would have been an obvious choice for a site in imminent danger, and had the PA chosen to submit its file, as many believed that they would, it would have presented a case much more compelling. The imminent danger in Battir, and in other Area C projects which could have been prioritized, stems from the direct threat of the wall's construction and its annexation of land. Prioritizing such sites would be a direct challenge to Israel's expansionist policies. Such a move would have forced attention to the occupation's ongoing destruction and its appropriation of Palestinian heritage and livelihood into Israel's "green" spaces and municipal boundaries. It would have challenged Israel's redrawing of borders, a process that attenuates Palestinian land on a minute-by-minute basis in Area C.

Under these conditions, one would have hoped and expected that sites in Area C would garner priority in the UNESCO recognition process. But predictably the PA chose the uncontroversial Church of the Nativity; predictably, Israel and the United States expressed disapproval; predictably, the PA scripted its deeply uncourageous choice as some sort of bold and defiant move.

I am not suggesting that the occupation could be ended with a simple formula of choosing one site over another for the top of a UNESCO list of heritage sites in danger. Nobody has any illusions about the limited role of the

UNESCO membership in the broader scope of Palestinian politics. But this is precisely the point: that PA decisions and statements about culture and heritage cannot be understood without the political context in which they are made. This political context is a regime that will not directly challenge Israel, and believes that it should keep law, order, and security to continuously indicate that it is ready and capable for statehood. But "security" under occupation is in reality maintaining Israel's security by force and eliminating any threat to the status quo through political repression. PA repression is not an occasional occurrence; it is a regular feature of the current regime's efforts to maintain and build power in the small enclaves of the West Bank that Israel and the United States have designated as expendable to Israel's expansion. It can be seen through the control of the population using the US-trained PA security forces (Dayton's men); through the neo-liberal policies of Salam Fayyad, which attempt to disable collective resistance by drowning West Bank Palestinians with individualized debt. And it can be seen in every aspect of state planning and development: tourism and the heritage industry is no exception.

In the following days, while celebrations took place in the Manger Square bubble, PA thugs beat and arrested Palestinians in a show of force that demonstrated to Israel their willingness to act as bodyguards for the apartheid minister Mofaz. These scenes are tied together by the PA's statehood bid. It is unclear what will be more deafening: the noise of the wall's construction as it seals in al-Walaja and Battir, or the racket of Abbas, Fayyad, and their cronies as they celebrate their triumph of justice at the UNESCO restored church. Maybe they will invite Mofaz as a guest of honor.

6 July 2012

Palestine at the United Nations?

Mouin Rabbani

The significance of the United Nations General Assembly vote to recognize Palestine as a non-member observer state has been exaggerated by opponents and proponents alike. It has no consequences for the status of the Palestine Liberation Organization (PLO) as the sole legitimate representative of the Palestinian people, nor does it undermine the rights of Palestinian refugees living in exile, the occupied territories, or indeed Israel as codified in international law and particularly UNGA Resolution 194 of 1948. By the same token, and as demonstrated by Israel's subsequent decision to build several thousand new settlement units, it does not make the West Bank (including East Jerusalem) and the Gaza Strip any less occupied or colonized, nor does it confer any additional powers upon either the PLO or Palestinian Authority (PA) that can be exercised within Palestinian territory.

Although it essentially changes nothing, it nevertheless has the capacity to contribute to a strategic transformation in Palestinian fortunes. This will depend primarily on how it is utilized by the Palestinians—all Palestinians—but also the actions of others.

To take the most obvious aspect, the United Nations initiative was strenuously opposed by Israel and the United States. For good reason, because it forms a flagrant violation of the Oslo framework pursuant to which they alone are empowered to answer the question of Palestine, without heed to either the international community or the corpus of resolutions and laws that collectively represent the will of that community with respect to a resolution of the Israeli-Palestinian conflict. The question for Palestinians is therefore whether the initiative is a first step towards referring the question of Palestine back to the United Nations—which after all created it and remains responsible for its resolution—or merely a tactical maneuver to resume bilateral negotiations with Israel under American supervision.

To point out that Mahmoud Abbas went to New York in an attempt to shore up his domestic standing and that he has every intention of rushing back to the negotiating table is in this context almost irrelevant. Abbas similarly wanted to host Shaul Mofaz in the center of Ramallah several months ago. Yet, popular revulsion at the prospect of a war criminal being feted at the scene of his crime put an end to the planned rendezvous. Similarly, in the wake of Israel's latest assault on the Gaza Strip, Palestinians across the political and geographic spectrum are with renewed vigor demanding the formulation of a meaningful national strategy and its implementation by a genuinely representative national movement. Ensuring that the UN initiative serves the internationalization of the struggle for Palestinian self-determination, rather than being a prelude to more negotiations that are but a fig leaf for deepening colonization, can hardly be considered an impossible task. It will require serious effort, and will not succeed overnight, but it can, and therefore should, be done. To dismiss and miss this opportunity strikes me as a dereliction of duty.

The first step in this direction must be to end the Palestinian schism on the basis of a rejuvenated PLO, particularly since the political programs of Fateh and Hamas are today all but indistinguishable and they are primarily engaged in a power struggle more about factional interest than ideology. Accusing either or both of these parties of having sold out their people is all well and good, but detractors need to get used to the fact that there can be no national movement without both of them, and that the most effective restraint on the excesses of either leadership is not Hamas but rather a rejuvenated Fateh. It may be too late for the latter, but the left and Islamic Jihad presently lack the capacity to play this role, and it will be years before a credible and sufficiently powerful alternative emerges from today's otherwise inspirational youth movements. Civil society, particularly that large swathe of it dependent on foreign funding, cannot substitute for a national liberation movement.

The UN vote taught us not only that Canada and the Czech Republic today have the most fanatically pro-Israel governments on the planet, and that there are a few more rocks in the Pacific than we thought, but also that Israel's position in Europe—and Europe's subservience to Washington on matters Palestinian—are in a state of flux. Here again, things are not going to develop of their own accord, and will be reversed if they are not actively promoted to their logical conclusion. For Palestinians not to capitalize on these opportunities—for at present they are only opportunities—and work to ensure that the EU policies and those of its member governments begin to more faithfully reflect Palestinian rights and European public opinion would be tantamount to criminal negligence.

The time is ripe, for example, to put an end to decades of efforts to ensure that settlement products are properly labeled and taxed, and seek to have them defined as contraband and prohibited from the European market altogether. Similarly, there is no reason why European arms sales to Israel are not now prominently on the agenda of every European parliament. In the context of decades of growing Arab disengagement from the conflict with Israel, the regional upheaval that commenced in late 2010 presents an almost unique opportunity to re-mobilize official Arab influence in support of the Palestinian struggle for self-determination, particularly in Europe.

The one concrete achievement resulting from Palestine's elevated status at the United Nations is the ability to join subsidiary organizations. Given credible US threats of sanctions against such institutions, Palestinians would do well to first join those, such as the World Intellectual Property Organization, that mean most to Washington and least to the Palestinians. Make those knaves on Capitol Hill publicly proclaim that their loyalty to Avigdor Lieberman precedes the interests of their constituents and corporate sponsors. The same principle applies to the International Criminal Court (ICC). But joining the latter and ending the African monopoly on its interests make little sense if existing legal instruments, such as the 2004 International Court of Justice (ICJ) Advisory Opinion on the West Bank wall, are not activated without further delay.

Indeed, using existing mechanisms to confront the massive settlement scheme Israel proclaimed the day after the UN vote, and which once implemented completes the encirclement of East Jerusalem through its isolation from the rest of the West Bank and effectively bisects the latter, should be considered an urgent priority. Sufficiently urgent to override and invalidate initial Palestinian statements that further recourse to international law is not imminent, and would be assessed in light of Israeli and US conduct in the coming weeks and months. With the Obama administration today enabling an Israeli plan that George W. Bush consistently opposed for eight years, the immediate priority for Palestinians is to compel their leaders to show no consideration toward American sensitivities—or threats—when it comes to defending and promoting Palestinian rights.

3 December 2012

[A shorter version of this article initially appeared as "UN Vote is Symbolic - Unless Palestinians Take Advantage" in The National (UAE)*]*

Colonial Planning of My Grandfather's Hilltop

Dana Erekat

Today, I walked onto an Israeli settlement for the first time in my life, one where most of the land it stands on once belonged to my grandfather. I needed the settlers' permission to walk onto this soil. As I walked down the sidewalk, I felt alienation and contentment all at once. The first for the utter disconnect between this land and me. The second for finally being able to set foot in a place that is rightfully mine.

"You see this hilltop? It all belongs to your grandfather." This phrase was a recurring one during our family drives from Abu Dis to Jericho. I heard it from the first moment that I could comprehend words. I cannot even remember who said it first. But it has been a constant refrain since childhood. Even today, at thirty-four years old, my mother, father, aunt, and grandmother repeat the statement as if they are saying it to me for the first time. The repetition is an assurance, a call, to never forget. They refuse to forget. And even after so many years, I still respond with a perplexed "all of it?" as if hearing the news for the first time. I refuse to forget. "All of it." Today, when I travel alone with no one to remind me, I repeat: "This land belonged to my grandfather."

Still, despite this historical bond with the land, despite the assurance of that history, despite the will to never forget, all that lies on that hilltop is as foreign to me as is the north pole. Today the settler at the gate only allowed me to enter a mere two hundred yards to the police station, which sits on the settlement's periphery, and back. He made it clear I could only spend the time necessary to finish my paperwork. I could not explore. I could not become familiar with my land. And, therefore, I continue to construct my familiarity with my ancestral heritage from a distance.

As I drive by, the settlement resembles the gorgeous green fields of the luxurious Napa Valley in California. Those fields, too, are compelling, and those fields, too, are often off limits, fenced off with a sign: "Beware. Electrical Fence." In my daydreams, I run up the hilltop of Ma'ale Adumim just as I imagined transgressing the Napa Valley fences and reveling in the green fields. In my

California daydreams, I may get a citation for trespassing. In my Palestine daydreams, I may be killed or at the very least detained. There are no signs that tell me so. It is knowledge that I, like so many Palestinians, understand viscerally.

There are other reminders of California here on my grandfather's land. Those red-tiled pitched roofs mimic the houses in suburban Fremont, where I lived for part of my adolescence. I used to sneak out the window with my cousins onto the steep roof; we gazed up at the stars and giggled about our latest crush. The possibility of being caught or sliding down and falling made it all the more thrilling. Glimpsing those same roofs lining Ma'ale Adumim, I have the urge to dismember the red tiles, one at a time, and toss them into the valley. This is not Fremont. It is my grandfather's land.

From a distance, Ma'ale Adumim appears perfectly planned, each house a replica of the next. The homogeneity is in direct contrast to Palestinian towns, where homeowners, unbridled by urban plans, each add a bit of inconsistency to create the irrational landscape. Perhaps this homogeneity is only true for the part I can see from the road, the settlement's oldest quarter dating all the way back to the late 1970s. Regardless of its prevalence, the pre-planned homogeneity, meant to give the sense of communal coherence, is the epitome of settler colonialism. It is colonial hegemony.

"Everything must be systematically settled beforehand," wrote Theodor Herzl in "The Occupation of the Land" section of his 1896 treatise, *The Jewish State*. The implications of Herzl's earnest are at the root of Israel's planning strategy. In 1948, only a few weeks following the Nakba, Arieh Sharon (not to be confused with Ariel Sharon), a Bauhaus graduate and architect, began working on a comprehensive master plan for Israel. Sharon, who was the head of the Government Planning Department at the time, worked with David Ben-Gurion and a team of European and Jewish planners, architects, and mapping experts to produce a single plan (scale: 1:20,000) for the entire state of Israel. Within a single year, Sharon and his team produced a master plan that became known as The Sharon Plan. Such scale and scope were unprecedented, as countries tend to grow over a longer period of time as opposed to cities, which are planned with such rapidness. However, Israeli leadership needed the plan quickly in order to forge the physical and developmental vision for Israel, and to ensure its control over Palestine.

The political agenda, including its time constraint, drove the development of the master plan. Thus, the outcomes of the Sharon Plan can be summarized as three-fold. First, it is an agglomeration of borrowed ideas and models, some of which were developed during the British Mandate and others taken from Europe "as ready made and abruptly naturalized."[1] Second, the plan answered the urgent need of providing fast housing for new Jewish immigrants, especially on the borderlands in order to prevent the return of Palestinian refugees. Third, the plan divided Israel into a number of districts that were planned mathematically, with modular neighborhoods, to house an equal number of residents. Thus, the Sharon Plan laid the foundation for the Israeli apartheid state today: architecture that echoes European designs; peripheral settlements that enclose Palestinian towns; and "New Towns," which are pre-planned and built in modules to facilitate rapid construction.

Less than twenty years after the Sharon Plan laid the foundation for Israel's design, the Israeli government augmented its vision for territorial expansion. Following Israel's victory of the 1967 War in June 1967, the Israeli government passed legislation incorporating East Jerusalem and adjacent parts of the West Bank into Israel, thus expanding its land expropriation project and settlement expansion. In order to meet this goal, Israel pursued a number of systematic policies that would help expand Jerusalem and secure Israel's hegemony over the city through demographic and physical control.

While Israel enacted the Land Acquisition for Public Purpose Ordinance and the Absentee Property Law in 1967 in order to legalize the confiscation of Palestinian land and limit Palestinians spatially, Israel also put into effect a set of urban and design guidelines aimed at attracting European Jewish settlers and further displacing Palestinians. To meet these goals, Israel placed much of the land annexed in 1967 under the jurisdiction of the Israel-Lands Administration (ILA) whose management had been merged with the Jewish National Fund. The charter of the Jewish National Fund restricted the developments and use of the land to the exclusive benefits of Jews: the ILA land, constitutionally, could not be "sold or leased or used" by or for Palestinian Arabs.

Second, following the vision of the Sharon Plan for Jerusalem, the Israeli municipality began a project of "evacuation and building," under the pretext of "modernization," which constituted the demolition of old Palestinian buildings, the construction of new streets, and the widening of Jaffa Street in the heart of Jerusalem. The widening of the street meant more demolitions of old Palestinian buildings. Thus, in its claim to "renew" the city, Israel erased the narrative of its Arab inhabitants.

Third, the municipality produced design guidelines that catered to the immigrating Jewish population. For the development of many of the neighborhoods in Jerusalem, the Israeli municipality set the height limit of buildings at six to eight stories, and required the buildings to be multi-units and "modern" looking. By modern here, I solely refer to the architectural era marked by the simplification of buildings. In other neighborhoods, Garden City patterns, borrowed from European designs of the Sharon Plan, were implemented. These designs consisted of red tiles, pitched roofs, and green spaces, and were intended to give the sense of a "planned community."

Based upon these design guidelines intended for Jewish colonial settlement of the West Bank, the Israeli municipality rejected most plans submitted by Palestinian residents. The Israeli municipality, considered the latter plans, usually characterized of stone-built one to two story single-family homes, as unacceptable for being "Arabic style." Furthermore, even when the Israeli municipality approved design plans for Palestinians, a permit could take up to four years to be issued. The Israeli authorities used this prolonged waiting period to determine if the land proposed for development could be useful for future Israeli projects. If they saw it as useful, they would apply the Public Ordinance Law, and confiscate the land for state use.[2]

I doubt my grandfather ever applied for a permit. He never had the chance.

In addition to the territorial expansion in 1967, Yigal Allon, the minister of labor at the time, drafted the Allon Plan to "secure" Israel's borders. The Allon Plan proposed that Israel would hand over the Arab populated areas of Palestine to Jordan, while no Jordanian troops would be allowed to cross the Jordan River westward. In addition, the plan proposed the creation of a "security belt"[3] of Israeli settlements along the Jordan Valley as well as a road connecting Jerusalem to the Dead Sea. In 1975, during Allon's tenure as foreign minister under the first Rabin government, Israel moved to a new stage of planning and began designing the "security belt."

Israel carried out the "security belt" urban planning strategy to preclude the expansion of any Palestinian housing construction, to implant a Jewish-Israeli population into the predominantly Palestinian population, and to further separate and segregate the Arab towns from one another. The former director of Jerusalem District of the Ministry of Housing, Shmaryahu Cohen, summarizes the process:

> We have made enormous efforts to locate state lands
> near Jerusalem and we decided to seize them before...
> the Arabs have a hold there. We all know that they

> remove rocks and plant olive trees instead in order to
> create facts in the fields. What is wrong with trying to
> get there before them? I know this policy is harmful
> to Jerusalem in the short run, but it guarantees living
> spaces for future generations. If we don't do it today,
> our children and grandchildren will travel to
> Jerusalem through a hostile Arab environment.[4]

My grandfather's olive trees, on the hilltop, were creating facts in the fields.

The process of creating the security belt included building settlements on hillsides, peaks, and near important roads in the municipal areas surrounding Jerusalem. The Israeli government planned to build three settlements within this belt: Ma'ale Adumim in the east, Givon in the north, and Efrat in the south.[5] With the help of the Israeli government, twenty-three Israeli families took over my grandfather's hilltop, marking it an Israeli settlement. Michael Dumper, a professor in Middle East politics at the University of Exeter, eloquently explains the location of Ma'ale Adumim in his book *The Politics of Jerusalem Since 1967*:

> Adumim was purposely situated on an exposed
> hilltop overlooking the Jericho road for both security
> reasons and to prevent the creation of a land corridor
> for Jordanian access to East Jerusalem in the event of
> a peace agreement.[6]

The decision to build Ma'ale Adumim on the hilltop was purely political. The land of Ma'ale Adumim did not lend itself to building a town settlement, as the morphology was uneven, and a great deal of excavation and flattening would need to take place. It was, on the other hand, ideal for the building of small villages.[7]

When Thomas Leitersdorf, the lead architect and planner of Ma'ale Adumim, expressed these concerns regarding the site to Gideon Patt, the minister of tourism at the time, he was told that "with all due respect, this was a government decision and that in 120 days the bulldozers had to begin work on the site."[8] Furthermore, when Leitersdorf presented location alternatives to the Ministerial Committee of Settlements, the only questions his government audience posed were: "Which of the alternative locations has better control over the main routes?" and "Which town has a better chance to grow quickly and offer qualities that would make it competitive with Jerusalem?"[9] Thus, Israel's political decision to "grab the hilltops" overrode any site, architectural, or planning considerations.

In 1979, Israel began the construction of Ma'ale Adumim. In following with Israel's planning strategy of producing "instant cities," Leitersdorf and his team designed and developed the first phase of Ma'ale Adumim within three years, which included 2,000 apartments, all built on "one system of construction and infrastructure."[10] In October of 1991, the Israeli government declared Ma'ale Adumim, with 15,500 inhabitants, "the first and largest Hebraic city in Judea and Samaria,"[11] despite the fact that it falls within the 1967 Green Line. Despite the fact that it cuts across, and onto, my grandfather's land. The population of Ma'ale Adumim has grown from twenty-three families in 1975 to around 40,000 people today. And it is growing.

On 30 November 2012, less than twenty-four hours after Palestine gained non-member status at the United Nations, and five days after I set foot on my grandfather's land for the first time, Israel announced its plan to build an additional three-thousand settler units. The E-1 Plan, as it is known, intends to expand Ma'ale Adumim from the west and connect it to Jerusalem, thereby accomplishing Israel's long-term vision. It must be noted here that the expansion of Ma'ale Adumim on the east to the Jordan Valley is an ongoing process. While Israel only made the E-1 plans announcement following the UN bid, it would be naive to believe that Israel came to this decision within twenty-four hours and only as retaliation to Palestinian "unilateralism." Israel approved the E-1 plan in 1999, but shelved it due to US and international pressure. Israel seized the moment of the UN bid to implement a plan that dates back much further than 1999.

Through examining the plans and maps that Israeli leaders had drafted over the last sixty-four years, it becomes evident that the historical processes of settlement and road construction led to the deliberate creation of Greater *Israeli* Jerusalem. The boundaries of the Greater Jerusalem that Israel is currently implementing are larger than those of the Greater Jerusalem under the 1948 UN Partition Plan, which declared Greater Jerusalem a *corpus separatum*. The expansion of settlements both eastward and westward, as well as the creation of bypass roads, all serve to connect Israeli settlements with Jerusalem and the rest of Israel, while further dividing the Palestinian areas into pockets of lands.

Furthermore, by comparing the Palestinian land classified as Area C, and therefore under Israeli control, under the 1993 Oslo Agreement to the Allon Plan, it becomes apparent that Area C fulfills Allon's vision of Israeli territory within the 1967 borders. This further puts into question the viability of the US-brokered "peace process" and Israel's good faith to establish a two-state solution. The building of E-1, which covers around 12,000 dunams, will be another step in fulfilling the Allon Plan, as it would divide the West Bank into two areas, north and south, and seal off East Jerusalem from other Palestinian cities.

Israel refuses to leave Ma'ale Adumim isolated, unconnected, and within the Palestinian territories. Perhaps, the only way for Ma'ale Adumim to be returned to its original owners is through a one-state solution. However, I know that no Israeli leader will voluntarily dismantle Ma'ale Adumim during my lifetime. It is a fortress guarding the occupiers. It is a watchtower overlooking the Jordan Valley. It is a symbol of colonial modernity. It is hegemony.

But I also know that I will never forget that the land on which this settlement stands belongs to my grandfather. A land I could have called my own. A land my children could have called their own. And I look forward to the day that I tell a daughter "You see all this hilltop? This is all your mama's grandfather's."

12 December 2012

---

[1] Zvi Efrat, "The Plan," *A Civilian Occupation: the Politics of Israeli Architecture*, Rafi Segal and Eyal Weizman, ed. (London: Babel, 2003) Chapter 4.

[2] Kate Maguire, "The Israelization of Jerusalem," *Arab Papers*, 7 (July 1981).

[3] Michael Dumper, *The Politics of Jerusalem Since 1967* (New York: Columbia Univ. Press, 1997)

[4] Ibid.

[5] Following the concepts of the Allon Plan, the Israeli governments built 21 settlements along the Jordan Valley and Eastern plains between 1967 to 1977.

[6] Dumper, 1997.

[7] Eran Tamir-Tawil, "To Start a City From Scratch: An Interview with Architect Thomas M. Leitersdorf," *A Civilian Occupation: the Politics of Israeli Architecture*, Rafi Segal and Eyal Weizman, ed. (London: Babel, 2003) Chapter 9.

[8] Ibid.

[9] Ibid.

[10] Ibid.

[11] Ma'ale Adumim Official Website

Conclusion

Nadia Hijab

Achieving Palestinian Rights in a Leadership Vacuum

Several of the essays in this book have discussed strategies for national liberation, with a special focus on representation, international law, and the statehood bid by the Palestine Liberation Organization (PLO) and Palestinian Authority (henceforth referred to as "the PLO/PA" given that the latter has subsumed the former).

Any strategies must be judged by their effectiveness in achieving one's goals. But even such a seemingly self-evident assertion is open to question in the Palestinian context. What are Palestinian goals and who sets them? Who defines the strategies? Who controls the resources to make strategies effective? In other words, goals, strategies, and representation—surely among the key components of a successful national liberation movement—have become a plague of questions for the Palestinian people, with each dependent on the others for answers.

And yet, Palestinians retain their boundless creativity and commitment. They manage to strive for their rights regardless of the decades-long leadership vacuum as well as the dire conditions created by sixty-five years of remorseless Israeli colonization, expulsion, and fragmentation. This concluding chapter reflects on Palestinian efforts to develop goals, strategies, and representation over the years in order to suggest ways forward.

Experiences in Setting Palestinian Goals

As is well-known, Palestinian national political goals shifted from liberating all of Palestine and creating a secular, democratic state in 1968, to establishing a national authority on any part of Palestine in 1974 as a transitional step, to a state in the West Bank and Gaza with East Jerusalem as its capital as adopted by the Palestinian National Council in 1988.

The relatively recent decision by the PLO to seek non-member observer state status at the United Nations is certainly in line with the declared 1998 goal of a

230

two-state solution, which was adopted at a time when a majority of the Palestinian people accepted the PLO as their sole, legitimate representative as did a majority of world nations.

The two-state solution is also still the internationally recognized solution to the problem, and elements of it are enshrined in international law, for example, the "inadmissibility of the acquisition of territory by war," which is the international law foundation for UN Security Council Resolution 242. Of course, had it ever been applied, this principle would have required Israel to withdraw from the territories occupied in 1967 without any "peace process" at all. The fact that this never happened supports the argument of those who say that international law is a weak tool that merely serves the existing powers.

However, the PLO/PA decision to embark on the statehood bid came at a time when Israel's relentless colonization was ever closer to killing off the two-state solution. In other words, as the possibility of achieving a sovereign Palestinian state steadily receded, the PLO/PA's attachment to it steadily grew.

Although the PLO/PA has not formally questioned the two-state goal despite changing circumstances, many Palestinians activists and intellectuals within and outside the land of Palestine have been doing so. There is now a solid literature around the one-state solution, a throwback to the PLO's 1968 political program of a secular democratic state. Still, this has not yet gained enough traction to become the demand of a critical mass of Palestinians.

A significant number of Palestinians, particularly those living under Israeli occupation, remain attached to the two-state solution, because they believe it will guarantee their national rights and enable them to have a place where they can "be" Palestinian. Moreover, a lot of cynicism remains about the one-state solution as a feasible national goal. The question often posed is: If Palestinians have not yet mustered the power to achieve two states how can they hope to achieve one state? Indeed, this is a question I also used to ask, though I have recently begun to question whether the one-state might have become more achievable than the two-state solution.

Put another way, what strategies and sources of power would be needed to achieve either goal, and which are the Palestinians in a better position to muster? This is an important analysis to undertake, and it may result in a strong case in favor of the one-state solution, although such an exposition is not the aim of this essay.

Disagreement about the ultimate political goal need not stand in the way of establishing other goals. For example, by putting the emphasis on a rights-based approach, the Palestinian Civil Society Call of 2005 that established the Boycott, Divestment and Sanctions (BDS) movement cleverly sidestepped the question of an ultimate political goal. The BDS call, backed by over 170 Palestinian associations, unions, and civil society organizations, sets out three rights-based goals that, together with the right of self-determination, cover all segments of the Palestinian people: an end to the occupation of all Arab lands, the right of the Palestinian refugees to return, and equality for the Palestinian citizens of Israel. The call urges that BDS be carried out against Israel until these rights are realized.

And yet, there is no getting away from the fact that the lack of an ultimate political goal behind which all Palestinians can align causes confusion and fragmentation of efforts and resources to advance the Palestinian cause. Rights cannot be achieved in the abstract: There must at some stage be a physical space in which Palestinian rights are realized. The confusion has not stifled Palestinian activism, but it does mean that much of this activism cannot be channeled towards a political end-goal.

Of course the Israelis, and previously the Zionist movement, calibrated their stated goals depending on how much power they had and what they felt they could get away with. They first secured the modest-sounding "national home" in the 1917 Balfour Declaration, then took advantage of the 1947 plan to forcibly acquire seventy-eight percent of historic Palestine, and finally exploited the 1967 conquests to settle the West Bank, including East Jerusalem, and the Gaza Strip, as well as the Golan Heights. When they occupied Palestinian and other Arab territory in 1967, the Israeli leaders may have initially intended to impose a peace on the Arabs on Israel's terms while acquiring some additional land. However, throughout the past century, enough Zionists/Israelis consistently held to the less publicly stated goal of a Jewish state in all of Mandate Palestine. By now, they have acquired enough power to make major strides towards attaining this goal.

Indeed, there is a growing consensus among right-wing Israelis that they can cope with the remaining Palestinian population in their midst, emptying it out a bit at a time. This is being done in the 60% of the West Bank defined as Area C under the Oslo Accords as well as in East Jerusalem. The settlements and outposts ringing Ramallah and Nablus show what will be done to these cities and others in the future if Israel's colonization project is not halted. One could even speculate that, if the Israelis succeed in their project to absorb the West Bank with a minimum number of Palestinians, those seemingly fringe elements who dream of an Israel from the Nile to the Euphrates could become as strong a force in the government as the settlers have become today. What would stop them?

As both the Palestinian and Israeli experiences show, there is nothing intrinsically wrong with changing the ultimate political goal based on a solid analysis of changes in the external environment together with a reassessment of available strategies. However, any revised goal should achieve the minimum of a people's aspirations. The two-state solution, which the PLO proposed, first implicitly in 1974 given its leaders' fear of assassination, and finally explicitly in 1988, promised, on paper, to ensure the rights of the entire Palestinian people despite its truncated geography.

The Palestinian citizens of Israel and the Palestinian refugees and exiles soon understood that this was far from a rock solid guarantee. Their fears were affirmed by the Oslo process begun in 1993 and reaffirmed by the 2002 Arab Peace Initiative, with its reference to an "agreed upon" just solution for the refugees and its silence on the Palestinian citizens of Israel. These two segments of the Palestinian people began organizing to address their respective situations. Exiles and refugees sought to ensure that their rights were not sold out, and the Palestinian citizens of Israel began to work for equality and recognition as a national minority within the State of Israel.

This brief review of the efforts to set a political end goal makes it clear that the Palestinian people are unlikely to be able to unify around a goal for the foreseeable future. Too much has been invested in the two-state solution for it to actually be declared dead, and there is nothing to replace it in the international arena or among the Palestinian leadership. This leadership has been unable to effectively strategize or lead since at least 1988. Moreover, since 2007, it has been split between an old guard in the West Bank and a newer guard in Gaza that has many of the same failings, albeit with more seriousness in strategic thinking, planning, and implementation.

In such a context, the most realistic approach is to focus on the rights that must be achieved whatever the final political outcome, whether one-state or two, as advocated by the 2005 Civil Society BDS Call. In either political configuration, the rights of the refugees must be realized, the colonization of Palestinian land must end and the Golan Heights returned to Syria, and the Palestinian citizens of Israel must become equal citizens of the state. The rights-based approach enables Palestinians and their supporters to organize effectively until an ultimate political goal can be agreed by a majority of the Palestinian people, even if this takes many years.

The Track Record of Palestinian Representation

Palestinians cannot agree upon an ultimate political goal without effective representation that is recognized by a majority of, if not by the entire, Palestinian people. The crisis of representation is now flagrant and Palestinians in the occupied territories, in exile, and in Israel are seeking alternatives. The youth movement in the occupied territories, having started in 2011 by calling for an end to the Fateh-Hamas split, now no longer minces its words regarding the leadership's lack of legitimacy. Palestinians in exile are spearheading a movement for elections to the Palestinian National Council where every Palestinian would have a vote, working together with Palestinians within the occupied territories. Other efforts seek to foster reconciliation and build on the promises made by Fateh and Hamas to reform the PLO into a more representative body that would be answerable to the Palestinian people.

The challenge facing Palestinians is twofold. Reconstituting the PLO from within is likely to lead to dominance by Fateh and Hamas, neither of which is known for their democratic tendencies. Palestinian civil society and the people at large would thus continue to be excluded from decision-making.

On the other hand, constituting a new national movement that is as representative of all Palestinians as the PLO was in its early days is a nigh impossible task. Fateh and Hamas sit on the resources and the levers of power over the local population. Even though their own levers are controlled by Israel, the United States, and Egypt, they can stymie any initiative toward a new Palestinian representation. Moreover the PLO, although it still excludes Hamas and is currently no more than an empty shell, is still recognized internationally as the Palestinians' legitimate representative. A new national movement may not be similarly recognized.

To be sure, a national political institution is crucial. Without national representation, it is not only impossible to set national political goals; it is also difficult to drive those goals forward.   Until it might become possible to reconstitute a national representative body, is it possible to think of different forms of national representation that are democratic and effective? Before addressing this question, it is useful to note that democratic representation can be achieved in ways other than through elections. Elections are ideal, of course, but they are difficult to implement in a meaningful way in the Palestinian context, given the dispersal and insecurity faced by many Palestinian communities, among other factors.

In its heyday, the PLO was not an elected body. Instead, political parties and mass organizations sent representatives to the Palestinian National Council (PNC) where they constituted the majority and where Fateh dominated. The PNC then "elected" an executive committee whose members had been negotiated in advance. Nonetheless, the Palestinian population believed the PLO to be broadly representative of Palestinian aspirations because it had a respected leadership as well as a clearly understood and broadly endorsed agenda. This type of unelected yet relatively democratic representation might be the best that can be achieved by a struggle for national liberation that is under constant threat of liquidation from many different quarters.

Other forms of representation have been developed by Palestinian communities in different parts of the world—the United Kingdom, Chile, and the US. These include community organizations that pull together at least some of the nationals in those countries, sometimes drawing on families from the same village or town of origin. An example of a more direct form of political organizing comes from the US, where, in 2008, a group of Palestinians brought together nearly 1,000 Palestinian Americans to reclaim the Palestinian voice and affirm the right of Palestinians in exile to participate fully in shaping the people's joint destiny. US-based activists affiliated with Fateh attempted to co-opt and/or split the organization, but it has maintained its independence. Nevertheless, this body has yet to take off as a strong representative body for the Palestinians in the US that can indeed participate in shaping the overall Palestinian people's destiny.

In thinking of different forms of representation, it is instructive to review the experience of the BDS movement. It has over time developed from a call with a large number of signatory bodies into a democratically representative body in the form of the BDS National Committee (BNC). The BNC includes representatives of all Palestinian political factions in the form of the Council of National and Islamic Forces in Palestine; the Palestinian General Federation of Trade Unions as well as the Federation of Independent Trade Unions; the General Unions of Palestinian workers, women, teachers, writers, peasants, farmers, and public employees; campaigns such as the Palestinian Campaign for the Academic and Cultural Boycott of Israel and Stop the Wall; civil society organizations including PNGO, the Palestinian NGO Network; and the Global Palestine Right of Return Coalition; among other groups within and outside Palestine. Decisions are made by consensus.

The BNC model is another effective form of democratic representation that has been achieved without elections. It brings together groups that find it hard to collaborate in other more politicized spheres to work on a specific strategy: inflicting economic pain on Israel and challenging its international image through boycotts, divestment, and sanctions. The BNC can be said to be a representative body at the national level—not the national representative by any means, but certainly a national representative. Moreover, it is a national representative that is providing guidance to an international following, albeit on a specific strategy for promoting Palestinian rights.

Indeed, perhaps the BNC works because it is focused on a specific strategy and not on seeking political representation of the Palestinian people in any shape or form. Perhaps during this phase of the Palestinian struggle and the fragmentation of the Palestinian body politic, it is simply not possible to have national political representation.

Palestinians should consider that the best way forward in terms of effective democratic representation to secure Palestinian rights may be to form bodies that are similar to the BNC but focused on other strategies, such as legal strategies. Such bodies would bring together political factions, mass organizations, and civil society organizations within and outside Palestine to collaborate on specific strategies that would challenge Israel's colonization and denial of Palestinian rights until a national political body can be reconstituted.

Sources of Power and Effective Strategies

As I noted at the start of this essay, one must judge the value of a strategy in terms of its effectiveness in achieving one's goals. Judged by this criterion, and assuming that the goal is to fulfill Palestinians rights in two sovereign states based on the 1967 lines, the PLO/PA bid for observer member state status has so far been an ineffective strategy because the PLO/PA has made no use of it whatsoever in advancing the goal.

Changing the letterhead from PA to State of Palestine does nothing to change the power dynamic that is so harshly skewed against the Palestinians. The PLO/PA did not follow up on the new state status by applying to join the International Criminal Court, by insisting that the European Union suspend its trade association agreement with Israel because of its international law violations in the occupied territories, or indeed any other action that could enable the Palestinians to muster the power to turn back the relentless settlement machine as a first step to securing other rights.

The PLO/PA statehood bid aside, what other strategies are there in the Palestinian arena that can serve as models for national level strategies, i.e. strategies that can be implemented and/or supported by the entire Palestinian people?

There is of course the longstanding strategy of armed struggle, enshrined in the 1968 national charter as the strategy to achieve Palestinian rights. In the early days this strategy helped to coalesce the Palestinian people and to put the Palestinian cause on the map.

In recent decades the strategy of armed struggle has had mixed results for several reasons. First, it places the Palestinians in the battlefield where Israel is strongest and the Palestinians are weakest. Second, Israel has learned to use Palestinian armed attacks to its advantage, both in the battle for international public opinion and as a pretext to launch heavily destructive assaults on Palestinians in Gaza and in the West Bank, killing and injuring far more civilians than armed fighters. And third, it often puts Palestinians in violation of international law, which clearly forbids indiscriminate attacks on civilians. Because Israel is a state, it is easier for it to get away with international law violations than armed groups, which can be seen as another failing of the system of international law.

The fact that the armed struggle has had mixed results is by no means a call for Palestinian groups to lay down their arms, which are important for self-defense, certainly in Gaza and arguably also among Palestinian refugees in Lebanon against other armed groups. In the West Bank, Palestinians are at the mercy of Israeli occupation forces. Moreover, the Oslo Accords have, tragically, introduced Palestinian security forces to police Palestinian civilians and suppress their resistance to occupation rather than to protect them from Israel's occupying forces.

However, I would argue for the need to distinguish between the terms "resistance" and "armed struggle" that are so often conflated to suggest that armed struggle is the only form of resistance. Armed struggle is just one form of resistance: others include economic, cultural, legal, diplomatic, and media. If one measures a strategy in terms of its effectiveness in securing Palestinian rights, it can be argued that armed resistance has in recent years served more as something of a deterrent to Israel rather than as a proactive strategy with the power or potential to secure Palestinian rights.

I have already discussed the BDS strategy of inflicting economic pain on Israel and challenging its claim to be a bona fide member of the community of nations by using cultural and academic boycotts to expose its apartheid policies. The BDS movement has had considerable success in these areas although, of course, there is still much to be done.

Palestinian intellectuals are fond of criticizing the BDS movement for what it has not achieved and for the occasional mistakes it makes. But who can work without making mistakes? It is, after all, the only way to learn and progress. Critics of the BDS movement spend less time on recognizing what it has achieved and on understanding its structure and functions. Whatever the caveats, it is undeniable that the BDS strategy is nurturing a major source of power for the Palestinians in their struggle against Israel and for human rights.

Other strategies worth highlighting include the hunger strikes adopted by Palestinian prisoners to win their freedom from Israeli jails, despite the great costs to their health and lives. It is possible to call this a strategy rather than a tactic (an act that is part of an overall strategy towards a goal) because it has achieved more than the freedom of individual prisoners. It has also, because of the prisoners' dedication and bravery, served to mobilize the Palestinian people at large as well as to galvanize international public opinion in support of Palestinian rights.

The public protests and mobilization of the burgeoning youth movement in the occupied territories, which has recently organized actions under the coalition Palestinians for Dignity, also have the potential to reach the level of a national strategy. Many questions would need to be addressed before this can be the case. For example, what are ways to further engage youth communities beyond the West Bank in joint actions? Have effective linkages been developed with a local boycott movement and efforts to promote a resistance economy? What are the movement's short or long-term goals? Is the goal to make the West Bank ungovernable or at least more expensive for Israel and/or the PA, or to ensure that the PA does not reengage in a peace process that undermines Palestinian rights? There may be answers to all these questions but they are not yet clear, although of course the movement is still in its nascent stage.

The diverse initiatives to tell the Palestinian story in words, film, visual arts, and performing arts can also be said to have the status of a national strategy. Especially in the past two decades, the many talented Palestinians have had remarkable success in telling the story on a world stage. Three such films, Divine Intervention, Paradise Now, and Five Broken Cameras, have secured Oscar nominations. They, and many other Palestinian films, have garnered other coveted awards. The implicit goal here is to communicate that the Palestinians are a people with an unshakeable attachment to the land of Palestine who have universal rights that are being violated, and that they will continue to tell their story until those rights are realized.

Legal and diplomatic strategies would potentially be very effective in achieving Palestinian goals. Unfortunately, the diplomatic strategy is in the hands of the PLO/PA and is not being used to good effect. The PLO/PA also controls legal strategies that require action within the state system, such as holding Israel accountable through the International Court of Justice or state sanctions at some level. Nevertheless, some legal strategies can be undertaken by Palestinian civil society on its own or in collaboration with the PLO/PA.

Lawsuits against Israelis accused of violating international human rights would be an example of legal strategies. Some have been successful in, for instance, preventing the travel of top Israeli officials like Tzipi Livni to Britain for fear they might be arrested for war crimes. Unfortunately the British government and other European states have changed their laws to limit the potential of universal jurisdiction. Legal strategies of this nature are potentially expensive unless pro bono legal help can be secured, or by combining money and pro bono activism. It would certainly be worth forging a global coalition of lawyers and activists around this strategy with goals of applying human rights and international law to the conflict.

What To Do About Goals, Representation, Strategy?

The Palestinian national movement may be the only liberation struggle that has to be conducted without a representative leadership, without a consensus on clearly stated national goals that have a chance of being achieved in the foreseeable future, and without nationally agreed strategies. What can be done?

In terms of goals, internationally recognized human rights offer a way forward that is short of a political outcome, and they can and do form the basis of many Palestinian strategies. Human rights can be fulfilled in either a one-state or two-state political outcome. Either political outcome will involve considerable efforts to secure refugee rights, given the potential of a sell-out by the PLO/PA; equality for the citizens of Israel, given Israel's structural racism; and even freedom from occupation, given how narrowly Israel defines the sovereignty of any potential Palestinian state.

In the meantime, Palestinian civil society at home and abroad, together with those members of political parties that care more about rights than about power, can and should methodically assess what sources of power and strategies can be mustered behind each of the two possible political goals—one state or two—and analyze likely changes in the external environment. A clear, unemotional decision grounded in facts could broaden the consensus around the political goal that is achievable in a meaningful time frame.

As for representation, Palestinians are unlikely to have a sole, legitimate representative for some time to come. Even if the PLO is expanded to include Hamas, among other reforms, it will likely "lead" in the same non-representative way it has in past decades.

Thus, in the meantime, Palestinians should seek to build legitimate representative bodies around specific strategies. These bodies should include representatives of political factions, mass organizations, and civil society organizations within and outside Palestine, as the BNC has done. Such representative bodies could even coordinate to achieve an umbrella body that could serve as a quasi-national movement and channel Palestinian energies, as was suggested by Palestinian-American professor Beshara Doumani as a workshop organized by the Crisis Management Initiative (CMI) and Masarat in November 2012.

Finally, even without a sole, legitimate national representative, the Palestinian people can still invest in a range of strategies—economic, cultural, legal, mass mobilization, among others—to nurture their sources of power and make progress in achieving their individual and collective human rights.

[Nadia Hijab is co-founder and director of Al-Shabaka: The Palestinian Policy Network]

VI | Appendix

Palestinian Statehood at the United Nations: An Information Resource

[The following is the latest from Quaker United Nations Office (QUNO) on Palestinian Statehood at the UN.]

Introduction

These pages aim to serve as an informal information resource for issues relating to the current discussions around the question of Palestinian Statehood at the United Nations. The resources contained here are not intended to be exhaustive or definitive; rather they are intended to serve as a bibliographic record of our own research around this complex issue. This is a political and emotional topic for many, and much of the commentary is also politicized: views expressed in the sources cited are those of the authors, not of QUNO. We hope to update this resource on a regular basis and welcome feedback and recommendations for supplementary materials, although we do not make a commitment to include all materials submitted. Please write to quno@afsc.org.

Background

It is currently anticipated that Palestinian officials will approach the United Nations (UN) this September with a request for formal UN membership. Palestinian statehood was unilaterally declared in 1988 and has been recognized by around 122 countries to date. In UN terms, becoming a UN member state requires a Security Council (SC) recommendation followed by a vote with a two-thirds majority (129 member states) in the General Assembly (GA). The Israeli leadership opposes the idea and the US has indicated they would likely use their veto to block the process in the SC. However, there are a number of alternative routes that the Palestinians could take to bolster their case for statehood, some of which are referenced below.

This current initiative for UN recognition follows efforts to strengthen diplomatic relations, support the Palestinian private sector and implement institutional reforms. In April 2011, the Ad Hoc Liaison Committee and the IMF joined the World Bank in stating that the Palestinian Authority (PA) has the institutions and economic policies required of a well functioning state. The backdrop to these developments is Prime Minister Salam Fayyad's two-year plan "Ending the Occupation, Building the State" (2009-2011), supported by the Quartet. The latest National Development Plan (2011-13) entitled "Establishing the State, Building the Future" has also secured international backing.

At the UN, considerations of Palestinian statehood can be seen in the context of the broader discussions of statehood, legitimacy and UN membership that have arisen in recent cases such as those of Kosovo and South Sudan, and even in the context of the recognition of Libya's rebel Transitional National Council.

Scenarios

A number of alternative avenues to pursuing UN membership are being discussed in the public domain. These include:

- Palestinian leadership requesting the GA to reaffirm the 1947 General Assembly Partition Plan Resolution 181, which called for the partition of British Mandate Palestine into a Jewish state and an Arab one.

- Resolution 377, 'Uniting for peace', being deployed. Uniting for peace is a rarely applied mechanism in which a two-thirds majority in the GA can potentially overrule the SC (and its veto) in certain circumstances. (See 'Specific Issues' for more information).

- Palestinian leadership requesting that the GA upgrades the status for Palestine from a 'non-member entity' to 'permanent observer'.

- The GA referring aspects of the issue to the International Court of Justice (ICJ). (For further
discussion see 'Specific Issues').

- Passing a GA resolution recognizing a Palestinian State, which would not be binding but which could have political and symbolic implications.

19 August 2011

Report on Palestine's Application for Admission to the United Nations

[The following is from the Columbia University-affiliated Security Council Report on the Palestine statehood bid.]

Expected Council Action

On Monday, 26 September, it is expected that the Security Council will meet in consultations at 3pm on the issue of Palestine's application for UN membership. However, at time of writing it remained unclear if or when the Security Council might vote on such an application.

Key Recent Developments

Palestinian president Mahmoud Abbas formally submitted Palestine's application for UN membership to the Secretary-General today (Friday, 23 September) before his address to the General Assembly. Ambassador Nawaf Salam of Lebanon, president of the Security Council in September, confirmed receipt of this application from the Secretary-General and reported that he had circulated the application to all Council members.

Also on 23 September, the Quartet—comprised of the EU, Russia, UN, and the United States—issued a statement noting Palestine's application and setting out a time frame for both the Israelis and Palestinians to resume direct negotiations to reach an agreement by the end of 2012.

The recent round of diplomatic activity by the Quartet began on Sunday, 18 September, as an attempt to find a formula for parameters satisfactory to both parties in order to resume direct negotiations and defuse tensions over the Palestinian membership bid. Today's statement covered a specific time frame but did not address any parameters for resuming negotiations. It seems many of the concerns from the 11 July Quartet meeting in Washington, DC still have not been sufficiently addressed. (The US draft from the July meeting referring to 1967 borders as the basis for negotiations was apparently weakened by omitting the notion of agreed land swaps and by the very broad reference to new demographic realities, i.e., settlements. Other aspects seem to have been contentious as well.)

US president Barack Obama met separately with both Israeli prime minister Benjamin Netanyahu and Abbas on Wednesday, 21 September, following his General Assembly address in which he reiterated the commitment to a two-state solution through direct negotiations and discouraged the Palestinian initiative for UN membership.

On 21 September, French president Nicolas Sarkozy also addressed the General Assembly recognizing that Palestine cannot immediately achieve full membership via the Security Council and advocating for a non-member state observer status by the General Assembly as a productive intermediary step. Sarkozy also noted that a veto at the Security Council could be a problematic signal to send to the region given the current political upheavals.

Robert Serry, the UN Special Coordinator for the Middle East Peace Process, prepared a report for the 18 September Ad-Hoc Liaison Committee meeting in New York. The report reiterated Serry's message from his 26 July briefing to the Security Council—that there was a dramatic gap between the maturation of Palestinian state-building and the failure of the peace process to deliver on the political track.

On 16 September Abbas made a speech to the Palestinian people outlining his approach to the UN to apply for membership.

On 12 September an Arab League committee met in Cairo to discuss the possible membership bid. The outcome of the meeting appeared to be broad enough to cover both a formal application for full UN membership—which would require a Security Council resolution—or an alternate strategy in the General Assembly—perhaps a General Assembly resolution to elevate Palestine's status to that of a non-member observer state—or conceivably even both, i.e., apply for formal membership first in the Security Council and if that fails pursue the General Assembly strategy. However, unlike the Doha meeting of this committee in July, it seemed there was a stronger sense that the Palestinians would pursue the Security Council option first.

Key Issues

The key issue is how the Council will treat the application by Palestine for admission to the UN.

A related issue is the application's possible impact on the peace process and the signals any subsequent Council action might send to the region given the current political upheavals.

In the context of Palestine's application for full UN membership, the following background is relevant.

Declaration of a State of Palestine

On 15 November 1988, Palestine unilaterally declared its independence. The declaration and accompanying political communiqué addressed the territorial dimension of Palestine indirectly. It inferred recognition of Israel and limited Palestinian territorial scope by affirming the terms of Security Council resolutions 242 of 1967 and 338 of 1973.

Palestinian recognition of the state of Israel was formalized in an exchange of letters between Palestine Liberation Organization (PLO) head Yasser Arafat and Israeli prime minister Yitzhak Rabin in the lead-up to the signing of the Oslo Accords on 13 September 1993, thereby giving greater specificity to the territorial scope of Palestine, with the Oslo peace process meant to agree on exact boundaries.

Current Status of Palestine in the UN

In 1974 the General Assembly, in resolution 3237(XXIX), approved the PLO (then seen as a national liberation movement) as an observer.

In December 1988, shortly after the proclamation of the state of Palestine, the General Assembly, in resolution 43/177, acknowledged "the proclamation of the State of Palestine" and decided "that the designation 'Palestine'" should be used in place of the PLO without prejudice to the observer status and functions of the PLO "in conformity with relevant UN resolutions and practice." The resolution came close to an acknowledgement that Palestine was a state, but stopped short of that and in effect maintained Palestine in the non-state observer category.

In July 1998, the General Assembly, in resolution 52/250, enhanced the participation privileges of Palestine in the UN system by defining better treatment for Palestine in terms of making proposals and seating. But again this resolution contained language which made it clear that Palestine was still being accorded a lesser status than a state. In effect the resolution elevated Palestine to a new sui generis observer status, still less than a state but higher than all other observers.

The General Assembly could change the status of Palestine at the UN from its current sui generis observer status to that of a non-member state observer.

Admission of a UN Member: Charter and Rules of Procedure

Applications to be admitted to the UN are submitted to the Secretary-General. The application must include a formal instrument as a declaration accepting the obligations in the Charter. The Secretary-General is required to "immediately place the application" before the Security Council (rule 59 of the Provisional Rules of Procedure of the Security Council) and to send a copy of the application to the General Assembly "for information" (rule 135 of the Rules of Procedure of the General Assembly).

Article 4 of the UN Charter is clear that only "states" may apply to be admitted to the UN. An application for admission therefore has to be from an entity which meets the criteria for statehood, including a defined territory and a recognized government. Past precedents confirm, however, that this does not rule out applicants in situations where there remain significant disputes about the territorial boundaries. Past precedents also confirm that applicants do not have to achieve universal recognition before they can be admitted. In 1950 Secretary-General Trygve Lei wrote a memo (S/1466) advising the Security Council that in effect admission to the UN could not be conditioned on recognition of the applicant by all member states.

Article 4 also requires that applicants be "peace-loving," that they accept the obligations contained in the Charter and that, in the judgement of the organization, they are "able and willing" to carry out the obligations. The decision on admission to the UN is for the General Assembly to make. But article 4(2) requires that this be "upon the recommendation of the Security Council." Past practice has shown numerous cases where applicants have not been able to achieve admission because of division between permanent members of the Security Council and the veto of draft resolutions recommending admission.

As indicated above, the application for admission must first be considered by the Security Council. Under rule 59 of the Provisional Rules of Procedure of the Security Council there is a standing Council Committee on Admission of New Members (comprised of all 15 members) which reports its conclusions to the

Council. The Council then, by resolution, takes a decision to make a recommendation to the General Assembly. This decision is subject to the veto. Under rule 60, if there is no recommendation for admission, the Council must submit a "special report" to the General Assembly.

In the General Assembly, under rule 83 of its Rules of Procedure, the admission of a new member is an "important question" which requires a two-thirds majority. Rule 137 allows the General Assembly, if the Security Council fails to recommend admission or postpones consideration, to refer the application back to the Council "for further consideration and recommendation or report."

Admission of a New Member: Process and Practice

Once a state submits an application the Secretary-General is expected to immediately send a copy of the application to the General Assembly and to the Council. However, in the past the Secretary-General has delayed transmission as in the case of the applications of the Democratic Republic of Vietnam (1948) and the Democratic People's Republic of Korea (1949). In both cases, the Secretariat circulated the applications "for the convenience of the Security Council" but "not in the application of rule 6 of the provisional rules of procedure of the members of the Security Council" (which requires the Secretary-General to immediately bring to the attention of the Council communications on any matter for the consideration of the Security Council). This prompted the USSR to allege that the Secretariat had not complied with its duties under Chapter 4 of the Charter. More recently, in the case of the former Yugoslav Republic of Macedonia in 1993, the Secretary-General only circulated the application after requesting the President of the Council to hold informal consultations on the "receivability" of the application (S/25147).

Following referral from the Secretary-General, the Council will consider the application at a formal closed meeting and adopt an agenda item usually entitled "Admission of New Members." At this session the Council could agree that the application should be referred by the president of the Council to the standing Committee on Admission of New Members. However, over the years, applications for membership have also been referred to the Committee by the president without discussion or a decision of the Council.

The Council could also choose not to refer the application to the Committee as Rule 59 states that "unless the Security Council decides otherwise, the application shall be referred by the President [of the Council] to a committee."

Over the years the practice of referring membership applications has varied. The first countries whose applications for membership were not sent to the Committee and received a direct recommendation from the Council were Pakistan (1947), Finland (1947), and Indonesia (1950). Between 1952 and 1968 the Council did not refer any applications to the Committee. However, since 1969, applications generally have been referred to the Committee.

Under Rule 59 of the Provisional Rules of Procedure of the Security Council the Committee is expected to examine the application and report its conclusions to the Council not less than thirty-five days before a regular session of the General Assembly or not less than fourteen days before a Special Session. Under Rule 60, the Council should then report to the General Assembly not less than twenty-five days or four days respectively. Although it appears that the time limits in Rules 59 and 60 are intended to give the General Assembly sufficient time to consider the Council's recommendation, in effect they do not require the Committee or the Council to make a decision within a certain time frame. In addition, the last paragraph of Rule 60 allows the Council to waive the time limits under "special circumstances."

This occurred most recently in 2000 when the Council waived the time limit for Tuvalu and the former Yugoslavia so that their applications could be considered by the General Assembly's 55th session. In the case of Yugoslavia the Committee recommended the Council use the "special circumstances" clause to waive the time limits and allow for an earlier submission to the General Assembly. The application was referred to the Committee on 31 October and the General Assembly admitted Yugoslavia on 1 November. In the case of Namibia, the Council adopted a proposal (S/PV.2917) to waive the time limit on the 6 April 1990 application as the General Assembly was going to be meeting on 23 April.

As with most Council subsidiary bodies, the Committee generally takes decisions by consensus, i.e., agreement among all fifteen members, although there have been instances in which it has done so by simple majority. In effect this means each member has an "informal" and "hidden" veto. (Committee meetings are not public.) If there is disagreement in the Committee on whether or not to recommend Palestine for UN membership it is possible that its application could remain in the Committee.

If the Committee recommends admission it usually presents the Council with a draft resolution recommending admission of the new member for consideration by the General Assembly. In recent years, if there is no disagreement over the Committee's recommendation, the Council has chosen to adopt this resolution "in accordance with the understanding reached in prior consultations" and without either a debate or a vote.

If there is a lack of consensus on whether to refer the application to the Committee or debate it within the Council, the President of the Council could propose to put the referral of the matter to the Committee on the agenda of the Council and call for a vote. This would be a procedural vote requiring nine votes and no vetoes would be applicable. If the proposal is not adopted the application would then be dealt with by the Council.

Generally the Council would then have to vote on a resolution on admitting the country that has applied for UN membership. As membership is a substantive issue, at least nine of the fifteen members of the Council, with no permanent members casting a veto, must agree to the admission of the new state. Past practice has shown numerous cases where applicants have not been able to achieve admission because of division between permanent members of the Security Council and the veto of draft resolutions recommending admission.

The P5 have used their veto against admission of new members fifty-nine times. The USSR vetoed fifty-one applications between 1946 and 1961 while the US vetoed six between 1975 and 1976. China has used its veto twice, blocking the admission of Mongolia (1955), and Bangladesh (1972). In 1961, when Mongolia was finally recommended for admission after reconsideration, China did not participate in the vote. In two more recent occasions (Nauru 1999 and Tuvalu 2000), China disassociated itself from the Committee report recommending admission and then abstained on the Council resolutions enabling their admission to the UN.

The last time the Council rejected a membership application due to a veto by a permanent member was on 15 November 1976 when the United States vetoed the application of the newly established Socialist Republic of Vietnam. Following the 1976 veto, the General Assembly expressed "deep regret and concern" that "one negative vote by a permanent member of the Security Council prevented the adoption of the draft resolution supported by 14 members" and asked the Council to reconsider the matter favorably in strict accordance with Article 4 of the Charter.

However, there have been exceptions to the Council adopting a resolution to recommend admission of a new member. In the case of Kuwait (1963) the Council did not adopt a resolution but instead unanimously agreed in its 1034th meeting that it should become a member. The Council president then declared that the statements made warranted the conclusion that the Council had recommended the admission of Kuwait and notified the Secretary-General.

In a rather unusual case related to the admission of Burundi and Rwanda, the General Assembly acted before the Council, recommending that both states be granted UN membership after their proclamation of independence. Following their independence on 1 July 1962, the Council complied with the recommendation contained in General Assembly resolution 1746 (XVI). Moreover, Rwanda actually filed its application for membership four days before independence (S/5137).

If the Council recommends admission, the recommendation is presented to the General Assembly for consideration. A two-thirds majority is needed in the General Assembly for admission of a new member, and membership is effective on the date that the enabling resolution is adopted.

In recent years the practice has been for the Council to complete its consideration of membership applications rather quickly. For instance, in the most recent case of South Sudan, the entire process took three days (11-13 July 2011). The first meeting of the Council to consider the application, the Committee meeting and the second open meeting of the Council to adopt its recommendation took two days. The General Assembly then approved the membership application the following day.

However, in the past there have been examples of this process taking many years. It took the Republic of Korea and the Democratic People's Republic of Korea forty-two years to become members (1949-1991). Most of the first applicants for UN membership were also placed on hold, only getting through the Council following a grand bargain reached on 14 December 1955 that paved the way for sixteen states.

Historically, there has also been a time lag between the Secretary-General's submission of the application and the Council's consideration. In the case of Kuwait in 1963 the Council took five and half months before it took it up for consideration.

If the Council decides not to recommend the new state for admission or postpones consideration of the application, under Rule 60 of its Rules of Procedure it has to submit a special report to the General Assembly. Having studied the special report, the General Assembly can then send the application back to the Council with a full record of its discussion for further consideration and recommendation. In the case of Israel (1949), its representative at the UN actually made a direct request (S/1267) to the Council to reconsider its application after it had failed to obtain the required number of votes from the Council on 17 December 1948.

The General Assembly is also able to recommend that permanent members of the Council consult to reach agreement as was the case in 1947 with the applications of Albania, Bulgaria, Hungary, Romania, and Mongolia (resolution 113(II)A).

The Council, however, can choose to postpone indefinitely the reconsideration of an application when it comes back from the General Assembly as was the case with 14 states between 1947 and 1950. In a number of cases the decision to postpone reconsideration of an application indefinitely was done in order to allow consultations among the permanent members.

Options

The Council has the following options:

- Referral by the President to the Committee without a decision of the Council
- Referral to the Committee by a decision of the Council
- Decide not to refer the application to the Committee and debate and vote on the application in a Council meeting
- Take no immediate action

Council Dynamics

It is widely thought among Council members that the United States would veto any Palestinian application for full UN membership. President Obama's address to the General Assembly underscored that position. However, the United States may not be the only Council member that could find the application premature, as none of the EU Council members (France, Germany, Portugal, and the UK) have explicitly signaled support for full UN membership. Such support might be unlikely given that none of the four EU countries have bilaterally recognized Palestine.

Colombia highlighted that a negotiated settlement is the only way forward in its 21 September General Assembly address.

Palestine is currently recognized by 128 states, nine of which are Security Council members (Bosnia and Herzegovina, Brazil, China, Gabon, India,

Lebanon, Nigeria, Russia, and South Africa). It is unclear if Bosnia and Herzegovina and Nigeria are prepared to support Palestine's membership bid in the Security Council.

The Palestinians have said that they do not view their bid for UN membership as contradictory with either the peace process or the parallel track of going to the General Assembly to seek non-member state observer status (which can be granted by a simple majority of the General Assembly).

UN Documents

Security Council Resolutions

- S/RES/1999 (13 July 2011) recommended South Sudan for UN membership.

- S/RES/702 (8 August 1991) recommended the Republic of Korea and the Democratic People's Republic of Korea for UN membership.

- S/RES/338 (22 October 1973) called for a ceasefire and the comprehensive implementation of resolution 242.

- S/RES/242 (22 November 1967) was a British-sponsored compromise between the three-power and US drafts, calling on all parties to end territorial claims, respect sovereignty, and for Israel to withdraw from occupied territories.

- S/RES/109 (14 December 1955) recommended Albania, Jordan, Ireland, Portugal, Hungary, Italy, Austria, Romania, Bulgaria, Finland, Sri Lanka (Ceylon), Nepal, Libyan Arab Jamahiriya (Libya), Cambodia, Lao People's Democratic Republic (Laos), and Spain for UN membership.

General Assembly Resolutions

- A/RES/65/308 (14 July 2011) admitted South Sudan as a member of the UN.

- A/RES/55/12 (1 November 2000) admitted the Federal Republic of Yugoslavia as a member of the UN.

- A/RES/52/250 (7 July 1998) elevated Palestine to a new sui generis observer status.

- A/RES/46/1 (17 September 1991) admitted the Republic of Korea and the Democratic People's Republic of Korea as members of the UN.

- A/RES/43/177 (15 December 1988) decided that the designation "Palestine" should be used in place of the designation "Palestine Liberation Organization."

- A/RES/31/21 (26 November 1976) was the General Assembly request for reconsideration of the application of Vietnam by the Security Council.

- A/RES/3237(XXIX) (22 November 1974) was the General Assembly approval of the PLO as an observer.

- A/RES/1746 (XVI) (27 June 1962) recommended the admission of Rwanda and Burundi after the proclamation of independence on 1 July 1962.

- A/RES/995 (X) (14 December 1955) admitted Albania, Jordan, Ireland, Portugal, Hungary, Italy, Austria, Romania, Bulgaria, Finland, Sri Lanka (Ceylon), Nepal, Libyan Arab Jamahiriya (Libya), Cambodia, Lao People's Democratic Republic (Laos) and Spain as members of the UN.

- A/RES/113 A (II) (17 November 1947) recommended that permanent members of the Security Council consult to reach agreement on the applications of Albania, Bulgaria, Hungary, Romania, and Mongolia.

Meeting Records

- S/PV.4215 (31 October 2000) was on the application of Yugoslavia.

- S/PV.4103 (17 February 2000) was on application of Tuvalu.

- S/PV.2917 (17 April 1990) was on the application of Namibia.

- S/PV.1972 (15 November 1976) was on the application of the Socialist Republic of Vietnam.

- S/PV.1034 (7 May 1963) was on the admission of Kuwait as a member of the UN.

- S/PV.503 (26 September 1950) was on the application of Indonesia.

- S/PV.386 (17 December 1948) was on Israel membership.

- S/PV.206 (1 October 1947) was on the application of Finland.

- S/PV.186 (18 August 1947) was on the application of Pakistan.

Other

- S/2011/420 (11 July 2011) was the report of the Committee on the Admission of New Members concerning the application of South Sudan for admission to membership in the UN.

- S/2011/418 (9 July 2011) was the application for membership of South Sudan.

- S/2000/1051 (31 October 2000) was the report of the Committee on the admission of new members concerning the application of Yugoslavia.

- S/2000/1043 (27 October 2000) was the application for membership of the Federal Republic of Yugoslavia.

- S/2000/70 (31 January 2000) was the report of the Committee on the admission of new members concerning the application of Tuvalu.

- S/25147 (22 January 1993) was a note from the Secretary General circulating the application of Macedonia.

- S/5137 (27 June 1962) was the application for membership of Rwanda.

- S/1267 (24 February 1949) was the application for membership of Israel.

- S/1247 (10 February 1949) was a note from the Secretary General circulating the application of DPRK.

- S/1238 (19 January 1949) was the application for membership of the Republic of Korea.

- S/2780 (22 November 1948) was a note from the Secretary General circulating the application of Vietnam.

25 September 2011

Text of Obama Address to the United Nations General Assembly

[The following statement was made by President Obama at the UN General Assembly on 21 September 2011. It was published on whitehouse.gov.]

Mr. President, Mr. Secretary General, fellow delegates, ladies and gentlemen: It is a great honor for me to be here today. I would like to talk to you about a subject that is at the heart of the United Nations—the pursuit of peace in an imperfect world.

War and conflict have been with us since the beginning of civilizations. But in the first part of the twentieth century, the advance of modern weaponry led to death on a staggering scale. It was this killing that compelled the founders of this body to build an institution that was focused not just on ending one war, but on averting others; a union of sovereign states that would seek to prevent conflict, while also addressing its causes.

No American did more to pursue this objective than President Franklin Roosevelt. He knew that a victory in war was not enough. As he said at one of the very first meetings on the founding of the United Nations, "We have got to make, not merely peace, but a peace that will last."

The men and women who built this institution understood that peace is more than just the absence of war. A lasting peace—for nations and for individuals—depends on a sense of justice and opportunity, of dignity and freedom. It depends on struggle and sacrifice, on compromise, and on a sense of common humanity.

One delegate to the San Francisco Conference that led to the creation of the United Nations put it well: "Many people," she said, "have talked as if all that has to be done to get peace was to say loudly and frequently that we loved peace and we hated war. Now we have learned that no matter how much we love peace and hate war, we cannot avoid having war brought upon us if there are convulsions in other parts of the world."

The fact is peace is hard. But our people demand it. Over nearly seven decades, even as the United Nations helped avert a third world war, we still live in a world scarred by conflict and plagued by poverty. Even as we proclaim our love for peace and our hatred of war, there are still convulsions in our world that endanger us all.

I took office at a time of two wars for the United States. Moreover, the violent extremists who drew us into war in the first place—Osama bin Laden, and his al-Qaeda organization—remained at large. Today, we've set a new direction.

At the end of this year, America's military operation in Iraq will be over. We will have a normal relationship with a sovereign nation that is a member of the community of nations. That equal partnership will be strengthened by our support for Iraq—for its government and for its security forces, for its people, and for their aspirations.

As we end the war in Iraq, the United States and our coalition partners have begun a transition in Afghanistan. Between now and 2014, an increasingly capable Afghan government and security forces will step forward to take responsibility for the future of their country. As they do, we are drawing down our own forces, while building an enduring partnership with the Afghan people.

So let there be no doubt: The tide of war is receding. When I took office, roughly 180,000 Americans were serving in Iraq and Afghanistan. By the end of this year, that number will be cut in half, and it will continue to decline. This is critical for the sovereignty of Iraq and Afghanistan. It's also critical to the strength of the United States as we build our nation at home.

Moreover, we are poised to end these wars from a position of strength. Ten years ago, there was an open wound and twisted steel, a broken heart in the center of this city. Today, as a new tower is rising at Ground Zero, it symbolizes New York's renewal, even as al-Qaeda is under more pressure than ever before. Its leadership has been degraded. And Osama bin Laden, a man who murdered thousands of people from dozens of countries, will never endanger the peace of the world again.

So, yes, this has been a difficult decade. But today, we stand at a crossroads of history with the chance to move decisively in the direction of peace. To do so, we must return to the wisdom of those who created this institution. The United Nations' Founding Charter calls upon us "to unite our strength to maintain international peace and security." And Article 1 of this General Assembly's Universal Declaration of Human Rights reminds us that "All human beings are born free and equal in dignity and in rights." Those bedrock beliefs—in the responsibility of states, and the rights of men and women—must be our guide.

And in that effort, we have reason to hope. This year has been a time of extraordinary transformation. More nations have stepped forward to maintain international peace and security. And more individuals are claiming their universal right to live in freedom and dignity.

Think about it: One year ago, when we met here in New York, the prospect of a successful referendum in South Sudan was in doubt. But the international community overcame old divisions to support the agreement that had been negotiated to give South Sudan self-determination. And last summer, as a new flag went up in Juba, former soldiers laid down their arms, men and women wept with joy, and children finally knew the promise of looking to a future that they will shape.

One year ago, the people of Côte d'Ivoire approached a landmark election. And when the incumbent lost, and refused to respect the results, the world refused to look the other way. UN peacekeepers were harassed, but they did not leave their posts. The Security Council, led by the United States and Nigeria and France, came together to support the will of the people. And Côte d'Ivoire is now governed by the man who was elected to lead.

One year ago, the hopes of the people of Tunisia were suppressed. But they chose the dignity of peaceful protest over the rule of an iron fist. A vendor lit a spark that took his own life, but he ignited a movement. In a face of a crackdown, students spelled out the word, "freedom." The balance of fear shifted from the ruler to those that he ruled. And now the people of Tunisia are preparing for elections that will move them one step closer to the democracy that they deserve.

One year ago, Egypt had known one President for nearly thirty years. But for eighteen days, the eyes of the world were glued to Tahrir Square, where Egyptians from all walks of life—men and women, young and old, Muslim and Christian—demanded their universal rights. We saw in those protesters the moral force of non-violence that has lit the world from Delhi to Warsaw, from Selma to South Africa—and we knew that change had come to Egypt and to the Arab world.

One year ago, the people of Libya were ruled by the world's longest-serving dictator. But faced with bullets and bombs and a dictator who threatened to hunt them down like rats, they showed relentless bravery. We will never forget the words of the Libyan who stood up in those early days of the revolution and said,

"Our words are free now." It's a feeling you can't explain. Day after day, in the face of bullets and bombs, the Libyan people refused to give back that freedom. And when they were threatened by the kind of mass atrocity that often went unchallenged in the last century, the United Nations lived up to its charter. The Security Council authorized all necessary measures to prevent a massacre. The Arab League called for this effort; Arab nations joined a NATO-led coalition that halted Qaddafi's forces in their tracks.

In the months that followed, the will of the coalition proved unbreakable, and the will of the Libyan people could not be denied. Forty-two years of tyranny was ended in six months. From Tripoli to Misurata to Benghazi—today, Libya is free. Yesterday, the leaders of a new Libya took their rightful place beside us, and this week, the United States is reopening our embassy in Tripoli.

This is how the international community is supposed to work—nations standing together for the sake of peace and security, and individuals claiming their rights. Now, all of us have a responsibility to support the new Libya—the new Libyan government as they confront the challenge of turning this moment of promise into a just and lasting peace for all Libyans.

So this has been a remarkable year. The Qaddafi regime is over. Gbagbo, Ben Ali, Mubarak are no longer in power. Osama bin Laden is gone, and the idea that change could only come through violence has been buried with him. Something is happening in our world. The way things have been is not the way that they will be. The humiliating grip of corruption and tyranny is being pried open. Dictators are on notice. Technology is putting power into the hands of the people. The youth are delivering a powerful rebuke to dictatorship, and rejecting the lie that some races, some peoples, some religions, some ethnicities do not desire democracy. The promise written down on paper—"all human beings are born free and equal in dignity and rights"—is closer at hand.

But let us remember: Peace is hard. Peace is hard. Progress can be reversed. Prosperity comes slowly. Societies can split apart. The measure of our success must be whether people can live in sustained freedom, dignity, and security. And the United Nations and its member states must do their part to support those basic aspirations. And we have more work to do.

In Iran, we've seen a government that refuses to recognize the rights of its own people. As we meet here today, men and women and children are being tortured, detained and murdered by the Syrian regime. Thousands have been killed, many during the holy time of Ramadan. Thousands more have poured across Syria's borders. The Syrian people have shown dignity and courage in their pursuit of justice—protesting peacefully, standing silently in the streets, dying for the same values that this institution is supposed to stand for. And the question for us is clear: Will we stand with the Syrian people, or with their oppressors?

Already, the United States has imposed strong sanctions on Syria's leaders. We supported a transfer of power that is responsive to the Syrian people. And many of our allies have joined in this effort. But for the sake of Syria—and the peace and security of the world—we must speak with one voice. There's no excuse for inaction. Now is the time for the United Nations Security Council to sanction the Syrian regime, and to stand with the Syrian people.

Throughout the region, we will have to respond to the calls for change. In Yemen, men, women and children gather by the thousands in towns and city squares every day with the hope that their determination and spilled blood will prevail over a corrupt system. America supports those aspirations. We must work with Yemen's neighbors and our partners around the world to seek a path that allows for a peaceful transition of power from President Saleh, and a movement to free and fair elections as soon as possible.

In Bahrain, steps have been taken toward reform and accountability. We're pleased with that, but more is required. America is a close friend of Bahrain, and we will continue to call on the government and the main opposition bloc—the Wifaq—to pursue a meaningful dialogue that brings peaceful change that is responsive to the people. We believe the patriotism that binds Bahrainis together must be more powerful than the sectarian forces that would tear them apart. It will be hard, but it is possible.

We believe that each nation must chart its own course to fulfill the aspirations of its people, and America does not expect to agree with every party or person who expresses themselves politically. But we will always stand up for the universal rights that were embraced by this assembly. Those rights depend on elections that are free and fair; on governance that is transparent and accountable; respect for the rights of women and minorities; justice that is equal and fair. That is what our people deserve. Those are the elements of peace that can last.

Moreover, the United States will continue to support those nations that transition to democracy—with greater trade and investment—so that freedom is followed by opportunity. We will pursue a deeper engagement with governments, but also with civil society—students and entrepreneurs, political parties and the press. We have banned those who abuse human rights from traveling to our country. And we've sanctioned those who trample on human rights abroad. And we will always serve as a voice for those who've been silenced.

Now, I know, particularly this week, that for many in this hall, there's one issue that stands as a test for these principles and a test for American foreign policy, and that is the conflict between the Israelis and the Palestinians.

One year ago, I stood at this podium and I called for an independent Palestine. I believed then, and I believe now, that the Palestinian people deserve a state of their own. But what I also said is that a genuine peace can only be realized between the Israelis and the Palestinians themselves. One year later, despite extensive efforts by America and others, the parties have not bridged their differences. Faced with this stalemate, I put forward a new basis for negotiations in May of this year. That basis is clear. It's well known to all of us here. Israelis must know that any agreement provides assurances for their security. Palestinians deserve to know the territorial basis of their state.

Now, I know that many are frustrated by the lack of progress. I assure you, so am I. But the question isn't the goal that we seek—the question is how do we reach that goal. And I am convinced that there is no short cut to the end of a conflict that has endured for decades. Peace is hard work. Peace will not come through statements and resolutions at the United Nations—if it were that easy, it would have been accomplished by now. Ultimately, it is the Israelis and the Palestinians who must live side by side. Ultimately, it is the Israelis and the Palestinians—not us—who must reach agreement on the issues that divide them: on borders and on security, on refugees and Jerusalem.

Ultimately, peace depends upon compromise among people who must live together long after our speeches are over, long after our votes have been tallied. That's the lesson of Northern Ireland, where ancient antagonists bridged their differences. That's the lesson of Sudan, where a negotiated settlement led to an independent state. And that is and will be the path to a Palestinian state— negotiations between the parties.

We seek a future where Palestinians live in a sovereign state of their own, with no limit to what they can achieve. There's no question that the Palestinians have seen that vision delayed for too long. It is precisely because we believe so strongly in the aspirations of the Palestinian people that America has invested so much time and so much effort in the building of a Palestinian state, and the negotiations that can deliver a Palestinian state.

But understand this as well: America's commitment to Israel's security is unshakeable. Our friendship with Israel is deep and enduring. And so we believe that any lasting peace must acknowledge the very real security concerns that Israel faces every single day.

Let us be honest with ourselves: Israel is surrounded by neighbors that have waged repeated wars against it. Israel's citizens have been killed by rockets fired at their houses and suicide bombs on their buses. Israel's children come of age knowing that throughout the region, other children are taught to hate them. Israel, a small country of less than eight million people, look out at a world where leaders of much larger nations threaten to wipe it off of the map. The Jewish people carry the burden of centuries of exile and persecution, and fresh memories of knowing that six million people were killed simply because of who they are. Those are facts. They cannot be denied.

The Jewish people have forged a successful state in their historic homeland. Israel deserves recognition. It deserves normal relations with its neighbors. And friends of the Palestinians do them no favors by ignoring this truth, just as friends of Israel must recognize the need to pursue a two-state solution with a secure Israel next to an independent Palestine.

That is the truth—each side has legitimate aspirations—and that's part of what makes peace so hard. And the deadlock will only be broken when each side learns to stand in the other's shoes; each side can see the world through the other's eyes. That's what we should be encouraging. That's what we should be promoting.

This body—founded, as it was, out of the ashes of war and genocide, dedicated, as it is, to the dignity of every single person—must recognize the reality that is lived by both the Palestinians and the Israelis. The measure of our actions must always be whether they advance the right of Israeli and Palestinian children to live lives of peace and security and dignity and opportunity. And we will only succeed in that effort if we can encourage the parties to sit down, to listen to each other, and to understand each other's hopes and each other's fears. That is the project to which America is committed. There are no shortcuts. And that is what the United Nations should be focused on in the weeks and months to come.

Now, even as we confront these challenges of conflict and revolution, we must also recognize—we must also remind ourselves—that peace is not just the absence of war. True peace depends on creating the opportunity that makes life worth living. And to do that, we must confront the common enemies of humanity: nuclear weapons and poverty, ignorance and disease. These forces corrode the possibility of lasting peace and together we're called upon to confront them.

To lift the specter of mass destruction, we must come together to pursue the peace and security of a world without nuclear weapons. Over the last two years, we've begun to walk down that path. Since our Nuclear Security Summit in Washington, nearly fifty nations have taken steps to secure nuclear materials from terrorists and smugglers. Next March, a summit in Seoul will advance our efforts to lock down all of them. The New START Treaty between the United States and Russia will cut our deployed arsenals to the lowest level in half a century, and our nations are pursuing talks on how to achieve even deeper reductions. America will continue to work for a ban on the testing of nuclear weapons and the production of fissile material needed to make them.

And so we have begun to move in the right direction. And the United States is committed to meeting our obligations. But even as we meet our obligations, we've strengthened the treaties and institutions that help stop the spread of these weapons. And to do so, we must continue to hold accountable those nations that flout them.

The Iranian government cannot demonstrate that its program is peaceful. It has not met its obligations and it rejects offers that would provide it with peaceful nuclear power. North Korea has yet to take concrete steps towards abandoning its weapons and continues belligerent action against the South. There's a future of greater opportunity for the people of these nations if their governments meet their international obligations. But if they continue down a path that is outside international law, they must be met with greater pressure and isolation. That is what our commitment to peace and security demands.

To bring prosperity to our people, we must promote the growth that creates opportunity. In this effort, let us not forget that we've made enormous progress over the last several decades. Closed societies gave way to open markets. Innovation and entrepreneurship has transformed the way we live and the things that we do. Emerging economies from Asia to the Americas have lifted hundreds of millions of people from poverty. It's an extraordinary achievement. And yet, three years ago, we were confronted with the worst financial crisis in eight decades. And that crisis proved a fact that has become clearer with each passing year—our fates are interconnected. In a global economy, nations will rise, or fall, together.

And today, we confront the challenges that have followed on the heels of that crisis. Around the world recovery is still fragile. Markets remain volatile. Too many people are out of work. Too many others are struggling just to get by. We acted together to avert a depression in 2009. We must take urgent and coordinated action once more. Here in the United States, I've announced a plan to put Americans back to work and jumpstart our economy, at the same time as I'm committed to substantially reducing our deficits over time.

We stand with our European allies as they reshape their institutions and address their own fiscal challenges. For other countries, leaders face a different challenge as they shift their economy towards more self-reliance, boosting domestic demand while slowing inflation. So we will work with emerging economies that have rebounded strongly, so that rising standards of living create new markets that promote global growth. That's what our commitment to prosperity demands.

To combat the poverty that punishes our children, we must act on the belief that freedom from want is a basic human right. The United States has made it a focus of our engagement abroad to help people to feed themselves. And today, as drought and conflict have brought famine to the Horn of Africa, our conscience calls on us to act. Together, we must continue to provide assistance, and support organizations that can reach those in need. And together, we must insist on unrestricted humanitarian access so that we can save the lives of thousands of men and women and children. Our common humanity is at stake. Let us show that the life of a child in Somalia is as precious as any other. That is what our commitment to our fellow human beings demand.

To stop disease that spreads across borders, we must strengthen our system of public health. We will continue the fight against HIV/AIDS, tuberculosis, and malaria. We will focus on the health of mothers and of children. And we must come together to prevent, and detect, and fight every kind of biological danger — whether it's a pandemic like H1N1, or a terrorist threat, or a treatable disease.

This week, America signed an agreement with the World Health Organization to affirm our commitment to meet this challenge. And today, I urge all nations to join us in meeting the HWO's [sic] goal of making sure all nations have core capacities to address public health emergencies in place by 2012. That is what our commitment to the health of our people demands.

To preserve our planet, we must not put off action that climate change demands. We have to tap the power of science to save those resources that are scarce. And together, we must continue our work to build on the progress made in Copenhagen and Cancun, so that all the major economies here today follow through on the commitments that were made. Together, we must work to transform the energy that powers our economies, and support others as they move down that path. That is what our commitment to the next generation demands.

And to make sure our societies reach their potential, we must allow our citizens to reach theirs. No country can afford the corruption that plagues the world like a cancer. Together, we must harness the power of open societies and open economies. That's why we've partnered with countries from across the globe to launch a new partnership on open government that helps ensure accountability and helps to empower citizens. No country should deny people their rights to freedom of speech and freedom of religion, but also no country should deny people their rights because of who they love, which is why we must stand up for the rights of gays and lesbians everywhere.

And no country can realize its potential if half its population cannot reach theirs. This week, the United States signed a new Declaration on Women's Participation. Next year, we should each announce the steps we are taking to break down the economic and political barriers that stand in the way of women and girls. This is what our commitment to human progress demands.

I know there's no straight line to that progress, no single path to success. We come from different cultures, and carry with us different histories. But let us never forget that even as we gather here as heads of different governments, we represent citizens who share the same basic aspirations—to live with dignity and freedom; to get an education and pursue opportunity; to love our families, and love and worship our God; to live in the kind of peace that makes life worth living.

It is the nature of our imperfect world that we are forced to learn these lessons over and over again. Conflict and repression will endure so long as some people refuse to do unto others as we would have them do unto us. Yet that is precisely why we have built institutions like this—to bind our fates together, to help us recognize ourselves in each other—because those who came before us believed that peace is preferable to war, and freedom is preferable to suppression, and prosperity is preferable to poverty. That's the message that comes not from capitals, but from citizens, from our people.

And when the cornerstone of this very building was put in place, President Truman came here to New York and said, "The United Nations is essentially an expression of the moral nature of man's aspirations." The moral nature of man's aspirations. As we live in a world that is changing at a breathtaking pace, that's a lesson that we must never forget.

Peace is hard, but we know that it is possible. So, together, let us be resolved to see that it is defined by our hopes and not by our fears. Together, let us make peace, but a peace, most importantly, that will last.

Thank you very much.

21 September 2011

[Originally published on whitehouse.gov]

Text of Abbas Speech to the United Nations General Assembly

[The following statement was made by President and Chairman Mahmoud Abbas at the UN General Assembly on 23 September 2011.]

Mr. President of the General Assembly of the United Nations, Mr. Secretary-General of the United Nations,

Excellencies, Ladies and Gentlemen,

At the outset, I extend my congratulations to H.E. Mr. Nassir Abdulaziz AI-Nasser on his assumption of the Presidency of the assembly for this session, and wish him all success.

I extend today my sincere congratulations, on behalf of the Palestine Liberation Organization and the Palestinian people, to the government and people of South Sudan for its deserved admission as a full member of the United Nations, wishing them progress and prosperity.

I also congratulate the Secretary-General, H.E. Mr. Ban Ki-moon, on his election for a new term at the helm of the United Nations. This renewal of confidence reflects the world's appreciation for his efforts, which have strengthened the role of the United Nations.

Excellencies, Ladies and Gentlemen,

The Question Palestine is intricately linked with the United Nations via the resolutions adopted by its various organs and agencies and via the essential and lauded role of the United Nations Relief and Works Agency for Palestine Refugees in the Near East - UNRWA - which embodies the international responsibility towards the plight of Palestine refugees, who are the victims of Al-Nakba (Catastrophe) that occurred in 1948. We aspire for and seek a greater and more effective role for the United Nations in working to achieve a just and comprehensive peace in our region that ensures the inalienable, legitimate national rights of the Palestinian people as defined by the resolutions of international legitimacy of the United Nations.

Excellencies, Ladies and Gentlemen,

A year ago, at this same time, distinguished leaders in this hall addressed the stalled peace efforts in our region. Everyone had high hopes for a new round of final status negotiations, which had begun in early September in Washington under the direct auspices of President Barack Obama and with participation of the Quartet, and with Egyptian and Jordanian participation, to reach a peace agreement within one year. We entered those negotiations with open hearts and attentive ears and sincere intentions, and we were ready with our documents, papers and proposals. But the negotiations broke down just weeks after their launch. After this, we did not give up and did not cease our efforts for initiatives and contacts. Over the past year we did not leave a door to be knocked or channel to be tested or path to be taken and we did not ignore any formal or informal party of influence and stature to be addressed. We positively considered the various ideas and proposals and initiatives presented from many countries and parties. But all of these sincere efforts and endeavors undertaken by international parties were repeatedly wrecked by the positions of the Israeli government, which quickly dashed the hopes raised by the launch of negotiations last September.

The core issue here is that the Israeli government refuses to commit to terms of reference for the negotiations that are based on international law and United Nations resolutions, and that it frantically continues to intensify building of settlements on the territory of the State of Palestine.

Settlement activities embody the core of the policy of colonial military occupation of the land of the Palestinian people and all of the brutality of aggression and racial discrimination against our people that this policy entails. This policy, which constitutes a breach of international humanitarian law and United Nations resolutions, is the primary cause for the failure of the peace process, the collapse of dozens of opportunities, and the burial of the great hopes that arose from the signing of the Declaration of Principles in 1993 between the Palestine Liberation Organization and Israel to achieve a just peace that would begin a new era for our region.

The reports of United Nations missions as well as by several Israeli institutions and civil societies convey a horrific picture about the size of the settlement campaign, which the Israeli government does not hesitate to boast about and which it continues to execute through the systematic confiscation of the Palestinian lands and the construction of thousands of new settlement units in various areas of the West Bank, particularly in East Jerusalem, and accelerated construction of the annexation wall that is eating up large tracts of our land, dividing it into separate and isolated islands and cantons, destroying family life and communities and the livelihoods of tens of thousands of families. The occupying power also continues to refuse permits for our people to build in occupied East Jerusalem, at the same time that it intensifies its decades-long campaign of demolition and confiscation of homes, displacing Palestinian owners and residents under a multi-pronged policy of ethnic cleansing aimed at pushing them away from their ancestral homeland. In addition, orders have been issued to deport elected representatives from the city of Jerusalem. The occupying power also continues to undertake excavations that threaten our holy places, and its military checkpoints prevent our citizens from getting access to their mosques and churches, and it continues to besiege the Holy City with a ring of settlements imposed to separate the Holy City from the rest of the Palestinian cities.

The occupation is racing against time to redraw the borders on our land according to what it wants and to impose a fait accompli on the ground that changes the realities and that is undermining the realistic potential for the existence of the State of Palestine.

At the same time, the occupying power continues to impose its blockade on the Gaza Strip and to target Palestinian civilians by assassinations, air strikes and artillery shelling, persisting with its war of aggression of three years ago on Gaza, which resulted in massive destruction of homes, schools, hospitals, and mosques, and the thousands of martyrs and wounded.

The occupying power also continues its incursions in areas of the Palestinian National Authority through raids, arrests and killings at the checkpoints. In recent years, the criminal actions of armed settler militias, who enjoy the special protection of the occupation army, has intensified with the perpetration of frequent attacks against our people, targeting their homes, schools, universities, mosques, fields, crops and trees. Despite our repeated warnings, the occupying power has not acted to curb these attacks and we hold them fully responsible for the crimes of the settlers.

These are just a few examples of the policy of the Israeli colonial settlement occupation, and this policy is responsible for the continued failure of the successive international attempts to salvage the peace process.

This policy will destroy the chances of achieving a two-state solution upon which there is an international consensus, and here I caution aloud: This settlement policy threatens to also undermine the structure of the Palestinian National Authority and even end its existence.

In addition, we now face the imposition new conditions not previously raised, conditions that will transform the raging conflict in our inflamed region into a religious conflict and a threat to the future of a million and a half Christian and Muslim Palestinians, citizens of Israel, a matter which we reject and which is impossible for us to accept being dragged into.

All of these actions taken by Israel in our country are unilateral actions and are not based on any earlier agreements. Indeed, what we witness is a selective application of the agreements aimed at perpetuating the occupation. Israel reoccupied the cities of the West Bank by a unilateral action, and reestablished the civil and military occupation by a unilateral action, and it is the one that determines whether or not a Palestinian citizen has the right to reside in any part of the Palestinian Territory. And it is confiscating our land and our water and obstructing our movement as well as the movement of goods. And it is the one obstructing our whole destiny. All of this is unilateral.

Excellencies, Ladies and Gentlemen,

In 1974, our deceased leader Yasser Arafat came to this hall and assured the Members of the General Assembly of our affirmative pursuit for peace, urging the United Nations to realize the inalienable national rights of the Palestinian people, stating: "Do not let the olive branch fall from my hand."

In 1988, President Arafat again addressed the General Assembly, which convened in Geneva to hear him, where he submitted the Palestinian peace program adopted by the Palestine National Council at its session held that year in Algeria.

When we adopted this program, we were taking a painful and very difficult step for all of us, especially those, including myself, who were forced to leave their homes and their towns and villages, carrying only some of our belongings and our grief and our memories and the keys of our homes to the camps of exile and the Diaspora in the 1948 Nakba, one of the worst operations of uprooting, destruction, and removal of a vibrant and cohesive society that had been contributing in a pioneering and leading way the cultural, educational, and economic renaissance of the Arab Middle East.

Yet, because we believe in peace and because of our conviction in international legitimacy, and because we had the courage to make difficult decisions for our people, and in the absence of absolute justice, we decided to adopt the path of relative justice - justice that is possible and could correct part of the grave historical injustice committed against our people. Thus, we agreed to establish the State of Palestine on only twenty-two percent of the territory of historical Palestine—on all the Palestinian Territory occupied by Israel in 1967.

We, by taking that historic step, which was welcomed by the states of the world, made a major concession in order to achieve a historic compromise that would allow peace to be made in the land of peace.

In the years that followed—from the Madrid Conference and the Washington negotiations leading to the Oslo agreement, which was signed eighteen years ago in the garden of the White House and was linked with the letters of mutual recognition between the PLO and Israel, we persevered and dealt positively and responsibly with all efforts aimed at the achievement of a lasting peace agreement. Yet, as we said earlier, every initiative and every conference and every new round of negotiations and every movement was shattered on the rock of the Israeli settlement expansion project.

Excellencies, Ladies and Gentlemen,

I confirm, on behalf of the Palestine Liberation Organization, the sole legitimate representative of the Palestinian people, which will remain so until the end of the conflict in all its aspects and until the resolution of all final status issues, the following:

1. The goal of the Palestinian people is the realization of their inalienable national rights in their independent State of Palestine, with East Jerusalem as its capital, on all the land of the West Bank, including East Jerusalem, and the Gaza Strip, which Israel occupied in the June 1967 war, in conformity with the resolutions of international legitimacy and with the achievement of a just and agreed upon solution to the Palestine refugee issue in accordance with resolution 194, as stipulated in the Arab Peace Initiative which presented the consensus Arab vision to resolve the core the Arab-Israeli conflict and to achieve a just and comprehensive peace. To this we adhere and this is what we are working to achieve. Achieving this desired peace also requires the release of political prisoners and detainees in Israeli prisons without delay.

2. The PLO and the Palestinian people adhere to the renunciation of violence and rejection and condemning of terrorism in all its forms, especially

271

State terrorism, and adhere to all agreements signed between the Palestine Liberation Organization and Israel.

3. We adhere to the option of negotiating a lasting solution to the conflict in accordance with resolutions of international legitimacy. Here, I declare that the Palestine Liberation Organization is ready to return immediately to the negotiating table on the basis of the adopted terms of reference based on international legitimacy and a complete cessation of settlement activities.

4. Our people will continue their popular peaceful resistance to the Israeli occupation and its settlement and apartheid policies and its construction of the racist annexation wall, and they receive support for their resistance, which is consistent with international humanitarian law and international conventions and has the support of peace activists from Israel and around the world, reflecting an impressive, inspiring and courageous example of the strength of this defenseless people, armed only with their dreams, courage, hope and slogans in the face of bullets, tanks, tear gas, and bulldozers.

5. When we bring our plight and our case to this international podium, it is a confirmation of our reliance on the political and diplomatic option and is a confirmation that we do not undertake unilateral steps. Our efforts are not aimed at isolating Israel or de-legitimizing it; rather we want to gain legitimacy for the cause of the people of Palestine. We only aim to de-legitimize the settlement activities, the occupation and apartheid, and the logic of ruthless force, and we believe that all the countries of the world stand with us in this regard.

I am here to say on behalf of the Palestinian people and the Palestine Liberation Organization: We extend our hands to the Israeli government and the Israeli people for peace-making. I say to them: Let us urgently build together a future for our children where they can enjoy freedom, security and prosperity. Let us build the bridges of dialogue instead of checkpoints and walls of separation, and build cooperative relations based on parity and equity between two neighboring States—Palestine and Israel—instead of policies of occupation, settlement, war, and eliminating the other.

Excellencies, Ladies and Gentlemen,

Despite the unquestionable right of our people to self-determination and to the independence of our State as stipulated in international resolutions, we have accepted in the past few years to engage in what appeared to be a test of our worthiness, entitlement and eligibility. During the last two years our national authority has implemented a program to build our State institutions. Despite the extraordinary situation and the Israeli obstacles imposed, a serious extensive project was launched that has included the implementation of plans to enhance and advance the judiciary and the apparatus for maintenance of order and security, to develop the administrative, financial, and oversight systems, to upgrade the performance of institutions, and to enhance self-reliance to reduce the need for foreign aid. With the thankful support of Arab countries and donors from friendly countries, a number of large infrastructure projects have been implemented, focused on various aspects of service, with special attention to rural and marginalized areas.

In the midst of this massive national project, we have been strengthening what we are seeking to be the features of our State: from the preservation of security for the citizen and public order; to the promotion of judicial authority and rule of law; to strengthening the role of women via legislation, laws and participation; to ensuring the protection of public freedoms and strengthening the role of civil society institutions; to institutionalizing rules and regulations for ensuring accountability and transparency in the work of our ministries and departments; to entrenching the pillars of democracy as the basis for the Palestinian political life.

When division struck the unity of our homeland, people and institutions, we were determined to adopt dialogue for restoration of our unity. We succeeded months ago in achieving national reconciliation and we hope that its implementation will be accelerated in the coming weeks.

The core pillar of this reconciliation was to turn to the people through legislative and presidential elections within a year, because the State we want will be a State characterized by the rule of law, democratic exercise and protection of the freedoms and equality of all citizens without any discrimination and the transfer of power through the ballot box.

The reports issued recently by the United Nations, the World Bank, the Ad Hoc Liaison Committee (AHLC), and the International Monetary Fund confirm and laud what has been accomplished, considering it a remarkable and unprecedented model. The consensus conclusion by the AHLC a few days ago here described what has been accomplished as a "remarkable international success story" and confirmed the readiness of the Palestinian people and their institutions for the immediate independence of the State of Palestine.

Excellencies, Ladies and Gentlemen,

It is no longer possible to redress the issue of the blockage of the horizon of the peace talks with the same means and methods that have been repeatedly tried and proven unsuccessful over the past years. The crisis is far too deep to be neglected, and what is more dangerous are attempts to simply circumvent it or postpone its explosion.

It is neither possible, nor practical, nor acceptable to return to conducting business as usual, as if everything is fine. It is futile to go into negotiations without clear parameters and in the absence of credibility and a specific timetable. Negotiations will be meaningless as long as the occupation army on the ground continues to entrench its occupation, instead of rolling it back, and continues to change the demography of our country in order to create a new basis on which to alter the borders.

Excellencies, Ladies and Gentlemen,

It is a moment of truth and my people are waiting to hear the answer of the world. Will it allow Israel to continue its occupation, the only occupation in the world? Will it allow Israel to remain a State above the law and accountability? Will it allow Israel to continue rejecting the resolutions of the Security Council and the General Assembly of the United Nations and the International Court of Justice and the positions of the overwhelming majority of countries in the world?

Excellencies, Ladies and Gentlemen,

I come before you today from the Holy Land, the land of Palestine, the land of divine messages, ascension of the Prophet Muhammad (peace be upon him) and the birthplace of Jesus Christ (peace be upon him), to speak on behalf of the Palestinian people in the homeland and in the Diaspora, to say, after sixty-three years of suffering of an ongoing Nakba: Enough. It is time for the Palestinian people to gain their freedom and independence.

The time has come to end the suffering and the plight of millions of Palestine refugees in the homeland and the Diaspora, to end their displacement and to realize their rights, some of them forced to take refuge more than once in different places of the world.

At a time when the Arab peoples affirm their quest for democracy—the Arab Spring—the time is now for the Palestinian Spring, the time for independence.

The time has come for our men, women and children to live normal lives, for them to be able to sleep without waiting for the worst that the next day will bring; for mothers to be assured that their children will return home without fear of suffering killing, arrest or humiliation; for students to be able to go to their schools and universities without checkpoints obstructing them. The time has come for sick people to be able to reach hospitals normally, and for our farmers to be able to take care of their good land without fear of the occupation seizing the land and its water, which the wall prevents access to, or fear of the settlers, for whom settlements are being built on our land and who are uprooting and burning the olive trees that have existed for hundreds of years. The time has come for the thousands of prisoners to be released from the prisons to return to their families and their children to become a part of building their homeland, for the freedom of which they have sacrificed.

My people desire to exercise their right to enjoy a normal life like the rest of humanity. They believe what the great poet Mahmoud Darwish said: "Standing here, staying here, permanent here, eternal here, and we have one goal, one, one: to be."

Excellencies, Ladies and Gentlemen,

We profoundly appreciate and value the positions of all States that have supported our struggle and our rights and recognized the State of Palestine following the Declaration of Independence in 1988, as well as the countries that have recently recognized the State of Palestine and those that have upgraded the level of Palestine's representation in their capitals. I also salute the Secretary-General, who said a few days ago that the Palestinian State should have been established years ago.

Be assured that this support for our people is more valuable to them than you can imagine, for it makes them feel that someone is listening to their narrative and that their tragedy and the horrors of Al-Nakba and the occupation, from which they have so suffered, are not being ignored. And, it reinforces their hope that stems from the belief that justice is possible in this in this world. The loss of hope is the most ferocious enemy of peace and despair is the strongest ally of extremism.

I say: The time has come for my courageous and proud people, after decades of displacement and colonial occupation and ceaseless suffering, to live like other peoples of the earth, free in a sovereign and independent homeland.

Excellencies, Ladies and Gentlemen,

I would like to inform you that, before delivering this statement, I, in my capacity as President of the State of Palestine and Chairman of the Executive Committee of the Palestine Liberation Organization, submitted to H.E. Mr. Ban Ki-moon, Secretary-General of the United Nations, an application for the admission of Palestine on the basis of the 4 June 1967 borders, with al-Quds al-Sharif as its capital, as a full member of the United Nations.

I call upon Mr. Secretary-General to expedite transmittal of our request to the Security Council, and I call upon the distinguished members of the Security Council to vote in favor of our full membership. I also appeal to the States that have not yet recognized the State of Palestine to do so.

Excellencies, Ladies and Gentlemen,

The support of the countries of the world for our endeavor is a victory for truth, freedom, justice, law and international legitimacy, and it provides tremendous support for the peace option and enhances the chances of success of the negotiations.

Excellencies, Ladies and Gentlemen,

Your support for the establishment of the State of Palestine and for its admission to the United Nations as a full member is the greatest contribution to peacemaking in the Holy Land.

I thank you.

23 September 2011

[Originally published by the UN]

Text of Netanyahu Speech to the United Nations General Assembly

[The following statement was made by Prime Minister Benjamin Netanyahu at the UN General Assembly on 23 September 2011.]

Ladies and gentlemen, Israel has extended its hand in peace from the moment it was established sixty-three years ago. On behalf of Israel and the Jewish people, I extend that hand again today. I extend it to the people of Egypt and Jordan, with renewed friendship for neighbors with whom we have made peace. I extend it to the people of Turkey, with respect and good will. I extend it to the people of Libya and Tunisia, with admiration for those trying to build a democratic future. I extend it to the other peoples of North Africa and the Arabian Peninsula, with whom we want to forge a new beginning. I extend it to the people of Syria, Lebanon and Iran, with awe at the courage of those fighting brutal repression.

But most especially, I extend my hand to the Palestinian people, with whom we seek a just and lasting peace.

Ladies and gentlemen, in Israel our hope for peace never wanes. Our scientists, doctors, innovators apply their genius to improve the world of tomorrow. Our artists, our writers, enrich the heritage of humanity. Now, I know that this is not exactly the image of Israel that is often portrayed in this hall. After all, it was here in 1975 that the age-old yearning of my people to restore our national life in our ancient biblical homeland—it was then that this was branded shamefully, as racism. And it was here in 1980, right here, that the historic peace agreement between Israel and Egypt wasn't praised; it was denounced! And it's here, year after year that Israel is unjustly singled out for condemnation. It's singled out for condemnation more often than all the nations of the world combined. Twenty-one out of the twenty-seven General Assembly resolutions condemn Israel—the one true democracy in the Middle East.

Well, this is an unfortunate part of the UN institution. It's the—the theater of the absurd. It doesn't only cast Israel as the villain; it often casts real villains in leading roles: Qaddafi's Libya chaired the UN Commission on Human Rights;

Saddam's Iraq headed the UN Committee on Disarmament. You might say: that's the past. Well, here's what's happening now—right now, today, Hezbollah-controlled Lebanon now presides over the UN Security Council. This means, in effect, that a terror organization presides over the body entrusted with guaranteeing the world's security.

You couldn't make this thing up.

So here in the UN, automatic majorities can decide anything. They can decide that the sun sets in the west or rises in the west. I think the first has already been pre- ordained. But they can also decide—they have decided—that the Western Wall in Jerusalem, Judaism's holiest place, is occupied Palestinian territory.

And yet even here in the General Assembly, the truth can sometimes break through. In 1984 when I was appointed Israel's ambassador to the United Nations, I visited the great rabbi of Lubavich. He said to me—and ladies and gentlemen, I don't want any of you to be offended because from personal experience of serving here, I know there are many honorable men and women, many capable and decent people, serving their nations here—but here's what the rabbi said to me. He said to me, you'll be serving in a house of many lies. And then he said, remember that even in the darkest place, the light of a single candle can be seen far and wide.

Today I hope that the light of truth will shine, if only for a few minutes, in a hall that for too long has been a place of darkness for my country. So as Israel's prime minister, I didn't come here to win applause. I came here to speak the truth. The truth is—the truth is that Israel wants peace. The truth is that I want peace. The truth is that in the Middle East at all times, but especially during these turbulent days, peace must be anchored in security. The truth is that we cannot achieve peace through UN resolutions, but only through direct negotiations between the parties. The truth is that so far the Palestinians have refused to negotiate. The truth is that Israel wants peace with a Palestinian state, but the Palestinians want a state without peace. And the truth is you shouldn't let that happen.

Ladies and gentlemen, when I first came here twenty-seven years ago, the world was divided between East and West. Since then the Cold War ended, great civilizations have risen from centuries of slumber, hundreds of millions have been lifted out of poverty, countless more are poised to follow, and the remarkable thing is that so far this monumental historic shift has largely occurred peacefully. Yet a malignancy is now growing between East and West that threatens the peace of all. It seeks not to liberate, but to enslave, not to build, but to destroy.

That malignancy is militant Islam. It cloaks itself in the mantle of a great faith, yet it murders Jews, Christians and Muslims alike with unforgiving impartiality. On September 11th it killed thousands of Americans, and it left the twin towers in smoldering ruins. Last night I laid a wreath on the 9/11 memorial. It was deeply moving. But as I was going there, one thing echoed in my mind: the outrageous words of the president of Iran on this podium yesterday. He implied that 9/11 was an American conspiracy. Some of you left this hall. All of you should have.

Since 9/11, militant Islamists slaughtered countless other innocents—in London and Madrid, in Baghdad and Mumbai, in Tel Aviv and Jerusalem, in every part of Israel. I believe that the greatest danger facing our world is that this fanaticism will arm itself with nuclear weapons. And this is precisely what Iran is trying to do.

Can you imagine that man who ranted here yesterday—can you imagine him armed with nuclear weapons? The international community must stop Iran before it's too late. That would be a tragedy. Millions of Arabs have taken to the streets to replace tyranny with liberty, and no one would benefit more than Israel if those committed to freedom and peace would prevail.

This is my fervent hope. But as the prime minister of Israel, I cannot risk the future of the Jewish state on wishful thinking. Leaders must see reality as it is, not as it ought to be. We must do our best to shape the future, but we cannot wish away the dangers of the present.

And the world around Israelis definitely becoming more dangerous. Militant Islam has already taken over Lebanon and Gaza. It's determined to tear apart the peace treaties between Israel and Egypt and between Israel and Jordan. It's poisoned many Arab minds against Jews and Israel, against America and the West. It opposes not the policies of Israel but the existence of Israel.

Now, some argue that the spread of militant Islam, especially in these turbulent times—if you want to slow it down, they argue, Israel must hurry to make concessions, to make territorial compromises. And this theory sounds simple. Basically it goes like this: Leave the territory, and peace will be advanced. The moderates will be strengthened, the radicals will be kept at bay. And don't worry about the pesky details of how Israel will actually defend itself; international troops will do the job.

These people say to me constantly: Just make a sweeping offer, and everything will work out. You know, there's only one problem with that theory. We've tried it and it hasn't worked. In 2000 Israel made a sweeping peace offer that met virtually all of the Palestinian demands. Arafat rejected it. The Palestinians then launched a terror attack that claimed a thousand Israeli lives.

Prime Minister Olmert afterwards made an even more sweeping offer, in 2008. President Abbas didn't even respond to it.

But Israel did more than just make sweeping offers. We actually left territory. We withdrew from Lebanon in 2000 and from every square inch of Gaza in 2005. That didn't calm the Islamic storm, the militant Islamic storm that threatens us. It only brought the storm closer and made it stronger.

Hezbollah and Hamas fired thousands of rockets against our cities from the very territories we vacated. See, when Israel left Lebanon and Gaza, the moderates didn't defeat the radicals, the moderates were devoured by the radicals. And I regret to say that international troops like UNIFIL in Lebanon and EUBAM in Gaza didn't stop the radicals from attacking Israel.

We left Gaza hoping for peace.

We didn't freeze the settlements in Gaza, we uprooted them. We did exactly what the theory says: Get out, go back to the 1967 borders, dismantle the settlements.

And I don't think people remember how far we went to achieve this. We uprooted thousands of people from their homes. We pulled children out of—out of their schools and their kindergartens. We bulldozed synagogues. We even—we even moved loved ones from their graves. And then, having done all that, we gave the keys of Gaza to President Abbas.

Now the theory says it should all work out, and President Abbas and the Palestinian Authority now could build a peaceful state in Gaza. You can remember that the entire world applauded. They applauded our withdrawal as an act of great statesmanship. It was a bold act of peace.
But ladies and gentlemen, we didn't get peace. We got war. We got Iran, which through its proxy Hamas promptly kicked out the Palestinian Authority. The Palestinian Authority collapsed in a day—in one day.

President Abbas just said on this podium that the Palestinians are armed only with their hopes and dreams. Yeah, hopes, dreams and 10,000 missiles and Grad rockets supplied by Iran, not to mention the river of lethal weapons now flowing into Gaza from the Sinai, from Libya, and from elsewhere.

Thousands of missiles have already rained down on our cities. So you might understand that, given all this, Israelis rightly ask: What's to prevent this from happening again in the West Bank? See, most of our major cities in the south of the country are within a few dozen kilometers from Gaza. But in the center of the country, opposite the West Bank, our cities are a few hundred meters or at most a few kilometers away from the edge of the West Bank.

So I want to ask you. Would any of you—would any of you bring danger so close to your cities, to your families? Would you act so recklessly with the lives of your citizens? Israelis prepared to have a Palestinian state in the West Bank, but we're not prepared to have another Gaza there. And that's why we need to have real security arrangements, which the Palestinians simply refuse to negotiate with us.

Israelis remember the bitter lessons of Gaza. Many of Israel's critics ignore them. They irresponsibly advise Israel to go down this same perilous path again. You read what these people say and it's as if nothing happened—just repeating the same advice, the same formulas as though none of this happened.

And these critics continue to press Israel to make far-reaching concessions without first assuring Israel's security. They praise those who unwittingly feed the insatiable crocodile of militant Islam as bold statesmen. They cast as enemies of peace those of us who insist that we must first erect a sturdy barrier to keep the crocodile out, or at the very least jam an iron bar between its gaping jaws.

So in the face of the labels and the libels, Israel must heed better advice. Better a bad press than a good eulogy, and better still would be a fair press whose sense of history extends beyond breakfast, and which recognizes Israel's legitimate security concerns.

I believe that in serious peace negotiations, these needs and concerns can be properly addressed, but they will not be addressed without negotiations. And the needs are many, because Israel is such a tiny country. Without Judea and Samaria, the West Bank, Israel is all of miles wide.

I want to put it for you in perspective, because you're all in the city. That's about two-thirds the length of Manhattan. It's the distance between Battery Park and Columbia University. And don't forget that the people who live in Brooklyn and New Jersey are considerably nicer than some of Israel's neighbors.

So how do you—how do you protect such a tiny country, surrounded by people sworn to its destruction and armed to the teeth by Iran? Obviously you can't defend it from within that narrow space alone. Israel needs greater strategic depth, and that's exactly why Security Council Resolution 242 didn't require Israel to leave all the territories it captured in the Six-Day War. It talked about withdrawal from territories, to secure and defensible boundaries. And to defend itself, Israel must therefore maintain a long-term Israeli military presence in critical strategic areas in the West Bank.

I explained this to President Abbas. He answered that if a Palestinian state was to be a sovereign country, it could never accept such arrangements. Why not? America has had troops in Japan, Germany and South Korea for more than a half a century. Britain has had an an air base in Cyprus. France has forces in three independent African nations. None of these states claim that they're not sovereign countries.

And there are many other vital security issues that also must be addressed. Take the issue of airspace. Again, Israel's small dimensions create huge security problems. America can be crossed by jet airplane in six hours. To fly across Israel, it takes three minutes. So is Israel's tiny airspace to be chopped in half and given to a Palestinian state not at peace with Israel?

Our major international airport is a few kilometers away from the West Bank. Without peace, will our planes become targets for antiaircraft missiles placed in the adjacent Palestinian state? And how will we stop the smuggling into the West Bank?

I bring up these problems because they're not theoretical problems. They're very real. And for Israelis, they're life-and- death matters. All these potential cracks in Israel's security have to be sealed in a peace agreement before a Palestinian state is declared, not afterwards, because if you leave it afterwards, they won't be sealed. And these problems will explode in our face and explode the peace.

The Palestinians should first make peace with Israel and then get their state. But I also want to tell you this. After such a peace agreement is signed, Israel will not be the last country to welcome a Palestinian state as a new member of the United Nations. We will be the first.

And there's one more thing. Hamas has been violating international law by holding our soldier Gilad Shalit captive for five years.

They haven't given even one Red Cross visit. He's held in a dungeon, in darkness, against all international norms. Gilad Shalit is the son of Aviva and Noam Shalit. He is the grandson of Zvi Shalit, who escaped the Holocaust by coming to the—in the 1930s as a boy to the land of Israel. Gilad Shalit is the son of every Israeli family. Every nation represented here should demand his immediate release. If you want to pass a resolution about the Middle East today, that's the resolution you should pass.

Ladies and gentlemen, last year in Israel in Bar-Ilan University, this year in the Knesset and in the US Congress, I laid out my vision for peace in which a demilitarized Palestinian state recognizes the Jewish state. Yes, the Jewish state. After all, this is the body that recognized the Jewish state sixty-four years ago. Now, don't you think it's about time that Palestinians did the same?

The Jewish state of Israel will always protect the rights of all its minorities, including the more than one million Arab citizens of Israel. I wish I could say the same thing about a future Palestinian state, for as Palestinian officials made clear the other day—in fact, I think they made it right here in New York—they said the Palestinian state won't allow any Jews in it. They'll be Jew-free—Judenrein. That's ethnic cleansing. There are laws today in Ramallah that make the selling of land to Jews punishable by death. That's racism. And you know which laws this evokes.

Israel has no intention whatsoever to change the democratic character of our state. We just don't want the Palestinians to try to change the Jewish character of our state. We want to give up—we want them to give up the fantasy of flooding Israel with millions of Palestinians.

President Abbas just stood here, and he said that the core of the Israeli-Palestinian conflict is the settlements. Well, that's odd. Our conflict has been raging for—was raging for nearly half a century before there was a single Israeli settlement in the West Bank. So if what President Abbas is saying was true, then the—I guess that the settlements he's talking about are Tel Aviv, Haifa, Jaffa, Be'er Sheva. Maybe that's what he meant the other day when he said that Israel has been occupying Palestinian land for sixty-three years. He didn't say from 1967; he said from 1948. I hope somebody will bother to ask him this question because it illustrates a simple truth: The core of the conflict is not the settlements. The settlements are a result of the conflict.

The settlements have to be—it's an issue that has to be addressed and resolved in the course of negotiations. But the core of the conflict has always been and unfortunately remains the refusal of the Palestinians to recognize a Jewish state in any border.

I think it's time that the Palestinian leadership recognizes what every serious international leader has recognized, from Lord Balfour and Lloyd George in 1917, to President Truman in 1948, to President Obama just two days ago right here: Israel is the Jewish state.

President Abbas, stop walking around this issue. Recognize the Jewish state, and make peace with us. In such a genuine peace, Israel is prepared to make painful compromises. We believe that the Palestinians should be neither the citizens of Israel nor its subjects. They should live in a free state of their own. But they should be ready, like us, for compromise. And we will know that they're ready for compromise and for peace when they start taking Israel's security requirements seriously and when they stop denying our historical connection to our ancient homeland.

I often hear them accuse Israel of Judaizing Jerusalem. That's like accusing America of Americanizing Washington, or the British of Anglicizing London. You know why we're called 'Jews'? Because we come from Judea.

In my office in Jerusalem, there's a—there's an ancient seal. It's a signet ring of a Jewish official from the time of the Bible. The seal was found right next to the Western Wall, and it dates back 2,700 years, to the time of King Hezekiah. Now, there's a name of the Jewish official inscribed on the ring in Hebrew. His name was Netanyahu. That's my last name. My first name, Benjamin, dates back a thousand years earlier to Benjamin—Binyamin—the son of Jacob, who was also known as Israel. Jacob and his twelve sons roamed these same hills of Judea and Samaria 4,000 years ago, and there's been a continuous Jewish presence in the land ever since.

And for those Jews who were exiled from our land, they never stopped dreaming of coming back: Jews in Spain, on the eve of their expulsion; Jews in the Ukraine, fleeing the pogroms; Jews fighting the Warsaw ghetto, as the Nazis were circling around it. They never stopped praying, they never stopped yearning. They whispered: Next year in Jerusalem. Next year in the promised land.

As the prime minister of Israel, I speak for a hundred generations of Jews who were dispersed throughout the lands, who suffered every evil under the sun, but who never gave up hope of restoring their national life in the one and only Jewish state.

Ladies and gentlemen, I continue to hope that President Abbas will be my partner in peace. I've worked hard to advance that peace. The day I came into office, I called for direct negotiations without preconditions. President Abbas didn't respond. I outlined a vision of peace of two states for two peoples. He still didn't respond. I removed hundreds of roadblocks and checkpoints, to ease freedom of movement in the Palestinian areas; this facilitated a fantastic growth in the Palestinian economy. But again—no response. I took the unprecedented step of freezing new buildings in the settlements for ten months. No prime minister did that before, ever. Once again—you applaud, but there was no response. No response.

In the last few weeks, American officials have put forward ideas to restart peace talks. There were things in those ideas about borders that I didn't like. There were things thereabout the Jewish state that I'm sure the Palestinians didn't like.

But with all my reservations, I was willing to move forward on these American ideas.
President Abbas, why don't you join me? We have to stop negotiating about the negotiations. Let's just get on with it. Let's negotiate peace.

I spent years defending Israel on the battlefield. I spent decades defending Israel in the court of public opinion. President Abbas, you've dedicated your life to advancing the Palestinian cause. Must this conflict continue for generations, or will we be able our children and our grandchildren to speak in years ahead of how we found a way to end it? That's what we should aim for, and that's what I believe we can achieve.

In two and a half years, we met in Jerusalem only once, even though my door has always been open to you. If you wish, I'll come to Ramallah. Actually, I have a better suggestion. We've both just flown thousands of miles to New York. Now we're in the same city. We're in the same building. So let's meet here today in the United Nations. Who's there to stop us? What is there to stop us? If we genuinely want peace, what is there to stop us from meeting today and beginning peace negotiations?

And I suggest we talk openly and honestly. Let's listen to one another. Let's do as we say in the Middle East: Let's talk "doogri." That means straightforward.

I'll tell you my needs and concerns. You'll tell me yours. And with God's help, we'll find the common ground of peace.

There's an old Arab saying that you cannot applaud with one hand. Well, the same is true of peace. I cannot make peace alone. I cannot make peace without you. President Abbas, I extend my hand—the hand of Israel—in peace. I hope that you will grasp that hand. We are both the sons of Abraham. My people call him Avraham. Your people call him Ibrahim. We share the same patriarch. We dwell in the same land. Our destinies are intertwined. Let us realize the vision of Isaiah—(Isaiah 9:1 in Hebrew)—"The people who walk in darkness will see a great light." Let that light be the light of peace.

23 September 2011

[Originally published by the UN]